T

Breaking Up the Euro

Also by Dimitris N. Chorafas

Household Finance: Adrift in a Sea of Red Ink (2013)

Quality Control Applications (2013)

Basel III, the Devil, and Global Banking (2012)

Sovereign Debt Crisis, the New Normal, and the New Poor (2011)

Business, Marketing and Management Principles for IT and Engineering (2011)

Energy, Environment, Natural Resources and Business Competitiveness (2011)

Education and Employment in the European Union: The Social Cost of Business (2011)

Cloud Computing Strategies (2011)

The Business of Europe Is Politics (2010)

Risk Pricing (2010)

Capitalism without Capital (2009)

Financial Boom and Gloom: The Credit and Banking Crisis of 2007–2009 and Beyond (2009)

Globalization's Limits: Conflicting National Interests in Trade and Finance (2009)

IT Auditing and Sarbanes-Oxley Compliance (2009)

An Introduction to Derivative Financial Instruments (2008)

Risk Accounting and Risk Management for Professional Accountants (2008)

Risk Management Technology in Financial Services (2007)

Stress Testing for Risk Control Under Basel II (2007)

Strategic Business Planning for Accountants: Methods, Tools, and Case Studies (2007)

International Financial Reporting Standards (IFRS), Fair Value, and Corporate Governance (2006)

Wealth Management, Private Banking, Investment Decisions, and Structured Financial Products (2006)

The Management of Bond Investments and Trading of Debt (2005)

The Management of Equity Investments (2005)

The Real-time Enterprise (2005)

Integrated Risk Management (2005)

Breaking Up the Euro

The End of a Common Currency

Dimitris N. Chorafas

palgrave
macmillan

BREAKING UP THE EURO
Copyright © Dimitris N. Chorafas, 2013.

All rights reserved.

First published in 2013 by
PALGRAVE MACMILLAN®
in the United States—a division of St. Martin's Press LLC,
175 Fifth Avenue, New York, NY 10010.

Where this book is distributed in the UK, Europe and the rest of the world,
this is by Palgrave Macmillan, a division of Macmillan Publishers Limited,
registered in England, company number 785998, of Houndmills,
Basingstoke, Hampshire RG21 6XS.

Palgrave Macmillan is the global academic imprint of the above companies
and has companies and representatives throughout the world.

Palgrave® and Macmillan® are registered trademarks in the United States,
the United Kingdom, Europe and other countries.

ISBN: 978–1–137–33326–1

Library of Congress Cataloging-in-Publication Data

Chorafas, Dimitris N.
    Breaking up the euro : the end of a common currency / Dimitris N.
Chorafas.
        pages cm
        ISBN 978–1–137–33326–1 (alk. paper)
        1. Monetary policy—European Union countries. 2. Bank
liquidity—European Union countries. 3. Bank reserves—European
Union countries. 4. Eurozone. I. Title.
HG930.5.C4596 2013
332.4'94—dc23   2013000413

A catalogue record of the book is available from the British Library.

Design by Newgen Knowledge Works (P) Ltd., Chennai, India.

First edition: July 2013

10 9 8 7 6 5 4 3 2 1

Contents

Foreword   ix

Preface   xiii

List of Abbreviations   xix

1 The Breakup of the Euro Is a Probable "Impossibility"   1
  1. The Start of Deglobalization   1
  2. Every Economy Is Sick in Its Own Way   4
  3. Two Little Caesars and a Template   8
  4. The "Template" Puts in Question the Very Nature of
    the European Union   10
  5. Was Political Action an Honest Brokerage or a Trap? 13
  6. Has Euroland Been a Big Political Mistake?   16
  7. Default on Debt Which Is No More "Domestic"   19

2 The Lack of Leadership Is Deeply Felt in Western Countries   25
  1. EMU and the Bubble of El Dorado Riches   25
  2. Europe Is Paying the Price for Mismanagement   28
  3. Spending Time and Money on Useless "Summits"   32
  4. If It's a Casino Society, Take Me to Las Vegas   35
  5. Mario Draghi and the Monte dei Paschi di Siena Scam 39
  6. Crisis Meetings of Chiefs of State without Tangible Results 41
  7. When the Economy Is Stalling, the Field Is Open
    to Folklore   45

3 The Nineteenth "Summit's" Miracle Weapons:
  June 28–29, 2012   49
  1. Throwing the Dice in Brussels   49
  2. Monti's Delight and Merkel's Sorrow?   52
  3. Troubled Countries Relief Program   56
  4. With Storm Clouds over Euroland, It's No Time for
    Miracle Weapons   60
  5. Euroland's Banking Union   63

6. The Great EU Bank Robbery Started with PSI   66
7. Private Involvement Might Be Good in Theory but Is
   a Huge Loophole in Practice   69

4 ECB, EFSF, ESM, Eurobonds, and Political Horse Trading   75
  1. The European Financial Stability Facility   75
  2. European Stability Mechanism   79
  3. Leveraging Euroland's Funds Is Wrong-Way Risk   84
  4. Dead Cat Walking: Eurobonds   87
  5. The French Connection   91
  6. Too Big to Jail   95

5 Throwing Money to the Four-Letter Wind: LTRO   99
  1. Long-Term Refinancing Operation: The Sarkozy Trade   99
  2. Euroland's Drift to Financial Mismanagement   103
  3. The Destination of LTRO Funds Is as Important
    as Their Amount   106
  4. LTROs Have Moral Hazard   110
  5. The Powerful Became Powerless   113

6 Fiscal Compact and Outright Monetary Transactions   119
  1. The Fiscal Compact Is an Upgraded Stability and
    Growth Pact   119
  2. What Might the Fiscal Compact Be Worth in the
    Longer Term?   124
  3. Economic Problems Mount as Sovereigns Lose Their Luster 128
  4. European Banking Industry and the Liikanen Committee 131
  5. Outright Monetary Transactions (OMT)   134
  6. Why OMT May End Up in a Fiasco   138

7 TARGET2: The Creeping Risk of a Financial Nuclear Bomb   145
  1. TARGET2 Imbalances Are Still on the Rise   145
  2. Breaking through the Austerity Wall with TARGET2   148
  3. The Creeping Risk of Financial Imbalances Can
    Destroy the Euro   153
  4. Without the German Economy, Euroland Is Off the Rails 157
  5. Aftereffect of Chronic Surpluses and Deficits in
    ECB Books   161
  6. Exit Germany?   166

8 Redenomination Risk Following a Euro Breakup   171
  1. The Euro Could Destroy the EU   171
  2. *Lex Monetae*: The Legality of Abandoning the Euro   176
  3. Redenomination Risk by Classes of Assets and Liabilities 180

4. Can a Fiscal Union Be the Solution?   184
5. What a Fiscal Union Cannot Do, a Political Union Might   187
6. Conclusion   191

Appendix   195
   1. The Pains of the Italian Economy   195
   2. The Pains of the Spanish Economy, Its Regions, and
      Its Banking Industry   198

Notes   203

Index   217

Foreword

And when I'm lying in my bed,
I think about life and I think about death...
And neither one particularly appeals to me.

—The Smiths, *Nowhere Fast* (Rough Trade Records), 1985

It is undoubtedly a cliché but the road to ruin is indeed paved frequently with good intentions. I don't think that anyone would disagree with the notion that the creators of the euro, the original road to "ever closer union," believed earnestly that monetary union would bring with it only harmony and prosperity. In the years leading up to its introduction, this belief was held with a religious zeal. It truly was faith.

And yet, just a few short years later, like a mediocre bond trader who only ever managed to make money in a bull market, the inherent design flaws in everything about the euro, its design, its operation, its very conceptual logic, were all laid bare as soon as the currency encountered its first economic downturn. One crash, one bear market, and it became apparent that the euro was not only half-baked in concept, it was also not fit for purpose. Far from driving ever closer union, ever more integrated economies, it was actually driving economies apart, as northern Eurozone countries stopped trading cross border, as banks in some member countries started running zero balances in banks in the southern Eurozone in case there was any overnight exit from the club.

Sports fans amongst us know the phenomenon. As the manager of their country's football team makes poor team selections, inexplicable formation choices and ineffective tactical substitutions, the cry around the stands goes up—does he know what he's doing? Can't he see what all of us up here can see? Why is he making decisions that just about all of us know are wrong?

It was no different with the euro. Anyone could have told the manager that one can't have monetary union without political union (or, at the very least, some form of integrated fiscal policy process). Professor Milton Friedman was just one of those "anyone." In a 1997 article entitled

"The Euro: Monetary Unity to Political Disunity?" he famously predicted that the euro would not survive its first economic recession. And although he has been proved to be not quite 100 percent right—the euro is still in existence and no member country has left it yet—he was still certainly very spot on, as he predicted exactly what the euro is suffering from now.

And suffering it is. The promise of the European Central Bank to do "whatever it takes" to save the euro doesn't actually address the currency's structural problems one bit, and is no more than a short-term expediency. The euro was always a political project, not an economic one, and as a political project it will command a lot of effort, expense, and head scratching before it is finally given up. But in the meantime, it will continue to cause a lot of economic misery and suffering. Long-term unemployment—a direct result of the impact of being in the euro—is never a pleasant thing for anyone at any time.

Because whatever way one looks at it, the outcome is not pleasant. Whether it continues on in current form, or experiences some members leaving, or it disintegrates completely, there is much more taxpayer money to be spent, higher unemployment to be endured, and welfare expenditure problems to be suffered. Neither outcome particularly appeals to me.

And yet it needn't have been like this. If the euro had been treated from the start as an economics project, and not a politics one, its operating framework could have been designed more robustly. Professor Chorafas points out all the insane thinking, the flawed concepts, and the very Alice-in-Wonderland ideas that lay behind the euro's design. The contradictions in this design were pointed out at the start—not least, as we have noted, by Professor Friedman—but ignored. The arrogance and conceit of the EU leadership at the time was, and continues to be, breathtaking. If one builds something with someone else's money, one will always take less interest in its design strength.

As has become apparent to Europhile and Eurosceptic alike, there is no painless outcome. Staying in the euro has painful consequences, for many years to come, for members such as Greece, Portugal, Cyprus, and Spain, while leaving it has equally, if not more, painful outcomes for every EU member. Is there a third option? Can the entire project simply not be unwound? Select a date in the future at which every member reverts overnight back to its domestic currency, Germany included. The legal, operational, and capital flight problems associated with exit or breakup would be less severe, as everyone moves at the same time. We should think about it.

This excellent, accessible, and incisive book actually makes for depressing reading. The EU's political leadership has succeeded in foisting problems on us that we needn't be suffering from, and there is no—repeat no—painless solution to the euro's problems. We will all suffer as the currency reaches its *denouement*. That's why this book should be read by every EU government leader. Sadly, we know it won't be.

March 14, 2013   PROFESSOR MOORAD CHOUDHRY FCSI
                                                  Department of Mathematical Sciences
                                                  Brunel University

Preface

The *euro* was planned as the common currency of a group of the European Union's member states. A dozen years of its implementation have shown that the planning was incomplete, at best. It was wrong to bring under one set of currency rules economically strong nations like Germany and Holland and weak ones like Greece, Spain, and Italy. To this has been added the weight of a deepening debt crisis among Western nations, which continues unabated.

The drama of the common currency is a hot topic. The method chosen for treating it starts with the global view of faltering economies the aftermath of which have been amplified by a lack of political leadership. The documentation is provided by a tandem of do-nothing "summits" and by initiatives that have thrown money at the problem. Some schemes, like the EFSF and ESM, have been put up by Euroland; and others by the European Central Bank. Examples are LTRO and OMT.

Another worry of creeping economic and financial risk is TARGET2, Euroland's settlement system at the ECB, which has turned into a mountain of bilateral debt. Conceivably, if its imbalances continue unabated, it will become the stuff of an economic and financial nuclear bomb. Therefore, the time has come to prepare for the foreseeable euro breakup and to confront the redenomination risk associated with it.

ESM, EFSF, LTRO, OMT, and plenty of other abbreviations are generally known and often used; TARGET2 less so. But there is, as well, a three-letter abbreviation PSI, which stands for *Private Sector Involvement* (chapter 1) and whose negative impact on banks and investors is much greater than the whole soup of new agencies, assistance funds, bailouts, and other ways of throwing away money. Yet little attention has been paid to it.[1]

PSI has been a milestone in Western finance: With the complicity of supranational authorities and international organizations, governments violated the sacrosanct guaranty of bank deposits. Many economists think that the first instance of violation of private financial property happened in Cyprus with *the mandatory taxation of private deposits*, including (for a brief time) insured deposits, which was a sacrilege that took place in March 2013 in Cyprus banks.[2] In reality, the strong-arm tactics by the EU, Euroland, ECB, Ecofin, and IMF in Cyprus have been the second episode that confirmed the first, namely, the 2011–2012 PSI. Taken together,

- They have been a blow and have caused injury to private property (chapter 1, chapter 2) and they are on the way to becoming the new norm, and
- Like the society of the 1920s and 1930s our economic, banking, and social travails are breeding "little Caesars." One of them has chosen domicile in Brussels, the other in Frankfurt.

Jim Rogers, the American investor, expressed all that mess in these terms: "It's pretty scary what's going on in Europe, especially when they're taking money out of people's bank accounts... with Cyprus, politicians are saying that this is a special case and urging people not to worry, but that is exactly why investors should be concerned... the IMF has said 'sure, loot the bank account', the EU has said 'loot the bank accounts' so you can be sure that other countries when problems come, are going to say 'well, it's condoned by the EU, it's condoned by the IMF, so let's do it too.'"[3]

*   *   *

Economists friendly to the idea of a common currency say that, despite Euroland's debt woes, one of the basic reasons for the euro's (apparent) relative stability is that the common currency area does not have a major external deficit. Its risks and challenges are largely internal because some of its member countries work hard, export, and save even as others—the profligate—depend on imports, spend more than they earn, and find no problem in getting deeper in debt.

Even if Euroland's crisis is largely internal, it is, however, too complex for a quick fix. Moreover, solutions will only make sense if the mounting problems are confronted within the perspective of the global economy. Seen from that viewpoint, the whole Western world is in a pretty bad shape and the deepening of the crisis may well carry along developing countries whose growth rested on exports to Western markets. Globalization worked as long as it worked, but it has now turned against the West:

- Relocating jobs from Western to emerging countries,
- Unraveling formerly great currencies like the US dollar,[4] and
- Confronting central banks with unspoken questions about their methods, their tools, and their effectiveness.

Economists and other experts who do not believe in miracles[5] argue that the European Central Bank can no longer cope with the economic divergence characterizing Euroland's 17 member countries. Neither can it halt the ineluctable demise of the common currency. Demise, however, is not just limited to the euro. Something similar, however, can as well be said about the yen and the dollar.

In America, the congressional super-committee charged with delivering solutions on how to control the US debt, reached no agreement. This left a public debt of over 16 trillion dollars—climbing at the rate of 100 billion dollars per month while, *as if* to make matters worse, the Federal Reserve continues printing money at an unprecedented pace.

In other terms, the so-often heralded and praised global economy had its victims. The IMF's chief economist sees the debt situation in America and Japan as worse than that in Europe.[6] Classically central banks thought that a debt crisis can be solved by siphoning out the red ink through rising inflation. But the fact of life has been that, with the exception of Britain, nowadays they cannot even pull that rabbit out of a hat.

Chapter 1 suggests that while many economists and most politicians look at the breakup of the euro as an impossibility, this is in reality a "probable impossibility" (though not a certainty). The text explains the reasons. One of the most important grounds for having reached this state of affairs is the lack of forward thinking and proactive action as well as political quarrels that flare up in Western countries—indeed, in all Western countries, not just in Euroland.

Chapter 2 makes the point that Europe is paying the price of several decades of mismanagement. This has been magnified by indecision on what to do; delays in working out reasonable solutions; the aforementioned interminable and controversial "summits," characterized as "last chance"; and Western *déclinisme*, which is the *alter ego* of the casino society that we live in.

Tragedy and comedy are the same thing, Socrates said, and should be written by the same authors. An example of the funniest outcomes of the different "summits" is the miracle weapon invented to solve Euroland's crisis; it is known as the Troubled Countries Relief Program (TCRP). Chapter 3 explains that this is nothing more than another case of money thrown to the four winds and wrapped up in folklore.

Chapter 4 looks at Euroland's financing mechanisms endowed with plenty of money: the ESFS and ESM, which have been accompanied by political horse trading all the way to cheat one's neighbor. For instance, the "eurobonds" and "banking union" ideas beloved to those squandering and most unwelcome by those working hard.

Chapter 5 presents to the reader one of the crowns of Euroland's money throw-away culture: the Long-Term Refinancing Operations (LTRO) by the European Central Bank. More than €1 trillion ($1.3 trillion) has been handed out to Euroland's banks, which used the money to buy sovereign bonds instead of restructuring their balance sheets and serving the economy with loans. There always exist exceptions. Some banks, the more virtuous, started repaying the ECB.

To bring some sense of financial responsibility, particularly with sovereign budgets, the Fiscal Compact has been invented to instill a sense of duty in the uneconomic member states of southern Europe, the so-called Club Med. This is the theme of chapter 6, which also brings to the reader's attention the likelihood that Euroland's member states will not treat the Fiscal Compact differently from its predecessor: the Stability and Growth Pact. That means with irrelevance.

Chapter 7 addresses a lesser-known abyss in Euroland's public finances: TARGET2, the European Central Bank's clearance and payments system that is characterized by rapidly growing imbalances to the tune of hundreds of billions of euros. TARGET2 has been the tool Euroland's waster member states have found to break through the austerity wall. By several accounts its imbalances and creeping risk could exceed previous extravagances in Euroland's financial squandering.

The subject of chapter 8 is redenomination risk following a euro breakup or exit by one of its member countries. Redenomination is a major risk that, so far, has not been given the attention it deserves. In addition, it is an issue that can only be examined by classes of assets and liabilities, and even then several uncertainties will remain.

A euro breakup, which could destroy the EU and not "only" Euroland, might be averted through leadership, not by do-nothing "summits," ill-studied and half-baked solutions like "fiscal union" and "banking union," or the inventiveness of Mario Draghi, the ECB's most recent boss, who always finds some new casting to throw away taxpayers' money. The text explains why.

Draghi's actions are in sharp contrast to the steady run of the European Central Bank by his predecessor, Jean-Claude Trichet. This shows how much a central bank's policies can change because of personalities. Compare the policies of the Fed under Paul Volcker and Ben Bernanke as another example. Draghi's appointment also begs the question why the Germans, whose turn had come to run the ECB, allowed Draghi to take over. Did they know that the ship was sinking and they did not care to be at the helm?

If Germany had decided to quit the euro (albeit when the time is right to do so), *then* Draghi's choice was correct. If not, it was wrong. His caricature by German cartoonists, with a Prussian helmet and the looks of a chocolate-box general, had no effect on his spend-away policies. It may be the reason that cash is a more potent weapon than lofty sermons about democracy.

* * *

Seen in unison, the interviews with experts on the wider range of issues covered by this and its companion volume *The Changing Role of Central Banks*, have been productive. They were conducted *on background*, meaning that it was possible to use the information but not identify its sources in the text.[7] This allowed each participant to express a blunt opinion without thinking of peer pressure. In the times which we live, this is the best way to obtain factual opinions about facts that don't cease to exist because they are denied or ignored.

The analysis of research results revealed many interesting aspects about the current economic situation as well as the behavior of central banks and the euro. The text is largely conceptual and it is written in a way that would be comprehensible to both economists and politicians. Its organization takes account of the fact that in the realm of their work economists can only point out choices and the consequences of choices. The final decision about what has to be done is political.

Critics, however, say that this modern society of ours is not really governed by the politicians but by the media. The media pull and push public opinion and by so doing set the conditions under which politicians must decide. This overwhelms the powers of parliamentary democracy, which have started to feint in the background.

* * *

I am indebted to a long list of knowledgeable people and organizations for their contribution to the research that made this book feasible. I am also indebted to several experts for constructive criticism during the preparation of the manuscript. Dr. Heinrich Steinmann, Dr. Nelson Mohler, and Eva Maria Binder have, as always, made a significant contribution.

Let me take this opportunity to thank Charlotte C. Maiorana for suggesting this project, for seeing it all the way to publication, and for the editorial work.

March 2013

DIMITRIS N. CHORAFAS
Valmer and Entlebuch

Abbreviations

AFDC	Aid to families with dependent children
BBVA	Banco Bilbao Vizcaya Argentaria
BMPS	Banca Monte dei Paschi dei Siena
CDO	collateralized debt obligation
CDS	credit default swap
CFTC	Commodity Futures Trading Commission
DIHK	Deutsch Industrie- und Handelskammertag
EBA	European Banking Authority
ECB	European Central Bank
ECCL	enhanced conditions credit line
ECJ	European Court of Justice
ECOFIN	Group of European Finance Ministers, who known as Eurogroup
EFSF	European Financial Stability Facility
EIB	European Investment Bank
EMS	European Monetary System
EMU	European Monetary Union
ERM	Exchange Rate Mechanism
ESM	European Stability Mechanism
EU	European Union
FC	Fiscal Compact
GAAP	Generally Accepted Accounting Principles
GDP	gross domestic product
GMU	German Monetary Union
ICB	Independent Commission on Banking
IFO	Munich Institute for Economic Research
IFRS	International Financial Reporting Standards
IIF	Institute of International Finance
IMF	International Monetary Fund
LMU	Latin Monetary Union
LTRO	Long-Term Refinancing Operations
MBS	mortgage-backed securities

MTO	medium-term objective
OMT	outright monetary transactions
PSI	Private Sector Involvement
QE	quantitative easing
ROE	return on equity
RWA	risk-weighted assets
S&P	Standard and Poor's
SGP	Stability and Growth Pact
SMP	Securities Market Program
SMU	Scandinavian Monetary Union
SPV	Special Purpose Vehicle
TARGET	Trans-European Automated Real-time Gross Settlement Express Transfer
TCRP	Troubled Countries Relief Program
UBS	United Bank of Switzerland
WTO	World Trade Organization

I

The Breakup of the Euro Is a Probable "Impossibility"

1. The Start of Deglobalization

Globalization has been both a process and a state of mind. In the course of the last three decades, global markets opened greater perspectives than regional or local markets for raw materials, agricultural produce, manufactured goods and services—and, to a more limited extent, for labor. Countries in a relatively early stage of development saw their gross domestic product grow. Some, by adopting tools and methods from developed countries, established themselves as manufacturing powerhouses.

The downside of the ascent of less developed countries to development status is that it has come at the expense of the developed countries, which found it more convenient (and cheaper) to import from abroad than to manufacture locally. As globalization grew, it hit its limits.[1] Over the last three decades, Western countries:

- Deindustrialized,
- Lost their competitive skills, and
- With few exceptions, they let their current account balance deteriorate till the West got deeply indebted to the East.

The words spoken by the prince in Giuseppe di Lampedusa's *Leopard* as he observed his own situation, perfectly describe the aftereffect on the Western economy: "Fire and flames for a year, ashes for thirty." In the case of globalization, largely because of their own mistakes, the developed countries have experienced 30 years of fire and flames. We simply don't know how long the time of ashes will last.

It is far from easy to reindustrialize. This requires not only strategic objectives, an ingenious plan, tight cost control (including labor and entitlements), price competitiveness, flexibility, adaptation, and marketing wizardry—but also difficult-to-recreate specialist manufacturing skills. Countries and companies that cannot meet the latter challenge remain deeply hurt by globalization.

In my book *Globalization's Limits* (2009), I have shown that globalization poses requirements and constraints; it is not a free lunch. As with any other complex and demanding process, *if* these requirements are not met and the limits are exceeded, globalization turns from friend to foe, and those who thought they would gain from it encounter a very rough weather. Two questions come up:

- Is this adversity an anomaly or the course of things? Without hesitation I would say that it is the new normal.[2]
- Which are the main worries now emerging, and why? The answer to this query is this chapter's goal, taking Euroland as an example.

The issue raised by the second question is part of a more general query on whether globalization's woes are the aftereffects of focusing too much on manufacturing and trade, with too little consideration of how it affects the people and the economy of Western countries. The answer to this query is that Japan, America, and the European countries have badly wounded themselves by relegating their future to globalization *as if* it were:

- The penicillin for every social pain, and
- The door to a permanent Nirvana.

One of the generally more acceptable idiosyncrasies of globalization is that it brings together the different cultures of those who outsource and those who insource. Better trade than war. But at the same time, the globalized world's uncertainties destabilized both common people and decision-makers in a way reminiscent of Goethe's "Faust" who, frustrated by the limits to his learning, makes a pact with the devil.

If two words could be sufficient to describe this pact with the devil made by Western countries they would be *abandonment* and *déclinisme*. In the developed world, only a few countries did not accept this curse and did what it takes to stand on their own—Germany, Norway, Sweden, and Switzerland. Unwisely, and in the most cowardly fashion, the self-wounded countries turned against them (particularly against the first and the fourth).

Switzerland is a small nation and so far it has only suffered a barrage of attacks by the US focused on its big banks (therefore on money) and on its banking laws. In contrast, Germany got demands for direct handouts to the profligates running into trillions of euros.

In a concentrated effort to get lots of money from the better-off countries in any way they could, the profligates attacked Germany for more and more funds via the ECB and in other ways, without even reading the statistics that talk volumes about who is responsible for their current plight:

- German unit labor costs rose by only 7 percent in the decade of the euro.
- By contrast, they soared by 30 percent in Italy, 35 percent in Spain, 42 percent in Greece, and so on and so forth.

To whom can we attribute this failure of control as money became cheap and debt spiralled during the days of the euro?Critics say that because of easy money and "the good life," the monetary union achieved the opposite of what was intended. Socialist and populist governments opened wide their financial gates, probably counting on a future bailout, even though they knew that the Stability and Growth Pact had no bailout clause.

The question that now arises is: What does all this have to do with globalization? The answer is simple: Globalization and regionalization in motion—Euroland being an example of the latter—provided the grounds and the excuse for a change in the Western work culture for the worse. Globalization is not only the different commercial treaties like the "rounds" of the World Trade Organization (WTO); it is much more than that.

Globalization and regionalization have evolved into a spirit that says: What is mine is mine, what is yours is mine because we share it. That's how to interpret the American and British pressure that the European Central Bank should do much more quantitative easing till it destroys the euro, just like the Fed did to downsize the dollar. Or the request by Spain for €100 billion for its banks without any supervision on how the amount is spent,[3] as well as the French push for eurobonds (another aberration).[4]

That is also how the attack on the city of London as a financial center by American lawmakers and regulators, who characterized it as a source of financial crises, must be interpreted. The accusation came in the wake of $6 billion of trading losses in one bet from the London operations of JPMorgan Chase. Gary Gensler, chairman of the US Commodity Futures Trading Commission (CFTC), said at a congressional hearing on JPMorgan's trading losses that the US was vulnerable to risky activity in London. Gensler added that AIG, too, had been hit by its financial products unit in London, Citigroup had been harmed by special purpose investment vehicles, and the list goes on.[5]

Till the crash of 2008, the globalization of financial services was heralded as the jewel in the crown of globalization at large. With huge losses came doubts. Now we hear that there are definitely clear flaws in the regulatory set-up in London that harm the operations of big US banks because they take too many risks—forgetting, of course, that the crisis we have been in for over five years started with subprimes in continental United States.

The covert call for deglobalization is not only an American-British affair but also French-British. David Cameron, the British prime minister, invited the French high-income earners to take residence in Britain rather than pay the 75 percent tax that François Hollande, the French president, has implemented. This enraged Hollande. Other Byzantine deals, too, are being discussed, not as jokes but in all seriousness.

Rather than calming the global financial market, François Hollande fuelled speculation when he bemoaned the fact that Spain was being targeted by markets in spite of the planned €100 billion bailout of its banks and its tough austerity measures, which in the end were not as tough as promised. Hollande also said the interest rates being paid by Spain and Italy on their debts were "not acceptable" because Italy's public finances were improving.

These statements were not made in London, Paris, or Brussels, but in Los Cabos, Mexico, during the G20 meeting. Why did all these gentlemen go all the way to Los Cabos (at taxpayers' expense) to talk about issues that should be treated in Europe is unclear. And the reason they did so in front of all the other G20s is even more obscure. Unless, of course, they wanted to provide hardcore proof that the EU's regionalization has frayed at the seams, and, consequently, it would not be long before globalization, too, falls apart.

2. Every Economy Is Sick in Its Own Way

Turning back the clock by 55 years allows us to take a closer look at the most important reason that motivated the Treaty of Rome. The reason was to reconcile France and Germany after nine decades of strife that had led to 30 years of devastating European civil wars from 1914 to 1918 and from 1939 to 1945. Examined under this objective, the Treaty of Rome, and therefore the European Union (not only Euroland), has failed.

The most deadly mistake has been that of the Common Market's expansion without end. Left to their own devices, the original six—France,

Germany, Italy, and the Benelux countries—might have cemented a solid basis of integration, first with fiscal union, then with budgetary and current account policies, as well as a banking union, and in the end with monetary union.

The priorities, however, have been unwisely reversed and, as a result, instead of European integration we are contemplating the consequences of a breakup. It's bad policy to target out-of-reach goals, for instance, a banking union, when the prerequisites are ill-defined and at a time when banking and finance are becoming more national and breakup forces are gaining momentum, even if the economies share a common currency.

Two conflicting schools of thought confront one another. According to one, the *fiscal compact*, jointly devised by the EU, the ECB, and IMF and first applied to the rescue of the Greek, Portuguese, and Irish economies, is the right step toward permitting greater control at European level. This is by no means an idle statement.

- Ireland decided to work hard to get out of the tunnel, and it seems to have progressed toward this end (Remember that Iceland, Latvia and Estonia have also succeeded).
- Greece, unfortunately, stalled. Austerity was only part of the so-called *Troika plan*. Growth would have come from restructuring the labor laws.[6] This failed because no government had the guts to push it through.
- In terms of results Portugal finds itself between Ireland and Greece. Little filters through in terms of results but as the saying goes, no news is good news.

The opposite school of thought maintains, against existing evidence, that money thrown at the problem will make the economy move even if the preconditions are not fulfilled and even if prevailing wages are too high and therefore uncompetitive in a global market. Regarding the fact that the government and the citizen spend the money they don't have, the credo of this school is: Let debt pile on debt and we will see later on what to do with this mountain of toxic waste.

This policy of "I see nothing, hear nothing, and sense even less" has been practiced by Western countries for over two and a half decades but it has its limits. When these are exceeded, as in Spain and Italy these days, they lead to results that are terrifying for the common citizen: Spanish statistics are 55 percent youth unemployment and 28 percent general unemployment. The young are paying for the excesses of their parents.

In the seventeenth century, La Fontaine wrote a fable of this state of mind in "La Cigale et la Fourmi."[7] The "we will see later on" profligate countries are "les cigales" who have set their sights on German money, which they consider to be ready and waiting for them. This is highly unwise because the hardworking "fourmis" will not give their wealth away. If "les cigales" were half as intelligent, they would have understood that Germany:

- Is unwilling to let the European Central Bank's presses run wild, and
- It might consider opening its purse strings only *if* and *when* strong rules are established and there are credible controls at the European level that are good for all sovereigns.

The talk that Germany would find itself obliged to pay because its industry depends heavily on Euroland's market is based on false statistics. In terms of export to other Euroland countries, Portugal's and (surprise, surprise) Holland's dependence is nearly 65 percent, Spain's 54 percent, and France's almost 50 percent. Compared to these countries, Germany's 41 percent and Ireland's 40 percent are more modest.

In addition, one-sided dependence is bad policy by both sovereigns and companies. When an economic area gets into trouble (as is now the case with Euroland), there is contagion. As an article in the *Financial Times* informed its readers, more than 75 percent of executives surveyed in mid-May 2012 in connection with the Euroland crisis had no contingency plans for a possible breakup of the single currency, even though the majority said that should this happen it would have a significant impact on their enterprises.[8]

Banks, including central banks, should also be prepared. The May 2010 first package for Greece saw to it that the ECB bought Greek bonds worth about €40 billion. In addition, the Bank of Greece owes the ECB around €130 billion in TARGET2 debt, which means internal obligations within the European central banking system. These would turn into real debt in the event of an exit. Adding this to the bailout credits, the Greek government owes the governments and institutions of Euroland over €290 billion, which represents about 3 percent of euro-wide GDP.

It is doubtful whether this money will be repaid after an exit by Greece. It would not be much different with Spain and Italy. The likelihood of a euro breakup is far from being zero. Some economists consider it inevitable given that the euro no more works as a common currency and the crisis has assumed greater magnitude than many people would have expected even in early 2012.

The argument starts being heard that it would be better to break up the monetary union, or at least that one or more states leave. The political irony of this solution is that as the euro was misconceived to be some sort of a super-Exchange Rate Mechanism (ERM), but the argument that its will have only a few more consequences than the ERM crisis is far from being documented. Other wrong arguments heard these days include:

- A strong economy can leave the euro without significant consequences.
- A weak economy can discharge the costs by going bankrupt.
- Any country will be able to stimulate growth by simply emphasizing growth policies.
- A country can be expelled from the euro by other members just by being told to get out.[9]

These statements are wrong because even if the euro has not been a success as a common currency, it did help to integrate diverse economies up to a point. Economically speaking, the majority of countries currently having big worries about their future are sick in their own way and a disorderly exit will make their economic, social, and financial situations much worse. To be done well, a euro exit will require:

- A lot of planning,
- Great discipline, and
- An iron fist in execution.

Neither the EU nor Euroland (with the possible exception of Germany, and even that is questionable) are known to have top-level planning skills or an iron first. That's too bad because a breakup could mean fragmentation even if it is secession by one state. Whether it takes place as a unilateral action or is the result of negotiations, a secession that fails can result in years of misery.

The finances of sovereigns and banks are so interdependent (particularly of banks in the sovereign's jurisdiction) that state bankruptcy will immediately mean the bankruptcy of banks. As an example, the Spanish government has aimed to recapitalize the country's banks.[10]According to the Institute of International Finance (IIF), the research lab and lobby of the global banking industry, some €240 billion of Spanish government bonds are held by Spanish banks, and this amounts to 6.5 percent of total Spanish bank assets.

- *If* the Spanish government had not used the country's banks as its piggybank,
- *Then* there would have been no need to massively recapitalize the banks and those near the abyss should have been left to fail.

Italy, too, suffers on account of its banks, but less than Spain. In good times, Italy was the most pro-EU and pro-euro of all European countries, but now that it totters at the edge of chaos, public sentiment has turned to apathy (though not to outright hostility). There exists as well the French connection. The political complexion has changed since the election of François Hollande. The new president is by no means radical, but there exists little popular support for "more Europe." Therefore, he wants "more money."

Where does all this diversity in backgrounds type of crisis and single-mindedness in getting more money out of the common purse leave the euro? It leaves the euro as a disorderly currency. In one of his arguments about the need for sound money, Daniel Webster has said that a disorderly currency is one of the greatest political evils.

3. Two Little Caesars and a Template

At the end of March 2013, when these lines were written, markets were still in the process of digesting the fact that to stabilize the banking system in Cyprus, the Ecofin (European Commission's group of finance ministers) and the ECB essentially confiscated private money. By all evidence, the IMF gave its approval. Economists criticized the fact that, in one act, with the Cyprus controls, the Ecofin and ECB struck down one of the most important characteristics of a monetary union:

- The ability to move money, without any restrictions, from one bank to another in the common currency area.

They also violated the sovereign's pledge of a *deposit insurance* of up to €100,000 ($128,000) since the first demand by the ECB—that has been rushed, unstudied in terms of consequences, and bordering on ridiculous—ordered that:

- The levy for all deposits up to €100,000 in a bank account in Cyprus will be 6.75 percent, and 9.9 percent beyond €100,000.[11]

Only two massive "no!" votes by the Cyprus parliament allowed the IMF, ECB, and Ecofin to save face, but neither Christine Lagarde nor Mario Draghi was even heard saying to the parliamentarians: "Thank you, you saved me from a snafu." Instead, they both pressed on even harder, paying no attention to the fact that:

- With capital restrictions, the value of a euro in Cyprus will no longer be the same as the value of a euro held by any other country in Euroland.

The *euro* has been the great sufferer and the *banking union* (chapter 3) became a joke. What's the sense of a banking union when the free transfer of euros from bank to bank in Euroland is no more feasible? Curiously, none of the decision-makers in the EU, Euroland, and ECB seems to have been aware of the fact that their rushed and totally unstudied Cyprus controls,[12] worsened by their money grab, led to two euros: one in Cyprus, the other elsewhere.

Interviewed on March 19, 2013, by Télévision Suisse Romande (TSR) about the ECB's decision, Andreas Höfert, chief economist of UBS, said that: "It risks to start a panic in the banking world in the South of Europe. There is no plan on how to handle bailouts and therefore the crisis is not inevitable. There have been already 5 solutions for 5 countries."[13]

Höfert is right. While we are now waiting for the Italian shoe to drop, at the same time we are wondering what has happened to the OMT (chapter 6) and to the great (and controversial) Draghi pronouncement that to save the euro he and the ECB are ready to do:

"Whatever it takes"

"Cyprus Lays Bare Euro's Flaws" was the headline of an article in the *Guardian Weekly*, which pressed the point that "those who say the monetary union has been a success must have an interesting definition of failure."[14] Mario Draghi, who had promised so much as to amaze the markets (and upset Berlin), simply disappeared from view in the crucial weeks of the Cyprus crisis. He reappeared only at the end of March 2013 with a hammer: an *ultimatum* to Cyprus: "Do it or else."[15]

The hammer was disguised as bailout in Draghi's toolkit: "Will do whatever it takes." Yet, while this dictatorial command has been a serious mistake, it is not the theme that attracted the attention of most economists. Their primary worry has been a statement made by Jeroen Dijsselbloem, the young Dutch finance minister, Angela Merkel's protégé,[16] and president of Ecofin.[17]

"The Cyprus solution is the template for future resolution of bailout problems."

By throwing his hat in the little Caesars' arena, the ecosystem of the EU's and Euroland's potentates, Dijsselbloem has shown that he is a rapidly rising young man in search of experience. An old hand in Ecofin like Jean-Claude Junker, the Luxembourg prime minister and longtime president of the Eurogroup of Finance Ministers, would not have made the mistake of a public "template" statement—unless it was not really a mistake but a trial balloon.

Whether through a slip of the tongue or Machiavellian calculation, Djisselbloem intensified market fears when on March 25, 2013, he said that the money of large depositors should be used elsewhere, too, to fill the gap in financial miscarriage. In effect, the Cyprus settlement officialized a precedent set by PSI (chapter 3). In its way, it complements the (also) poorly studied forced private capital involvement creating another and stronger framework. Economists are worried that this can have knock-on effects.

While Cyprus lays bare the euro's flaws, a couple of ECB board members found the opportunity to make lightweight statements. Benoit Coeure flatly refuted the template statement saying: "Cyprus is not a model for the Eurozone."[18] Others "clarified" that Cyprus was a "specific case." Notice that all that was done through oral statements, which are quickly forgotten. As far as the market is concerned, this verbal rigor has been counterproductive, as it identified:

- A clear lack of process in bailouts, including fiscal and political institutions able to efficiently resolve Euroland's internal crisis, and
- The fact that the risk of a next bail-in of senior unsecured bondholders is underappreciated by analysts, wealth managers, and the market.

Prior to the recent flare-up of Cyprus blues, the island state had asked Russia, the source of most of the foreign-owned bank deposits, for a €5 billion loan and was refused. In early March 2013, there was an attempt at a bilateral agreement also with Russia. The Cypriot finance minister flew to Moscow to negotiate. The mission failed.

Within the EU, Cyprus was accused of being an offshore tax haven. If so, Luxembourg is an one of a bigger magnitude. Malta, too, is on the list of offshore havens, and to a lesser extent Slovenia. Cyprus harbors a guestimated €20 billion of the money of Russian oligarchs. This is a small fraction of €300 billion ($338 billion) of Russian oligarchs' money in other Euroland countries, most of it in Luxembourg.[19]

4. The "Template" Puts in Question the Very Nature of the European Union

As Christopher Pissarides, a Nobel Prize-winning economist wrote in *The Economist*: "The way Cyprus has been treated by its eurozone partners shows that far from the currency bloc acting as a partnership of equals, it is a disjointed group of countries where the national interests of the big nations stand higher than the interests of the whole."[20] Critics add that the Cyprus settlement is:

- Wrong,
- Undemocratic, and
- Irrational.

It is as well counterproductive. From now on, who is going to have confidence in the banks? In the euro? Has it been *really* necessary to confiscate the deposits of the clients of Cyprus's banks, beyond the €100,000 of deposit insurance—and this at the high rate of 60 percent, as announced on March 31, 2013?[21] Where is the evidence? There is none that is written, or at least officially available in the public domain. Everything has been done in secrecy, and secrecy breeds plenty of scams—evidently reflecting on the reputation of all involved:

- European Central Bank (ECB),
- International Monetary Fund (IMF),
- Eurogroup of Finance Ministers (Ecofin), and
- The Government of Cyprus.

No thought has been given to the fact that the Bank of Cyprus and Cyprus Popular Bank (Laiki) were in a derelict state because of their mistake of lending money to the sinister Greek government of George Papandreou Jr. (and previous useless Greek prime ministers), losing 73.5 percent of their loans' worth with PSI. The private sector involvement was imposed by the IMF, EU, and ECB, and the same is true of the second disaster: the Cyprus restructuring and bailout.

Here we have an artificial common currency with plenty of reputational and stability problems to which are added political plots and economic machinations without anybody counting the consequences. We are past the times when governments tailored their economic policies to the needs of the common citizen. Now the kings are big banks, big governments, and big grabs—with the "template" statement opening the gates to this new policy.

All this points to an unprecedented change and also to power struggles. Which one of the two little Caesars will profit to become a big Caesar? One is the little Caesar of the "template"; the "other" little Caesar hides in Frankfurt. He has been involved in what *Bloomberg News* characterized as "chicken game in bailout test run."[22] The name is Mario Draghi of the ECB.

Draghi's CV could not be more different from that of Jeroen Dijsselbloem. He has a large amount of experience, but also reputational problems (chapter 2). He also has shown a curious stance with Cyprus, practically disappearing from sight, then issuing his infamous *ultimatum* (that exceeded his rights by a margin). Respect for democratic values does not seem to be one of his attributes. Curiously, he was not dictatorial with Monte dei Paschi die Siena (chapter 2).

The alternative to ECB's ultimatum to Cyprus, to commit to a €10 billion ($12.8 billion) rescue, was to *starve for liquidity*. It showed Mario Draghi playing more hardball than in any previous bailout. The talk that this was a test for Spain and Italy does not sell. What's easy enough with a small country may become akin to the detonation of an economic nuclear bomb when a big economy comes into play.

- *If* Italy was in the position of Cyprus, *then* the tsunami resulting from the financial earthquake in Europe would reach America's shores and shake down Wall Street.
- PIMCO calculated that *if* France faced the same problem that Cyprus did, just for the €7.5 billion bail-in demanded by Draghi's strong-arm tactics, *then* France would need €200 billion ($256 billion) to qualify for help by the IMF, EU and ECB.[23] Try to find it.

In fact, the little Caesar from Frankfurt may not know it, but he has lost a wonderful opportunity. The Cyprus banking and economic problems did not start overnight. The first time they were seriously discussed was in March 2012. A year provided plenty of time to make a thorough study, analyze, and understand the causes of the Cyprus economy's crisis, and come up with a factual and documented solution—instead of choosing the template-in-a-rush.

The most curious part of this story of "little Caesars and a template" is that denial has been slow to come. Nothing has been officially written; what was heard was little, oral, and informal. "The Cyprus program is not a template for future crises in Euroland," said one voice from the EU. The way another one had it, "European governments would not use a template. This was only a measure for Cyprus."[24]

Just a hair more formal was a short article by James G. Neuger distributed by *Bloomberg News* with the title: "Cyprus Program Isn't 'Template' for Euro-Area Bailouts, EU Says."[25] According to Neuger: "The swoop on bank accounts to finance Cyprus's aid package won't set a precedent for future rescues, pushing back against the impression given by Dutch Finance Minister Jeroen Dijsselbloem." That's according to a confidential document obtained by *Bloomberg News*, which is not publicly available.

"Within hours, Mr. Dijsselbloem was back to calling Cyprus a one-off," said an article in *The Economist*.[26] Yes, but nothing official has been published denying dependence on this template as a future policy instrument. There is no evidence it has been published for internal use. Anyway, it has not been made public. Words, words, and words—leading to ever greater instability rather than providing confidence to the common citizen, investors, and the market.

This absence of written confirmation may be due to the classical mismanagement of EU and Euroland affairs. But there is as well another hypothesis that cannot be rejected outright. We are entering an era of *banksterism, state gangsterism*, and *too-big-to-jail* policies (chapter 4). History shows that these are softly introduced by little Caesars without even asking parliaments to give an opinion. Then, before we know it, we wake up as slaves of a new economic fascism while Orwell's thought police is watching.

5. Was Political Action an Honest Brokerage or a Trap?

A senior investment advisor with whom I was talking on positioning one's assets against the forces of the coming years,[27] with particular emphasis on the euro's future, said: "The only way to hedge against a euro breakup scenario is to own no euro assets at all." Yet, a couple of years ago, on the tenth anniversary of the euro, the common currency was looking like being an unmitigated success. How and why did it fall in the crevasse?

To find the answer we must turn back to the days of the Maastricht Treaty. At that time, the more clear-eyed economists expressed doubt that a monetary union of very different economies could stand in the longer term, let alone be successful. They pointed out that in the past the only efficacious monetary unions were associated with fiscal unions and this was not the case with the euro.

In the background of this reaction has been the worry that open-ended goodwill deals don't end well. The doubters and critics added that no one would dispute that fiscal discipline is essential to any long-term common monetary solution while the Stability and Growth Pact was a paper tiger. Eventually the doubters proved to be right, the proof being that the absence of fiscal discipline—and of discipline at large—led to the euro crisis.

As the critics correctly pointed out, Euroland's rules and regulations were flawed from the start. There were no checks and balances and no real royalties. The Stability and Growth Pact was a piece of paper for which nobody would give a penny and which has been repeatedly revised downward. Briefly stated, Euroland lacked the appropriate policy framework to deal with its imbalances.

In the course of the first ten years of the euro euphoria, the pros argued that getting the monetary union on tracks was enough as a first step. Some brought up the United States as an example. This confusion between the *united* states of America and the *disunited* European states continues to the present day. Even an otherwise serious person like Georges Osborne, the British chancellor of the exchequer, said in an early 2012 EU gathering that salvaging Greece was like the US coming to the rescue of Arkansas—which is, most evidently, inaccurate, at best.

The United States was a political union project from day one, though it can be stated that it was not quite a monetary union. Some states had their own currency and were responsible for their finances and their deficits. When some states of the union drove themselves against the wall because of their financial excesses, the federal government in Washington refused to pull them up from under.

- Profligates and other big spenders were left to stew in their own juice, and
- This taught them a good lesson on the need for a steady economic and financial prudence.

It is indeed surprising that François Mitterrand and Giulio Andreotti, who took Helmut Kohl to the cleaners with the promise of a Stability and Growth Pact, did not study history's lessons. Their victory over Kohl was the victory of dissolution over prudence. It was bound to be ephemeral because the trio, particularly the duo of France and Italy, was unwilling to give up sovereignty to create a true political union.

To his credit, Helmut Kohl had spelled out his conditions just ten days prior to the Maastricht Treaty, when he said: "Political and economic and monetary union are inseparably linked. The one is the unconditioned (partner) of the other. We cannot and will not give up sovereignty over monetary policies if political union remains a castle in the air."[28] To his discredit, however, Kohl let himself be trapped in the Mitterrand/Andreotti net and then allowed Jacques Chirac[29] to push him aside while the French president was trimming the clauses of the Stability and Growth Pact.[30]

A worst-case analysis would have shown what might happen, but such a study was not done. If it were, it would have brought to attention the likelihood of a two-speed Euroland, a combination of cascading cross-border defaults, soaring risk premiums, currency dislocations, and collapsing banking system. A worst-case analysis would have as well examined what might happen to the common currency if the European and/or the world economy found itself in deep recessions.

The framers of an unstable euro also overlooked the absence of their own political will, and that of others, for tighter integration that could eventually allow economically weaker peripheral countries to be linked in a currency union. Back in 1992 when the euro was being negotiated, Jacques Attali, a trusted consultant of Mitterrand, and others said that a monetary union will not work without a political union. François Mitterrand and Helmut Kohl's answer was that "for the moment" the monetary union was enough.

But Attali and the other doubters were right. The absence of a political union allowed diverse economies to drift, each in its own way, with incompatible fiscal policies, employment policies, and social policies, culminating in a loss of confidence in the system. This loss of confidence was aggravated by the fact that different EU political leaders say things that are not true. The public knows that and therefore it does not believe them even if they happen to say the truth.

Things did not improve as the attention of Euroland's chiefs of state was absorbed by bickering about which nation will get the presidency of the ECB. Also missing from the agenda that surrounded the birth of the euro was a total absence of written confirmation, voted by the parliament of each member nation, of the willingness to give up a part of its sovereignty in exchange for benefiting from the common currency.[31]

Back in the late 1950s, asked by a journalist what in politics creates problems and opportunities, Harold Macmillan, the then prime minister of Britain, answered: "Events, dear chap events." Events that took place a dozen years after the euro's introduction proved that its critics and doubters were right. It was a mistake to introduce a monetary union ahead of a political union. As it were, bickering, resistance to change, short-termism, and cheating with statistics has destroyed the longer term.

That much about the lightweight statements made in an article by one of the best newspapers in Europe that the EU represents the world's most advanced experiment in interstate co-operation and in the pooling of national sovereignty. *If* this was the case, *then* we would not have had for most of 2012 the crisis of *Drachmageddon*,[32] followed by similar crises in Spain, Italy, and eventually France.

This pessimistic view of Euroland's future (and that of the EU) is written in full understanding that each single country on its own is a lightweight in the present-day global political and economic landscape. In addition, the problems confronting the old continent are by no means only financial. They appear predominantly economic because sovereigns are being crushed under mounting public debt due to:

- A long history of poor judgments, and
- The mismanagement of public affairs beyond reasonable doubts and bounds.

Any country that cannot, or will not, balance its public accounts, as well as continues running a current account deficit is a profligate country. No so-called fiscal austerity will be enough to eliminate deficits until the country restores external price competitiveness and generates trade surpluses to document that the competitiveness of its products and services has stopped eroding.

Such a turn for the better will in no way be automatic. Structural reform will be needed, as well as a change in the country's creditworthiness, even if this means a temporary fall in living standards (that definitely accompanies reforms and is inseparable from deleveraging).

The problems resulting from budgetary and current account deficits have only partly been created by the euro and easy-money policies. Many of the problems are deep-seated. It is better to tackle the reasons behind the problems rather than having to commit to the tough terms of bailouts.

In the go-go 1990s, the term "creative destruction" was used to identify a proactive form of innovation that could lead to job creation overtaking jobs lost because of decay in old product lines or intense foreign competition.[33] Failure to keep up with proactive policies can, in no time, switch a country from a winning streak to the camp of those who are uncompetitive and from there to hell.

6. Has Euroland Been a Big Political Mistake?

John Maynard Keynes was an early supporter of Franklin D. Roosevelt but he did not appreciate the gyrations of the dollar under the Roosevelt administration, characterizing them as "more like a gold standard on the booze." Keynes also castigated as foolish the idea that "there is a mathematical relation between the price of gold and the price of other things."[34]

Over the last three years, a common currency "on the booze" is a good enough description of euro's life. The late British economist's second aphorism is also an appropriate description of the touted banking union: "There is no mathematical relation describing how weak governments and weak banks are pulling each other down."[35] Yet this is an observed fact.

"We affirm that it is imperative to break the vicious cycle between banks and sovereigns," the European Union's leaders declared in their Miracle Weapon "summit" of June 28–29, 2011,[36] forgetting that it was they and George W. Bush who had established, in the first place, this unholy alliance between big banks and sovereigns.

- The vicious cycle between banks and sovereigns is very bad indeed, and
- The ill-conceived and poorly defined fiscal union will most likely reinforce it.

Here is how *The Economist* looked at this issue: "The National regulators have too often buried skeletons, not least to avoid intrusion by the commission's competition watchdog, which demands restructuring of banks that receive state aid. The talk in the commission is that of 45 banking cases it has looked into, 44 involved overestimation of assets by national regulators."

That's another sort of big-size transborder cheating in the EU. When the watchdogs are not permitted to examine the files and bring the wrongdoers to justice, the road is open to all sorts of trickery. In addition, discipline is wanting, important rules of behavior are missing, and the few which exist are brittle. It is not even possible to establish iron-clad conditions for new members pressing to be admitted to the EU.[37]

Member states of a monetary union should be very careful about whom they admit. New members always present challenges, particularly countries that lack in quality of skills and have mass unemployment or high labor costs, which make them uncompetitive. Yet several were welcome in Euroland. Taking Germany as the frame of reference, between 2000 (the year of euro's sweep) and 2011, its labor costs increased only 5 percent, but:

- Estonia's increased by 170 percent,
- Slovenia's by 154 percent, and
- Slovakia's by 135 percent.[38]

It is not only Spain, Italy, and Greece that goofed up cost control. Estonia, Slovenia, and Slovakia were welcomed to Euroland though they had patently failed to control their costs and did not immediately face a debt meltdown (Slovenia is considered to be next on the list).

Since new member countries to the EU get all sorts of subsidies when they sign up, it is easy to understand the rush for membership. But nobody pays attention to risk-weighted assets. From the viewpoint of countries needing funds and those providing them, the way to look at accumulated unfunded liabilities—from subsidies to bailouts—is as a *legacy cost* largely due to mismanagement of:

- Each individual member country,
- The common currency itself, and
- The institutions and watchdogs supposed to look after its wellbeing.

These legacy costs have a special price attached to them. They led to Greece, Portugal, and Ireland losing access to private market funding and are threatening to do the same for Italy and Spain (eventually for France as well). At the same time, in spite of bailouts, or because of them, hope has faded that there will be a quick, let alone lasting solution to the debt problems of member states. Doubts are mounting about the euro's ability even to survive. Worst of all, this has become a self-feeding process as Europe's economy will not see a sustained recovery until a credible solution is found to solving the fiscal problem.

Investment houses advice their clients to carefully weigh whether they want to expose themselves to the euro risk. As the fog of uncertainty is not likely to lift on its own, capital protection is the name of the game, to be achieved through a well-diversified portfolio. Be careful with euro-based investments, said the CEO of Standard Life in an interview by *Bloomberg News* on February 13, 2012. This warning reflects as much on the euro as on the leadership of Euroland's member states.

The answer to the question, "What should Euroland's sovereigns do on priority basis?" is, "They should restore confidence." The answer to the query, "How do you restore confidence in a very nervous market?" is far more complex. To do so, Euroland's politicians have to solve two problems at the same time:

- The immediate crisis, and
- The architecture of a new and better integrated common currency area.

To change the answer to "Has Euroland been a big political mistake?" from a "yes" to a "no," a no-reserves-made political union is a "must." It is time to recognize that what was agreed in 1958 about a Common Market and in 1992 about the euro has fallen woefully short of reaching announced aims. Neither will the addition of fiscal measures targeting budget overruns mean a great deal since everybody is cheating. Sovereign accounts are definitely unreliable and they will continue being so.

This being the current state of affairs, it does not make sense to have good money run after bad money while the profligacy continues. Neither is short-termism a solution. The curious thing with the economic and banking crisis is that nobody talks about how to avert the next crisis, just like nobody thinks of restoring confidence and competitiveness as being the core of the problem. Yet, this is precisely the case.

Several reasons suggest that a poorly planned and even badly managed Euroland is not anybody's pride—or profit. Even with a second austerity plan Greece had reached the limits of what it could do in terms of budget stringency. Portugal is not too far behind. Spain and Italy are right on track to the same end. To contain the risk of contagion to other countries, the European Central Bank may be forced to start a new wave of money printing, leading to more economic weakness—surely not to strength.

- If profligacy is rewarded by rich bailouts, and
- The "easy life" continues as if nothing has happened,

then there will be unexpected consequences as well. With the LTRO (chapter 5), providing liquidity, banks have used the ECB's ready cash to enter, at the taxpayers' expense, a profitable carry trade. They borrow for three years from the ECB at 1 percent and they purchase Spanish and Italian bonds of similar maturity at 4 percent, 5 percent, or more. With official complacency, the euro ends up becoming an instrument of the casino society.

Euroland might not have been, to start with, a fair-weather project. But the results are much worse than expected. There is a clear sense that some of the countries in Euroland simply don't belong there. They were not prepared for having a strong currency; they only wanted rich subsidies and low interest rates for their new debts.

7. Default on Debt Which Is No More "Domestic"

The status quo is clearly unsustainable but political integration is not on the cards for Euroland's member states. The opportunity for political union presented itself back in 1958, at the time of the Treaty of Rome. What is now left is a club of 27 member states based in Brussels with a highly expensive bureaucracy and an equally ineffectual monetary union characterized by very substantial interregional transfers. That's nothing to crow about.

What the profligate members of Euroland have missed in their calculations is that sharing a currency default on debt is no more a domestic affair. Default by one member country may shake the common currency by its roots at a time when the influence of globalization and regionalization is already waning. The enthusiasm prevailing in the pre-crisis years has faded away.

Not only are big interregional money transfers anathema to those who would advance the funds, but they also don't make sense. In addition, the scale of capital flows between economies as direct investments has leveled off. Heightened uncertainty has been a key factor in rendering these outcomes.

To instill some discipline in the way Euroland's rescues are being made, Germany tried to develop, postmortem, some rules of dependable financial behavior,[39] but other members do not go along; they simply want the money "no questions asked." For its part, Germany is fiercely opposed to the use of the ECB as a lender of last resort because it risks triggering a much higher price inflation along with:

- Monetary policy bias, and
- Major central bank losses later on.

This situation is difficult to untangle because in the early 1990s important issues related to a common currency were poorly examined or failed to get wider political backing. According to learned opinions, the political target has been guiding Germany since the beginning, and the common currency that it accepted was part of a strategy to reach that goal but now seems to be increasingly remote.

On June 26, 2011, George Soros was quoted by *Bloomberg News* as having said that amidst the debt crisis that hit Euroland's peripheral countries, a "euro-exit" mechanism is inevitable. Such a mechanism should have been part of Euroland's statutes, but does not exist. Today, even the fact that this option is discussed is enough to induce industrial and merchandizing companies to withhold their investments and keep their strategic plans tentative.

With the crisis in Euroland gaining momentum and the impact of currency movements on basic notions of what would happen if the single currency itself were to collapse, nobody can blame global companies for making contingency plans. At the very least, they are holding off entering into long-term contracts or placing big orders until there is more certainty in what happens to Euroland. While this is rational from the companies' viewpoint, it makes the peripheral countries fragile.

Any business that takes the disruption in economic activity and its aftermath seriously, has to take action to minimize risk, placing cash reserves in safer currencies (which explains the surge of the dollar)[40] and controlling nonessential investments. Some firms are looking for ways and means to protect themselves from a collapse of the euro with political risk insurance by buying two types of policies:

- Instruments protecting against expropriation or nationalization of an asset they own in countries under mountains of debt, and
- Instruments allowing to guard against the nonpayment of money owed because of government intervention, currency devaluation, or insolvency of the borrower.

At the other end of this protection strategy lies the fact that some underwriters have begun to include clauses excluding claims arising from the collapse of Euroland from nonpayment of insurance policies. As such actions are in their formative years and there is uncertainty about the probability of extreme events, it is too early yet to say what sort of risk may be covered and under which conditions.

Some multinationals buy an insurance known as currency market inconvertibility (non-transfer insurance). Its purpose is to guard against the risk of not being able to transfer locked assets in an overseas currency into a company's home currency. The downside is that it does not protect against devaluation of the euro or of the new national currency to be adopted by a country abandoning the euro.

In the background of these policies lies the fact that Euroland's member countries no longer have the luxury of a domestic default. Contagion will spread at no time. This is a dramatic change from the way the market was looking at the euro prior to the crisis, and the reference to retain is that in a currency union that includes no political integration, the troubles of one country hit all member states in the union.

- There is no way to provide a better support in countries not yet hit by the debt crisis.
- Default on debt which is denominated in the common currency no more domestic.

Some economists have suggested that one way to improve the market psychology would be a firm assurance that a troubled or exiting country's common currency partners would ease its departure from the euro by contributing to a large international financial support package. According to that opinion, such a package will be put together to build confidence in the newly introduced currency. Even if finding the money is not a problem, I don't think that this approach will work.

- First, because it is unclear from where the initiative will come, and
- Second, for the simple reason that nothing can assure that the members of the common currency will be parting as friends.

As far as default on domestic debt is concerned, a Euroland member state that chooses to leave the euro has essentially three choices ahead. One is to default on all its obligations like Argentina did in 2001. This is doable, but the defaulting country will be closed off the capital markets for a considerable length of time.

The second choice is forced conversion of euro-denominated debt into debt in the new national currency.[41] The way to bet is that this, too, will be judged as a default on the sovereign debt, an action generating lasting economic costs. The long-term cost of capital for the government would increase, and might lead to default under the first alternative.

The third choice is to leave its sovereign debt euro-denominated. This would mean that the entire debt is in a foreign currency over which the debtor country has no influence. Only if a country is earning plenty of euros through trade and tourism can it afford to pay in euros, but in such a case it does not have to leave the common currency in the first place.

Hence, essentially the first and second alternatives are those confronting Euroland countries with weakened economies. Since 2010, they have the added option of a bailout, but the way to bet is that not all of them will be able to comply with an austerity plan. It will take a miracle to come back on their own to a stable and affordable debt trajectory, unless their current debt is again and again significantly reduced. But who pays?

It is, therefore, time to recognize that what was agreed in 1992 about the euro's constitution, sustenance, and future has fallen awfully short of reaching its announced aims. Neither will the addition of fiscal measures targeting budget overruns mean a great deal since:

- Sovereign accounts are definitely unreliable and they will continue being so, and
- Imitations of the Maastricht agreement make no sense. Who cares to work on a plan that has already failed once?

Instead of targeting a holistic approach out of the current crisis in which no one believes and therefore nobody cares to follow, it is better that the different "summits" that have become nearly monthly affairs at taxpayers' expense,[42] take one country at a time and produce a focused, solid plan for economic recovery with:

- Timetables for deliverables,
- Well-defined responsibilities, and
- Sources of financing looking to the future, not at the past.

This does not need to be a voluminous text. Quite to the contrary, it should follow the advice by Campanella in *Cita Solaris* that rules and laws must be few but clear and focused. This is precisely the opposite of what bureaucracy is accustomed to produce. Here is an example. An article in the *Financial Times* pointed out that the British tax code is 11,500 pages long, and the American one ranges from 7,500 to 74,000 pages, depending on whether related regulations are included.[43]

It needs no explaining that a poorly planned and worst-managed growth plan for Euroland cannot be the pride of any chief of state, just like betting only on an austerity plan without restructuring for growth leads to deception. Austerity alone without restructuring followed by growth has failed. Restructuring means challenging ourselves and the system; also giving back some of our entitlements that are unsupportable and unsustainable. If we don't keep challenging ourselves, we will waste away.

The Lack of Leadership Is Deeply Felt in Western Countries

1. EMU and the Bubble of El Dorado Riches

From time to time, the Brussels-based European Commission outlines proposals that would allow Euroland's *rescue mechanism* to directly bail out member states or their banks. For instance, lending €100 billion ($130 billion) to Spanish banks whose bad loans are over €300 billion, and lending to governments at the same time. The common characteristic of these proposals is that they end up in the wastebasket (where they belong) shortly after they have been formulated.

Recently the European Union's executive body stated that the 17 countries using the common currency should consider setting up a banking union (chapter 3), but it did not bother to lay down prerequisites and rules. Details have been absent and the devil is in the details. Old hands have learned from experience that they should not bother asking Brussels-based European institutions for details; these raise unspoken questions about the future of projects whose failure is assured in advance for lack of leadership.

This is the present chapter's theme. It describes how leadership's substitution by unsubstantiated promises about a powerful "European Union" and an "almighty euro" lasted way too long, and then wore out. This substitution legacy is the economic damage inflicted by the trickery an interminable procession of European "summits" has created.

The Maastricht Treaty provides good evidence of how trickery works and how descent from the main line—whether this is the party line or the decisions favored by the dominant group of EU politicians—is muffled through massive propaganda. Writing on Stalin, Leonard Shapiro, the political scientist, stated,

> The true object of propaganda is neither to convince nor even to persuade, but to produce a uniform pattern of public utterance in which the first trace of unorthodox thoughts reveals itself as a jarring dissonance.[1]

Indeed, in Soviet Russia, dissent was regarded as lunacy; something similar can be said in our time about the EU, Maastricht, and the common currency (particularly during the latter's incubation and the first ten years of its life). Yet, clear spirits could see the dangers that at first hibernated but are now are on an explosive course.

At the time of the Maastricht Treaty negotiations, Martin Feldman, professor at Harvard and distinguished economist, wrote an article that castigated the agreement leading to the common currency. Feldman predicted not only economic but also political calamity if it came to pass.[2] It did pass and we all know that what followed years later has been a deep European debt crisis that proved Martin Feldman right.

A brief flashback will help bring to the reader's attention the building up of what I will call the El Dorado bubble. The El Dorado has been the euro, expected to bring riches to everyone. The race started with the creation of the European Monetary System (EMS) in 1978, which essentially was the work of Helmut Schmidt, the German chancellor, and Valéry Giscard d'Estaing, the president of France, assisted by Roy Jenkins, president of the European Commission. A dozen years later, in 1990, François Mitterrand, the French president, and Helmut Kohl, the German chancellor, created the scenario of the next step to El Dorado: the European Monetary Union (EMU).

The themes originally addressed by the EMU saw the light in 1989 when a committee headed by Jacques Delors produced a document generally known as the Delors Report. This advocated a three-step development toward a common European currency. Maastricht generally followed these lines, but it also added its own twists and clauses.

Karl Otto Pöhl, then Bundesbank president and signatory of the Delors Report, had this to say on the eventual impact of the European Monetary Union: "If the idea spread and the German population understood what it is about—namely, that it centers on their money, and that decisions on it will be taken not by the Bundesbank but by a new institution—then I would imagine that considerable resistance would arise."[3]

Back in 1990, the German public might not have known what the EMU meant for its savings, pensions, and generally its economic future, but any political leader who was not senile knew the facts. The most important of these facts (for the future) has been that several signatory countries did not have a hope of respecting the EMU's criteria, but neither did they want to be left out of the party.

Only second-class politicians could not have understood that there was money to be made by joining Euroland, while the Stability and Growth Pact of Maastricht and its constraints were only smoke and mirrors—a show set up by Mitterrand and Andreotti[4] to trap Kohl. Moreover, even governments that might have wanted to abide by the pact (they were not many) knew that the economy of their country would not have been able to follow-up.

- For Italy, Spain, Greece, and Portugal, among others, it was a race against time, and
- Seen from the perspective of events that took place in 2010–2012, the worst possible fears materialized.

For instance, in 1990, Portugal featured a 13 percent inflation rate as well as a 10 percent growth. The country badly needed to have and administer its own currency including the freedom to devalue it until its economy caught up with others in western Europe. The same was true of Greece as well as of Spain and Italy. The governor of the Bank of Italy had good reasons for being opposed to joining the euro, saying that the Italian economy was not ready for a common currency. But the then Italian prime minister would hear nothing of it.

It is not always easy to understand the murky economic reasoning of politicians, but neither is it impossible to appreciate that there have been conflicts of interest. One of them was the pressure by industry for joining the euro. Another, the illusion that merging a globalized, mass-production economy with nineteenth-century socialism and its nanny state is going to be beneficial to all.

The results are shown by the sclerotic and inflexible economic structure these incompatible bedfellows have left behind in Europe. No other political regime than the majority of those running Euroland's member states has led to so much useless spending[5] while structure and infrastructure have become dilapidated. Economists who still believe in the socialist international have recently renamed themselves neo-Keynesians[6] *as if* by changing their stripes they can mask their true selves.

The best proof that can be provided from real life of the fact that the structure of the European economies is ossified, inefficient, and out of joint with global competition—like the attempts to jump-start the economy through easy money and budgetary deficits. Take as an example the early 1980s' glaring failures in France under the presidency of François

Mitterrand that ended with three devaluations of De Gaulle's *franc lourd*:

- The first in October 1981 stood at a hefty 8.5 percent though it was presented as a 5.5 percent revaluation of the German mark.

No economist worth his salt believed that lie or its repetition.

- The third devaluation in early 1983 was also of 8 percent against the German mark, with statistics kept in disguise.

To save face for the third time in three years, the French regime asked, and the German agreed, to present it as a 5.5 percent revaluation of the mark against the franc and "only" a 2.5 percent franc devaluation. In exchange, the German government demanded measures to be taken to redress the French economy and the Mitterrand government was happy to oblige.[7]

The story of France in the early 1980s is the story of Italy, Spain, Portugal, and Greece (and eventually France all over again) in the second decade of this century. The bubble of El Dorado riches that were stockpiled and ready to be showered on nations sharing the common currency has been punched. Its aftermath has created nothing but trouble.

2. Europe Is Paying the Price for Mismanagement

The political mistakes made in the course of the formative years of the European Union, and of Euroland after the early 1990s, had economic, social, as well as political implications. The most important has been the loss of public confidence in the institutions set up to serve the purpose of European integration at large, and in rather similar solutions to be provided to uneven economic issues.

The organization responsible for overseeing economic integration in Euroland and for considering measures to reach that goal is the Council of Ministers for Economic and Financial Affairs (Ecofin). Its deliverables are trivial while its decisions are made in haste. As the careful reader will recall, to examine whether to approve a loan of €100 billion to self-wounded Spanish banks, Ecofin's chairman and members did not bother to conduct an audit and carefully study the banks' books and double books. On the basis of a couple of telephone conversations they agreed to throw the money to the four winds.

This is plain mismanagement evidently aggravated by the lack of leadership, the absence of which is felt not only in the European Commission but also in every Western country from America to Europe, except perhaps Germany and Britain (but even that is not sure). In the meantime the problems do not cease to exist and superficial summits (section 3) make matters worse.

Who can forget that since the beginning of the great debt crisis, which started in mid-2007 in America with the collapse of the subprimes, on both sides of North Atlantic governments have essentially used two ways to stop the drift of Western economies into deep recession:

- Uncontrollable deficit spending, and
- Nonstop money printing by central banks.

Worse yet, as time passed by, they repeated this wrong-way policy in ever bigger amounts, with the result that today we have a flat or shrinking Western economy along with a growing public debt and a never-ending banking debacle.

While one might accept that, as a one-off exception, the injection of liquidity into a self-wounded banking industry was necessary to avoid a complete collapse of the financial system, there is no doubt that this should have been a temporary solution. In addition, once the liquidity problem turned into a solvency problem, throwing public money into private companies should have stopped then and there.

- There is nothing wrong with some banks going bust, and
- The bankruptcy of high stakes and/or mismanaged institutions would have been an example to others of what to avoid.

Leaders have the stamina to adopt radical measures; the second-raters who run most governments don't. Even when there is plenty of evidence to prove that salvaging bankrupt banks, launching hugely expensive government stimulus programs, and engaging in the biggest money printing saga in history through quantitative easing, Twist,[8] LTRO (chapter 5) is counterproductive, they don't stop because they don't have anything else to offer.

Neither is the economic failure the only factor working against the Western world. Misorientation in higher education is another dark point. In the United States, three million unfilled positions search for the right skills and don't find them. In Germany that number is 500,000; in France, 400,000. The US has an unemployment rate of 7.8 percent, Germany 6.8 percent, and France 11.2 percent, with many of the unemployed, including university graduates, lacking the required skills. This is a flagrant failure in career planning.

When things turn out to be bad, only radical action has a chance of success. This requires not only leaders with a strong personality but also laws giving these leaders undisputed authority to bring a country up from under. Precedents from ancient Athens include two lawgivers: Drakos and Solon; in ancient Sparta the lawgiver was Lycurgus. According to Plutarch, the historian, as lawgiver, Lycurgus developed and applied a system of strict laws aimed at cleaning up a corrupt society whose wealth had centered upon a very few.[9]

Typically, ancient law setters (not parliaments or bureaucrats) have been persons of virtue[10] who have trained themselves to see very far and judge the outcome and the aftereffects of events well before they come to pass. "Once the mind is set on something, any challenge can be met," said Johann Wolfgang von Goethe. Setting the mind is the most important ingredient of sound management.

One of the foremost management skills is to see the challenges that are coming, and plan for them, positioning the organization in a way to meet them. In contrast to this, the most destructive management weakness is indecision and vacillation, along with the uncertainty and lack of trust they produce;these destabilize everybody else around the second- or third-class "leader."

Waiting for more data or a greater spread of opinions and muddling through is an excuse for failing to plan forward and make cutting decisions. The disaster that follows ranges from acting without a strategy to confusing the means with the end. Thinking ahead of the curve and focusing on the improbable but destructive events is fundamental. As a Wall Street adage has it: "What is most expected to happen is least likely to take place. The unexpected has a better chance."

Prognostications involve risks, but leaders are ready to assume them. They are set to control their exposure through careful treatment, executive ability, personal discipline, hard work, and skill in managing—that means in forecasting, planning, organizing, staffing, directing, and controlling. Our society has not produced many people with these qualities in this modern age.

Leaders look for solutions to problems; they don't run away from them. They like to be confronted by problems because they appreciate that without problems a person, a company, or a country is decadent. Trying to hide the problems from public view is the typical reaction of politicians because their mind is not set on solving problems involving social, political, and economic factors all at the same time. If it were, they would have appreciated that in 99 out of 100 complex cases, nobody, not even the ablest, can get the approach right the first time round because:

- Each case is different from those that preceded it, and
- Each has too many variables considered to be essential.

Only by planning, experimenting, testing, modifying plans, and experimenting again we might discover the right approach. Now compare this to what the typical average politician does, including the president-to-be of a republic. On May 2, 2012, in his televised interview with Nicolas Sarkozy—a duel for the French presidential elections—François Hollande, the socialist candidate, identified four sources of money to be scattered to the four winds under his leadership. In themselves these amounted to another socialist plan to bankrupt Europe:

1. Issuing *Eurobonds*, or, essentially, making the German taxpayers pay for other people's follies.
2. Involving the *European Investment Bank* (EIB), which should finance infrastructural projects (It was not clear whether Hollande understood the statutes of the EIB).[11]
3. Commandeering the European Central Bank (ECB), which, "instead of lending money to banks at 1 percent should lend directly to the states" (which, of course, is a violation of the statutes of the ECB).
4. Robbing the French common citizens of their savings as well as the patrimony of enterprises, to finance infrastructural and other ill-defined projects and also to cover part of the widening public deficits.[12]

It was amusing when during the televised debate François Hollande, the big spender, said that he was indeed for a balanced budget. He plans to achieve it by 2017, precisely the year his presidency ends, and he expected the viewers to believe him. That's the depth to which political short-termism has descended. For the last 40 years—that is, since 1974 when George Pompidou, a former banker and university professor, was president—year after year, France has had a budget deficit.

It is indeed curious that present-day French politicians pay no heed to the advice of the great nineteenth-century French physicist, mathematician, and astronomer, Pierre Simon de Laplace. In his *Essai Philosophique sur les Probabilités*, Laplace wrote: "Present events are connected to preceding ones by a tie based upon the evident principle that a thing cannot occur without a cause that produces it." What produced the big public debts is a lack of leadership that translated into spending, spending, and spending.

3. Spending Time and Money on Useless "Summits"

In early December 2011, Standard & Poor's (S&P), the independent rating agency, added its bit to the pressure on chiefs of state and prime ministers of the European Union to come up with a convincing deal on the ongoing economic and financial crisis. It did so by placing every member country of Euroland on a negative credit watch. That was a clear sign of the likelihood of reducing their credit ratings (that hit some of them later on).

S&P cited continuing disagreements among European politicians on how to respond immediately to the crisis of market confidence and, in the longer term, on how to ensure a better economic, financial, and fiscal convergence among Euroland's 17 members. The reminder was timely because, as a tandem of so-called "summits" demonstrated, EU political leaders were not around the corner of establishing a firm economic plan. S&P's pressure, however, went over their head even if nobody was denying that the European Union faces an agonizing dilemma.

- It absolutely needs to produce a plan to stop the accumulation of public debt and amortize the deep red ink, and
- Simultaneously, while keeping on the emphasis on austerity, have a program for growth that is able to attract new investments.

Confronting austerity and growth simultaneously can only be done by people who are both of high caliber and have the guts to express their contrarian opinion. Senator Carter Glass, former Treasury secretary under Wilson and coauthor of the famous Glass-Steagall Act,[13] is an example. When President Roosevelt called him to the White House to reveal his plans to profit through the official revaluation of gold bullion, Glass ridiculed that notion. *If* the president believed that by upping the dollar price of gold the government would have a profit of some two billion dollars *then*, Glass said, he was wrong.

> "That isn't a 'profit' as you call it—it is nothing more than a bookkeeping mark-up.
> "Furthermore, the gold you are proposing to confiscate belongs to the Federal Reserve Banks, and the Treasury of the United States has never invested a penny in it. You are proposing to appropriate something that does not belong to the government, and something that has never belonged to the government."[14]

Are today's politicians able to use such critical language when talking to the chief of state? I doubt it. (Glass was not alone in expressing his opinion without ambiguities. John Maynard Keynes did so with Lloyd

George when the latter was chancellor of the exchequer and Keynes worked for him.)

If in these useless "summits," the Euroland's chiefs of state who have maintained financial discipline in their jurisdiction clearly stated that they will not continue supporting sovereigns reneging on their promises[15] to put their house in order, it would have expended the argument of the beggars once and for all. This would have also been timely because the deficit-reduction momentum appears to be fading. While Spain is finger-pointed for its large budget deficit, it is just one of 12 (out of 17) Euroland member states that have asked the European Commission to change their recently agreed deficit-reduction targets—a perfectly unacceptable request, but permission was granted.

The irony is that even Holland, considered by some people as a model member of Euroland, is showing signs of slacking on its own deficit-reduction drive. In a race to avoid austerity (a dirty word in France), the recently elected president François Hollande[16] wanted to renegotiate Euroland's *fiscal compact*. Instead of coming forward with cost cuts, which would have strengthened his hand, he did the opposite— he put the retirement age at 60 (from a meager 62) while Germany, which is expected to foot the bill for French socialist festivities, has set the retirement age at 67.

Prior to François Hollande, Jacques Chirac, and after him Nicolas Sarkozy, led the quest for more money in the different "summits." "The EU has learned nothing about the shortcomings of the previous Stability and Growth Pact," said Simon Smith, chief economist at FxPro, a foreign exchange broker. "Investors would be correct in doubting the EU's ability to enforce any debt or deficit rules."[17] Even worse, investors doubt the willingness and ability of politicians to go ahead with needed painful readjustments of the economy.

In the now famous but ineffectual torrent of "summits," where politicians are talking about everything and nothing, the only thing sure is that the bill will be paid by the taxpayer. These slow-moving "summits," are held with little if any consideration of saving the old continent that is sinking under unaffordable debt,

- Restoring the economy, and
- Channeling the productive capacity of member states toward a growth path.

Public opinion in Euroland's member countries has turned against these expensive "summits" without results, as, little by little, the common citizen perceives that, except handshakes, the elected chiefs of state and prime ministers did not really know which way they were going. As confidence was lost, public opinion blamed the national leadership, including the economic and industrial leadership, for *not* setting:

- Clear,
- Realistic, and
- Reachable goals and objectives.

The early December 2011 EU summit spread wide the deception because of its lack of deliverables. This was already the fifth "last-chance" gathering labeled by its organizers as the "most important summit to the save the euro." In fact, it was no different from the previous summits, with very short-term decisions aimed to calm the markets for a while. This, however, did not change the fact that the summit failed to solve both the:

- Short-run funding issues, and
- Those of long-run fiscal sustainability.

This dual failure did not discourage European Council president Herman Van Rompuy from calling the result of the summit a "Fiscal Compact Treaty." Simply forgotten was the fact that it was not a real treaty agreed upon by all countries, but rather an intergovernmental treaty to which Britain objected and from which it decided to abstain.

The "intergovernmental" nature of the December 2011 "summit" was no random event. It was chosen because it allowed many countries to bypass their parliaments—a policy questionable from a democratic standpoint. The goal was to have it signed by early March 2012, before the next scheduled European "summit." Democracy took leave and virtue went along.

For its part, France learned nothing from the Mitterrand years, in early 1980s, when the government pushed very hard for economic growth during an economic trough. As we already saw, this led to devaluations of the franc. Today, supercharging for growth would have even worse results, since France already has a high level of government debt. Economists say that France cannot afford to spend €1.40 for each €1.00 collected in taxes. Some economists suggest that this has become a secret policy aimed at sustaining the French *social model*.

On the other side of North Atlantic, America is confronted by a deficit higher than that of any European country except Greece, which led a US congressman to suggest in an interview that the road his country has taken is that of Greece with a six-year difference. Worst of all, according to economists, since 2006, the US government debt has been growing roughly at the rate of 15 percent per year.

From currency stability to budget deficits and unaffordable entitlements, short-termism has been the order of the day both in Europe and in America. Back in 2008–2009, the US was in a worse position with its banking industry's meltdown. By 2013, the European Union, and most particularly Euroland, had been shaken by the accumulation of risks—from an on-and-off expectation of a Greek default, a Cyprus default, you name it—to ambiguity about debt reduction and a stream of ratings downgrades.

It is *as if* both sides of the North Atlantic decided to get into trouble simultaneously and then give the impression of *solving* the problems through "summits." As Andreas Höfert, chief economist of UBS, put it: "Since Greece ignited the European crisis 18 months ago, we have seen these last-chance summits come and go, along with politicians' plans to resolve the crisis once and for all. When Standard & Poor's announced it would put 15 of the 17 eurozone countries' ratings under review, the head of Standard & Poor's in France specifically mentioned investors' disappointment that none of the numerous European summits over the last two years has produced lasting results."[18]

In conclusion, in a desperate effort to buy time, rather than for any specific reason, during the last four years, "summits" have been the order of the day but like the euro's Stability and Growth Pact, they have failed to control deficits. Euroland's member countries have been required to keep to an upper deficit limit of 3 percent of GDP, on pain of sanctions, which were always waived. Therefore, nobody ever paid attention to this 3 percent limit, and deficits of 8 percent, 10 percent, and 12 percent became common.

4. If It's a Casino Society, Take Me to Las Vegas

The attitude taken in the course of these different "summits" can be generally characterized as one of *reflexible pullback*, retreating after asking for money from heaven. In contrast to this policy of the weak, what needs to be done to get the old continent out of the current mess is *forward leaning*: coming forward with imaginative projects while those member states who would do part of the financing ask critical questions about every plan and every detail.[19]

- Is the proposed project or plan believable?
- Is its goal achievable?
- What will be the required investment?
- How long will it take to recover the capital?

- From where will the funds come?
- What is the projected return on investment?
- Is it really worth the time and money?

Answers to these queries must be factual and documented, while arguments of convenience and reasons for delays should not be welcomed. In addition, both those asking for funds and the examiners must keep in mind that it is far easier to get into a project than to get out of it. Quite often, projects originally started for political purposes never die, nor do they deliver.

Solid management principles should not be violated.[20] This is the way to interpret Angela Merkel's hardening stand against a wild and uncontrollable debt sharing in Euroland. The attitude she has adopted makes sense. She understands what lies behind the different requests for "more money" and will not move till member states receiving the bailout have a responsible attitude. This, most evidently, runs against the culture of a *casino society*.

There is no better evidence than the deadly embrace between the banking industry and sovereigns. Big banks have transformed finance into a game of chance through bets using derivative financial instruments. Win or lose, the bosses shower themselves with bonuses, but when they lose they ask for taxpayers' money to avoid bankruptcy and governments are ready to oblige. As for punishment, forget it. The bosses who shower themselves with bonuses are *too big to jail*.

What Merkel essentially says in regard to Euroland's member states, is that Germans, Dutch, and Finns must not pay forever the debts of the big spenders in the Euroland countries. The same reservations also explain ECB's reluctance to be a lender of last resort. Still it:

- Allowed banks to secure funding for three years at 1 percent rather than using the capital market for private funding, and,
- Subsequently, turned a blind eye to the fact that the banks have used the larger part of a trillion euro not to lend but to buy government bonds.

Critics say that what has happened with LTRO is an abdication of central bankers' duties and responsibilities and it leaves the private sector dry of funds. By offering Euroland's banks access to cheap funding on a medium- to long-term basis, the ECB has reduced their pace of deleveraging—which is precisely the opposite of a sound solution.

The background reason may well be that the persons in charge have changed. In late November 2011, right after the dual event of Mario Draghi's appointment as ECB's president and Mario Monti's as Italy's prime minister of a government by technocrats, the *Canard Enchainé* published a prophetic article, "Le Complot des Super Marios." It is worth taking a look at. (Contrary to what many people think, the *Canard Enchainé* is a political, liberal weekly, not a satirical paper even if satire is its basic tool.)

Vil affairiste[21] was this article's underlying theme. The article pointed out that both Marios have been Goldman Sachs executives, and Goldman is the biggest investment bank in the US (and in the world) as well as one of the banks primarily responsible for the deep economic and financial crisis we are in. The two Marios' new mission, the political weekly stated, is to bring Europe back to financial health with a recipe that seems to be a mixture of:

• More debt, and
• More liquidity, but under respectable cover.

The article in the *Canard Enchainé* also reminded its readers that inter alia Goldman Sachs helped the Greek government in hiding its deficits. Moreover, right after he started to work in the investment bank's London office, Draghi signed an article with a Nobel Prize winner that justified the practice of dissimulation of debts. With this the French political paper concluded: "Nothing guarantees that the two Marios and their consorts are today for Europe more a good placement of values than a toxic product."

The European political leaders, this article says, did not want to refuse Mario Draghi the governorship of ECB because of his Wall Street connections. This is precisely the same position they took toward Lucas Papademos, a former Greek prime minister, who was the governor of the Bank of Greece between 1994 and 2002, and allegedly collaborated with Goldman Sachs in hiding big chunks of Greek public debt.

Two years later, the revelation that the governor of the Bank of Italy and boss of its powerful Ispettorato, Mario Draghi, turned a blind eye to the multibillion euro scam of Banca Monte dei Paschi di Sienna, Italy's third largest, reinforced that feeling (see section 6).

As for Monti, he became a celebrity for having opposed, as competition commissioner of the European Community,[22] the merger of General Electric and Honeywell, for which he was nicknamed "the Saddam Hussein of business," and for having imposed an antitrust fine of €479 million (worth $750 million at the time) on Microsoft, for which he was baptized by the *Financial Times* as "the antitrust czar." In 2004, as the French government poured taxpayers' money into Alstom to save it from bankruptcy, Monti got tangled with Nicolas Sarkozy, who was then minister of finance.

Once he became prime minister and took upon himself the task of balancing the budget of the Italian republic, Monti made a 180 degree turn in his aversion for subsidies and monopolies. Suddenly, subsidies to the budget of the Italian state through German taxpayer money became sacrosanct (see also in chapter 3 the twists of the June 28–29, 2012, Brussels "summit" and the Rome meeting that preceded it). To the Italian government[23] inflation is to life what tomato sauce is to spaghetti, said a critic.

In an article in the *International Herald Tribune*, Hugo Dixon expressed similar concepts in a milder form: The markets and the banks have jumped for joy in response to all this liquidity unleashed by the €1 trillion LTRO by the ECB. Italy and Spain rejoiced as their borrowing costs dropped and their banks took cheap cash from the ECB and invested it in their governments' bonds—making a profit on the round trip."

Critics asked some rather simple questions: "Is Draghi justified by his mandate in spending ECB funds as he does?" (The answer is far from being unambiguously positive.) "Have these spending extravaganzas brought confidence into the market?" (To this the answer is negative though Draghi has his fans.) Or was big spending needed to make some people (heads of state, bankers, traders) feel good?

Money is, of course, the central theme and, contrary to what the big spenders think, money does not grow on trees. If evidence is needed that handouts of large sums without appropriate controls are a waste as well as counterproductive, it has been provided in December 2011 and February 2012 with the Long-Term Refinancing Operations. The trillion euros waves of money injected into the banking system by the European Central bank helped only in the very short term. Banks in Spain and in Italy have hundreds of billions of bad loans on their books. With LTRO,

- The *liability* side of their balance sheets continues to grow, and
- There are less and less *assets* with strong valuations on those balance sheets.

The same is true at the level of national economies. Part, but only part, of the underlying disagreements and prevailing confusion among European politicians,[24] is due to the fact that as far as agreement on restructuring the balance sheet of each member state is concerned, it is simple utopia to say that "expenses will be reduced sometime in the future." Expenses will not be reduced without identifying the expense chapters that:

- Must be closed down altogether, or
- Be subjected to very severe cuts.[25]

This should have been the subject of the "summits." Careful observers however comment that all one hears are big words, empty of content. Critics also question whether Euroland's member states will reinforce the excessive deficit procedure by accepting "automatic consequences" if they breach the 3 percent ceiling. It is always easier to talk of the longer term than of solutions whose deliverable must be available in a short time,[26] such as fiscal discipline in crisis-ridden Euroland.

5. Mario Draghi and the Monte dei Paschi di Siena Scam[27]

The first people to reveal that the world's oldest bank (founded in 1472), and Italy's third largest, was cooking its books were not the bank's senior executives, regulators at the Bank of Italy, or independent auditors (KPMG), though all of them had a duty to keep the place honest. Those who rang the alarm bells were journalists, based on documents from another bank suggesting there had been a scam with derivative financial instruments.

Financial scandals are interesting not only because they reveal the honesty of people at "high places," but also because they tell us a great deal about the capacity of a company—and most particularly of a big bank—to reform itself, raise needed capital, make profits, create jobs, reward its investors, and secure its place in the financial market. There exist disturbing parallels between today's scandals and the corruption uncovered by prosecutors over the last three decades, not in one but in scores of big banks.

At Monte dei Paschi, investigators and prosecutors are confronted by complex financial transactions that appear to have been devised for the purpose of concealing losses incurred as a consequence of gambling with the bank's money. There has been, as well, plenty of poor governance in Italy's third largest bank, as leftwing politicians exploited its treasury like a cash cow to consolidate their hold on the city of Siena.

- Theoretically, at the start of 2013, the Monte dei Paschi had €224 billion ($266 billion) in assets.
- Practically, how much of these "assets" was real money and how much murky deals hiding derivatives losses, nobody would venture to say.

But there has been agreement on *responsibilities.* Mario Draghi led the Bank of Italy from December 2005—when he replaced the then governor Antonio Fazio—till late 2011 when he succeeded Jean-Claude

Trichet as president of the European Central Bank. According to what has been reported, under Draghi's watch, the Bank of Italy first became concerned about Monte dei Paschi's finances when in 2008 it reviewed a bank takeover.[28]

This was an alarm bell signaling to the reserve institution and bank inspectorate to be extra careful in auditing the commercial bank's balance sheet. Indeed, the 2008 findings led to two full inspections of Monte dei Paschi, starting in 2010—but, curiously enough, Banca d'Italia notified prosecutors only in March 2012, taking years to bring the scam to light and from there to justice.

The fact that murky deals are overlooked while the Bank of Italy is alerted, is suspicious. Further damaging to Draghi's reputation as supervisor and controller of financial entities (a duty he automatically assumed as governor of Bank of Italy) is that he did not make Monte dei Paschi disclose that information on the scam. Neither did he call the prosecutors. Only in 2012, under Ignazio Visco, Draghi's successor as governor of the central bank, did Italian prosecutors open a criminal investigation that included looking into the Bank of Italy's role.

Critics say that the Monte dei Paschi financial-and-political scam totally disqualifies Mario Draghi, as president of the European Central Bank, from being the superregulator of Euroland's banking industry. If he could not do a clean job in his own country that he presumably knew well, how could he be successful in:

- Transborder bank control over 17 different jurisdictions, and
- Nearly as many different organizational procedures, as well as languages.

Furthermore, as one piece of bad news never comes alone, there exists another financial scam that, as critics see it, is a classical case of a banking regulator turning a blind eye. In 2007 under Draghi's watch, Monte dei Paschi paid a high (and totally unjustified) premium for Antonveneta, a banking group based in Venice. Monte dei Paschi bought Antonveneta from Santander, a Spanish bank, for a cool €9 billion (then $12 billion). But Santander had forked out only €6.6 billion ($8.8 billion) to buy Antonveneta a few months earlier.

Now Italian prosecutors are investigating if kickbacks account, at least in part, for the extraordinary difference characterizing these two acquisition prices for the same financial institution within a short timeframe, the second having taken place under depressed market conditions but at a much higher price. Where did the €2.4 billion ($3.2 billion) go?

The early December 2011 so-called last-chance summit, supposedly organized to save the euro, also documented the persistence of significant differences of opinion among the main EU member states. It is nobody's secret that the relationship between Britain and France has been, for some time, characterized by mistrust on each side.

It is difficult to say how the bout of accusation and counteraccusations started, except that politicians in London and Paris traded several barbs up to the time David Cameron, the British prime minister, voted against the intergovernmental treaty, as he found himself between a rock and a hard place. If he abandoned London's City, the Tory party would have abandoned him. Immediately, however, his Brussels colleagues accused him that his veto did not allow a change to the Lisbon Treaty.[29]

The same thing happens with global summits. For example, in the late February 2012 gathering at Mexico City, G20 chiefs of state representing the world's leading economies *deferred* key decisions once again as they awaited more Euroland action to fight the old continent's debt crisis. They also soft-pedaled till they received confirmation that in the future the weight of different countries in the IMF reflects the developing world's financial might. These same themes were again debated in the course of the G20 "summit" of chiefs of state in Los Cabos, in mid-June 2012, without specific results other than the increase in IMF's war chest.

Whether we talk of G20, G8, EU, or Euroland, the "summits" pattern is totally negative as if the people participating in them are powerless. The usual EU political line that "summits" improve European integration is a red herring. "I have always found the word 'Europe' on the lips of those who wanted something from others which they dared not demand in their own names!" said Otto von Bismarck 133 years ago, in 1880.

6. Crisis Meetings of Chiefs of State without Tangible Results

"Greece is not the headline anymore," said one of the EU chiefs of state who, on March 1 and 2, 2012, participated in still another Brussels "summit." This has been only half true, as one of the most important decisions taken during that meeting was about Greece, confirming the €130 billion ($171 billion) of the second rescue package divided into two tiers:

- The first, of up to €35 billion ($46 billion), got immediate approval.

This was scheduled to be made available without delay, earmarked for settling the accounts with creditors in the so-called private sector involvement (PSI) deal and recapitalizing Greek banks deeply hurt by its

73.5 percent haircut. This supposedly private initiative by bondholders of Greek public debt severely punished private sector creditors (banks and other investors) while leaving official creditors untouched.

- The second part consisted of the balance of €95 billion ($125 billion) with disbursement to be decided on a later day depending on several factors.

Interviewed by CNN, the Swedish prime minister said that Greece still needs to do more to get itself out of the crisis.[30] In another interview held the same day, the Czech prime minister commented that Europe is made of diversity and he does not believe a fiscal streamlining across the board is doable. At the same time, however, he expressed his disappointment because the second Greek bailout had taken a weak position on the important theme of how a country should manage its debt.

According to financial analysts, a number of statements that followed the March 1—2, 2012, Brussels "summit" left much to be desired in terms of reporting what was going on during the different meetings. Most important, in their opinion, was the fact that decisions being made did not truly eliminate the risk of financial contagion. The risk was and is still present.

A second decision made during that meeting required that Euroland funds from the €130 billion earmarked to pay debt servicing costs be set aside in an escrow account. In that way they could not be used to beef up the general budget of the Greek government. And while banks hurt by the PSI made provisions to reflect the 73.5 percent haircut to net present value, important issues did remain, notably how the small number of private debt holders who refused the "voluntary" debt reduction would be forced to accept.

Even if the participants in the early March 2012 Brussels summit felt that the Greek debt crisis had been taken care of (which was not true by any means), they could not forget that the situation in Italy and Spain was unstable, and the region's financial system could be dragged down by its overindebted member states. "We have not exited the economic crisis but we are turning the page," said Nicolas Sarkozy, the then French president. "The strategy we put in place is bearing fruit."[31] Really?

Also in the course of this early March 2012 summit, European Union members approved new fiscal rules to curb government borrowing, expressing confidence that "the worst of the crisis was over" (a false estimate). But before the ink of Spain's signature on the accord sealed in that particular EU summit was dry, Mariano Rajoy, the Spanish prime minister, delivered the bad news: Spain could not live within the implied debt limit for 2012. Rajoy made no apologies for his defiance, saying that the 2012 deficit target was no longer realistic given the country's sinking economy.

Mariano Rajoy also disclosed that he had not informed fellow leaders or the European Commission, the EU's executive arm, of his plans, saying *he had been under no obligation to do so* (emphasis added). "This is a sovereign decision that Spain has taken," the prime minister told reporters after the summit.[32] In one stroke, this statement turned to ashes any sense of coordination in Euroland, and also explained why the EU had been such a failure.

Every European Union chief of state wants to be a prima donna in common decisions, but common decisions have to be observed by the others, not by him, because he is the leader of an independent nation. Hence, even though it had been a part of the common accords, Spain decided to breach the EU goals. In the words of its prime minister, Spain expected the 2012 deficit to be 5.8 percent of gross domestic product, well above 4.4 percent, the level it had previously agreed with the European Commission. (By July 2012, even the 5.8 per cent self-imposed goal upper limit had been exceeded.)

No wonder that Spain's plight had become a growing source of worry for European officials in the run-up to the next "summits." Bending supposedly "ironclad" budget rules so soon after their introduction tarnishes the credibility of the EU and of its "summits." To make matters worse, the European Commission has been pressing other countries, including Belgium and Hungary, to correct their finances but Spanish behavior makes this pressure look like a laughing matter.

"He seems to have forgotten there are some strict rules," an EU official said. "It makes no sense to declare right at the start that the deficit-reduction goals aren't valid anymore," commented Angela Merkel, Germany's chancellor. Merkel had probably expected the coming anticlimax as, prior to the Rajoy feux d'artifice, she cautioned that Euroland governments had to use what remained of the breathing space to restore their credibility in the financial markets. She had also pressed the point that Euroland governments must act on three fronts:

- With fiscal discipline to control borrowing,
- With institutional reform to improve their capacity to act, and
- With structural reform to boost growth and competitiveness.

During the same March 1–2, 2012, Brussels "summit," Mario Draghi, the ECB president, was reported telling political leaders that the recovery remained fragile, urging them not to let up their efforts. Yet this is precisely what they did, judging by the contents of another Brussels "summit" that took place nearly four months later, on June 28–29, 2012.

Theoretically, but only theoretically, the purpose of all this bickering at the different "summits" is to save the euro. This theory, however, is skin-thin. The real reason behind the crisis meetings and "summits of last chance" is that each member state wants to contribute the least possible to the common purse but take the most out of it. It is a show:

- Of selfishness,
- Of lack of concrete results, and
- Of propensity to continue profligate policies.

The cash cow is supposed to be Germany, and evidently Germans reject this role. After all, the per capita public debt in Germany is a notch higher than Euroland's average. Let's first recall the outstanding debt of the larger Euroland countries, translating it thereafter into a per capita debt:

- Italy: €2.1 trillion
- Germany: €2.0 trillion
- France: €1.9 trillion
- Spain: €900 billion

Correspondingly, the per capita public debt is:

- Italy: €38,180
- Germany: €24,390
- France: €29,000
- Spain: €28,350

The highest per capita public debt in Euroland, and unaffordable for that matter, is in Greece. It stands at €39,000. Note that the difference between the public debt of Greece and Italy (per capita) is only 2 percent.

Published statistics indicate that the average per capita public debt for Euroland is €25,000. This is not necessarily accurate because Euroland's public debt stands at €8.35 trillion and its population at 310 million, giving an average per capita of €26,930.

Nevertheless, because what is important is the order of magnitude, not precision, either of these two Euroland averages will do. Interestingly enough, Germany is below the average but not by much. Germany is hardly the country that can afford to pay for the public debt of other common currency members, unless it gets overindebted.

The per capita public debt averages look bleak, and they are so. However, when compared to the American per capita public debt, Euroland's averages shine up, because the US stands at €38,500 (according to published statistics), that is, at the level of Italy and Greece, Euroland's most indebted member states.

Order of magnitude statistics play an important role in analysis. In this particular case they document three things. First, that the Stability and Growth Pact has been a joke. Second, if the monitoring of public deficits of Euroland's member states has been a scam, the same will happen with the touted monitoring of fiscal policy. Third, the formerly "rich countries" have been singularly unable to exercise budgetary discipline.

7. When the Economy Is Stalling, the Field Is Open to Folklore

The bickering and horse trading taking place in the EU's and in Euroland's "summits," are evidence of a morose economic environment. The probability that the different deals being made will not lead to concrete results is augmented by the fact that a lot of funding has to be done to get them off the ground. The first big question therefore is: Will the European Central Bank be pulled into the storm of these unpayable debts by member countries?

With Mario Draghi at the helm, theoretically at least, the European Central Bank wants to make money cheaper, thereby facilitating the task of governments that want to borrow. Practically, through covert ways, it also buys the bonds of Euroland countries that are at or near bankruptcy. (This became evident as far back as early December 2011 with ECB's sovereign bond purchases in excess of €205 billion. Today, in all likelihood, the corresponding losses on these bonds are in excess of the ECB's original capital.)

The next crucial question, which is not even addressed in the different "summits," is for how long will the public be patient with the mismanagement of the EU and the euro's growing risks. Anecdotal evidence suggests that three out of four German citizens believe that they would have been better off if the euro had not seen the light. In Holland and Finland, too, powerful centrifugal forces exist.

For evident reasons, the reaction of weaker economies is different. Polls in France and Italy, which asked common citizens if they would like to continue with the euro, gave interesting outcomes. In Italy, which is near bankruptcy, 56 percent of the people answered "yes" to the question "Do you like the euro?" But in France, where the common citizen doesn't think that his country's economy approaches the precipice, the "yes" answer got only 36 percent.

Public opinion can, of course, change, as in Western countries today the majority of citizens are not emotionally attached to any one position. But people start having had enough of persistent mismanagement at both national and regional levels. Initiatives aimed to make the old continent a better place have been among the worst planned and executed in Western history. Among other negatives, this has given wings to folklore.

In the background of recent folklore has been the fact that France[33] lost its AAA sovereign debt rating. In a newspaper interview, Christian Noyer, the governor of Banque de France, commented that, based on economic fundamentals, the credit rating agencies should first downgrade Britain because it has higher deficits, more debt, bigger inflation, and less growth than France. François Fillon, the then French prime minister, supported this argument.

The answer came swiftly. In Britain, Mervyn King, the governor of the Bank of England, made some downbeat observations about the health of the single currency. Then, George Osborne, the chancellor of the exchequer, outraged the French by directly comparing their economy with that of Greece.

Christian Noyer answered that the British were ill-advised to weigh in with a series of unflattering assessments about the health of the French economy. François Baroin, the then French finance minister, followed up when he said France's economic situation was preferable to Britain's, and the loss of the AAA rating did not make France a peripheral country.

Many EU observers enjoyed the exchanges. In London, people close to David Cameron declared that he rises above the attacks from Paris. One aide said: "It's not something we are troubled about at all. We are fully confident that the policies we are adopting are the right ones and that's why we have a triple A rating."[34]

Forgotten in the folklore is the fact that credit rating agencies have to be watchful because at the end of the day a country's debt burden determines its creditworthiness. A higher debt:

- Requires governments to raise taxes simply to service interest payments, and
- Absorbs a huge amount of tax money in debt servicing—money that could have been used in innovation, education, and health care.[35]

In addition, many European countries suffer from low growth. Britain and France have similar levels of gross and net debt and a similar burden of interest payments. Britain has longer maturities on its debt, which is important in the current crisis because it makes it less vulnerable to rising interest rates, but its fiscal deficit is higher. In short, *match null.*

There exists as well an illusion France and Britain share between themselves and with America: the illusion of *riches* and *grandeur*. Today, the worst lie Western politicians can say, and citizens tend to believe, is to repeat the illusion that Western countries are "rich." They are not. Quite to the contrary, they are indebted at levels unprecedented in the last 200 years.

Few politicians have the brains to understand that, and the honesty to say so. Harold Macmillan, the late British prime minister, was one. "Mr Khrushchev," Macmillan said in a meeting with the Soviet Union's CEO, "England is no longer able to take an independent stand on issues of international politics. It used to be that Great Britain was the ruler of the seas and could determine policy towards Europe and the whole world. But that era has passed."[36]

The majority of politicians, however, lack Macmillan's honesty and penetrating mind, which reduces their ability to make realistic appraisals. They are deprived of the strength of personality that permits them to say aloud what they think. Hence, the empty "summits" that follow one after another with increasing frequency, and the make-believe that it is possible to change the current depressing economic and financial situation by making promises while keeping things as they are. The present system is:

- Too old in concept,
- Too unstuck from reality, and
- Too inefficient in its methods.

With the possible exception of Germany (and even this is not sure), America's and Europe's current status brings to mind the last years of communism before its fall. Paraphrasing Oscar Wilde, the tragedy of *déclinisme* is not that Western countries are no more rich and grand, but that they live in the utopia of old glory.[37]

Right after his confirmation, François Hollande, the new French president, flew to Berlin to convince Merkel on the issue of Eurobonds (chapter 4). He did not. More bad news was in the pipeline. On July 3, 2012, La Cour des Comptes, the French government's audit authority, published its findings: The French government would need an extra amount of €6 to 10 billion in 2012 to close its books,[38] and €33 billion in 2013 for precisely the same purpose.[39]

The message could not be more explicit. Deficits are unsettling many plans and other Euroland members have no money to throw around.

In addition, even *if* money was abundant, it would not have helped the unemployment issue all by itself. "More money" thrown at the problem will not create jobs. With the exception of Germany, Holland, Finland, and, to a lesser extent, Britain, European countries have not adapted themselves to the global economy. Therefore, their employment is clobbered by globalization's forces to the tune of an average 40 percent unemployment among those under 30 years of age.[40]

The irony is that youths who today suffer from lack of employment have been co-responsible because (as already stated several times) the education they choose—essentially soft subjects—is not at all in demand. By contrast, technical skills are in short supply. One in three German companies is reporting a shortage of skilled workers, double the number in 2011, according to the German chamber of trade and industry (DIHK).[41]

Let's look at this issue from a different perspective. The economic crisis alone would not have created the currently estimated 17.8 million Europeans without a job, statistically representing 11.2 percent of the working population.[42] The crisis has amplified the fact that Europe is no more the source of innovation and new ideas that are decisive for jobs, productivity, and economic growth. A structural change is most urgently needed, but embedded interests fight against it and resistance is fierce.

None of the existing capitalist or socialist theories and their offshoots[43] provide any help in confronting the problems the West at large, and most particularly Euroland, faces these days. As if this was not enough, the theories behind capitalism and socialism have failed. The former did so twice: in 1929–1933, and nearly eight decades later in 2007–2013. As for socialism, the crash of the Soviet Union (after seven decades of socialism) and China's switch from communism to state capitalism nicely document that the theory that underpinned these regimes rested on weak, unproved theories (and terror), ill-thought-out implementation, and poorly planned governance.

With hindsight, capitalism, socialism, and communism made the same fatal error: their deep misunderstanding of how individual and collective human nature works.

3

The Nineteenth "Summit's" Miracle Weapons: June 28–29, 2012

1. Throwing the Dice in Brussels

The politicians who nowadays run the different Western governments have not necessarily understood that if their electoral promises materialize, the result would be catastrophic particularly for their country. The economic realities are those that they are and it is counterproductive to deny them. Therefore, it is better to press on the decelerator of debt issuance than on the accelerator, as the latter leads straight to bankruptcy.

Even a US bankruptcy is no more off the table. Interviewed on July 2, 2012, by *Bloomberg News*, David Cote, chairman of Honeywell, had a word of advice for the US government. The monitor asked him: "As a successful businessman, given Honeywell's stellar results, if you were running the government what would you have done to redress the American economy?" Without a glimpse of hesitation, Cote answered: "I will declare bankruptcy."

The bureaucrats of the European Union don't think in the same way. For them it is unimportant to clean up the system, debts included, so that the economy starts growing again. At the top of their priorities is the preservation of the status quo with all the benefits it has in store. To keep change under lock and key, from time to time they come up with some big concept that, they know in advance, will be most difficult to materialize. On June 26, 2012, on behalf of the European Commission, Manuel Barroso, its president, proposed three issues to be taken up and acted upon by the "summit" of June 28–29, 2012.

1. Banking Union

The subject of a banking union in Euroland (section 6) was first raised by Mariano Rajoy, the Spanish prime minister, when he saw that the salvage of his country's credit institutions had reached an impasse. Banking union is an ill-defined concept, most particularly in terms of the prerequisites to be met before it can materialize. It is also highly unlikely that the 27 member states of the EU will accept a *unique* regulator with the right to look into their banks' books as this constitutes a breach of sovereignty (more on this later).

2. Fiscal Union

This has been defined in brief as including budget enforcement, which is only part of the problem. Here again, details are missing, and as for the "big plan" there is only a slim probability that EU member states will accept somebody from a supranational authority looking over their shoulder—let alone forcing their hand on how to make their budget, including what to incorporate in it and what to leave out.

Besides that, a fiscal union includes much more than balancing the budget. Its remit is the whole catchment area of what should be taxed, and by how much. Other issues, too, come into it. Therefore, it is not for reasons of absentmindedness that the communiqué from the June 28–29, 2012, Brussels "summit" spoke of a *budgetary union* (whatever that means) and not of a fiscal union.

3. Political Union

If the definition of the previous two goals is wanting, the one concerning a political union ranges from chaos to uncertainty. Significantly, the aforementioned communiqué makes no mention of one and only one parliament for the entire EU, which should be endowed with EU-wide full legislative powers like the US Congress.[1] Neither has anything been said about the pan-European election of a president with full executive powers, also along the US model.

Curiously enough, when, in Brussels parlance, there is talk of a "political union," emphasis is placed almost exclusively on the "mutualization of debt," which means passing the debts of the profligate to those who have been working harder—thereby annihilating the savings of the industrious citizen. And as one catastrophe never comes alone, the next Brussels-made claim to convergence toward political union is that of Eurobonds—which is anathema to the Germans.[2]

To make matters more complex, even those political leaders who are rather favorably inclined toward some form of political union are not going to have an easy time convincing their voters. François Hollande, for instance, should know that he will not be able to pull the rabbit of a political union out of the hat, even if he wants to. On June 27, 2012, in an interview of French deputies along the whole political spectrum, left to right, by Television Suisse Romande (TSR), opinions ranged:

- From "The French public rejected political union in the famous referendum,"
- To "There is no question to go through political union to find a solution to economic problems,"
- And "It is beyond doubt that the euro is dead, so why bother resurrecting it?"

The French government itself seems to be divided on this subject. Some like Pierre Moscovici, the minister of finance, are not against giving up a little sovereignty to deblock the use of Euroland's funds. Others, led by Laurent Fabius, the foreign minister, are against such a move. They do not want to hear anything about bending French sovereignty even if, according to the pros, this would benefit Euroland's economy.

Barroso's plan has not been the only game in town. Besides it, Brussels saw another initiative with more political savvy and the goal of trapping Angela Merkel into agreeing that Germany must pay. Allegedly, this was engineered by Herman Van Rompuy,[3] the president of the European Council, working closely with Mario Monti.[4]

Anecdotal evidence suggests that in June 2012, Mario Monti, the Italian prime minister, went to Brussels with a plan. Italy and Spain would block all agreements in Euroland until their colleagues, including the German chancellor, allowed the bailout funds to provide a great deal of immediate support for the two countries.

- The stated goal was to relieve their high borrowing rates.
- Insiders suggested that this was only a smoke screen and behind it was relief for the whole debt burden of the two countries that amounted to €3 trillion ($3.9 trillion).

This was a bold approach that seems to have taken the uninitiated by surprise. In its way it confirmed what several political analysts believed: that the players of the European Executive in Brussels have many tricks up their sleeve. In the opinion of these same political analysts, *if* summiteers in Brussels continue with trickery *then* the situation in the European Union is unlikely to improve.

Besides trickery there has been confusion. An example of that confusion is the fact that (as we will see in section 2) on June 28–29, 2012,

Euroland's presidents and prime ministers agreed that as long as they comply with the European Commission *consolidation targets*, member countries can receive support from bailout funds without agreeing to additional austerity measures. Lost from the radar screen was the fact that "consolidation targets" have been awfully manipulated in the past and this will continue happening.

Markets rose on this news, but the euphoria proved short-lived and rightly so since the Brussels "summit" set no measurable goals for consolidation targets and established no penalties for missing them. For instance, if Spain and Italy miss them, there will still be pressure for a full bailout program, which will be way underfinanced since it will take until mid-2014 for the ESM (chapter 4) to be able to use its maximum resources of €500 billion. Neither is that amount enough to salvage Italy and Spain whose total public debt is in the trillions.

An even greater uncertainty surrounds the gaping holes in the treasury of Spanish banks. Pseudo-stress tests and studies commissioned to consultancies have provided no reliable clue of how deep the holes are in their finances, because the banks are masters in keeping the most vital information close to their chest. On October 26, 2012, Bankia, the badly wounded, third biggest bank in Spain, declared a €7 billion ($9.1 billion) loss just as Euroland was preparing a bailout plan for Spanish credit institutions.[5]

2. Monti's Delight and Merkel's Sorrow?

François Mitterrand, the late French president, once said: "You get out of ambiguity only to your own disadvantage." The Brussels "summit" of June 18–19, 2012, has been a master of ambiguity, as if it had followed Mitterrand's dictum to the letter. The chiefs of state decided upon some general lines, which gave rise to delights and sorrows. In addition, it has been officially announced that the agreement they reached must still be:

- Made more precise, and
- Completed in its clauses.

Either and both points mean greater detail, and that's where divergent interests—all the way from financial matters to organization, staffing, and management of a complex multinational programs—show up and clash. Conflicts of interest are rarely visible in the general lines but they become powerful factors in the course of subsequent negotiations.

But is the summit's real outcome worthy of the attention it attracted? Did all major Euroland member states move toward tying their fates more inextricably together? Or were there excuses and pretexts?

In most peoples' minds a key question is how far Germany's position shifted from seemingly ruling out any massive help to Italy and Spain to a proactive stance with new money. Insisting that any assistance must be through the funds already in place (EFSF, ESM) is no evidence of a change in position. That's money already earmarked to go down the drain.

Moreover, Angela Merkel conceded nothing on the need of discipline *if* it were to come up with new aid. Explicit conditions and the institution of controls remained in the framework, an example being the decision to give the European Central Bank power over the regulation and supervision of Euroland's banks.

The devil's question of course is how much of their sovereignty will Euroland's member countries give up to make a reality out of this vaguely projected cross-border banking supervision by a unique Euroland regulator. For the time being, an answer to this query is not available. All that can be said is that both the longer term and the shorter term are important.

This is the crux of the debate that took place in Brussels, at end of June 2012, between chiefs of state, and led to the so-called Troubled Countries Relief Program (TCRP, section 3). The TCRP addresses itself to 13 countries of Euroland sharing the "troubled" label and having asked for relief for the sovereign and/or the country's banks. Those expected to advance the money are, as usual, Germany, Holland, Finland, and probably Austria.

- *If* this is indeed what Monti and company had in mind,
- *Then* the June 28–29, 2012, decision is one-sided.

As a Swiss market analyst commented in the course of our discussion, the TCRP decision was taken just to relieve the pessimism that reigns in Euroland. The analyst added that the financial markets at large would have loved to see the adoption of Eurobonds but this was not even mentioned as a possibility—which means that there has been no definite decision on deficits.

"A great deal of work remains to be done," the analyst said. "For instance whether the rescue fund will be used to buy Italian bonds is still unclear." The Swiss analyst also believes that interest on Italian bond is not going to drop permanently because the guarantor is the Italian state. (With Eurobonds it would have been different as the transparent lender of last resort would have been Germany.)

According to opinions expressed by other financial analysts, the talk of giving the EFSF and ESM banking license to boost their firepower—allegedly one of the issues discussed in the late June 2012 Brussels "summit"—remained just talk. As for the banking union, lots of uncertainties continue to prevail and *if* some of the chiefs of state rush for a decision *then* the banking union will be stillborn.

As they knew that they may be asked to foot the bill, the Germans were uneasy about what they believe to be *euro-concessions*. This explains why while the June 28–29, 2012, "summit" decided to allow that the two bail-out funds (EFSF and ESM) are tapped more easily and used to help ailing banks without requiring the involvement of national governments—but-there are still conditions to be met. No carte blanche has been issued to anybody or any subject.

If this opinion, which is shared by a lot of financial analysts, is retained, *then* Merkel did not deserve the shower of criticism in her homeland, as many Germans felt that the chancellor and her government have over-stepped their bounds. The reaction of common citizens was swift and negative. Several hundreds gathered on a lawn outside the German par-liament ahead of the vote on the ESM:

- Demanding that it be postponed, and
- Decrying that it would cost them their rights.

The German press did not treat Angela Merkel kindly. She was "a hostage of the South" for *Der Spiegel*, while *Die Welt* judged the Brussels "summit" as a unique defeat. The chancellor made risky concessions, said the *Stern*, while *Süddeutsche Zeitung* saluted the success of Rajoy and Monti (essentially in trapping Merkel) in the small hours of June 29, 2012, after the marathon talk in Brussels.

Monti, Rajoy, and Hollande were not the only parties Angela Merkel had to confront on June 29, 2012. That same day she addressed the Bundestag and to carry the day she needed the votes to approve two crisis-related measures:

- The European fiscal compact, and
- Euroland's rescue fund, the European Stability Mechanism.

On the one hand, she was lucky to get enough backing from the opposition Social Democrats and Greens to obtain the necessary two-thirds majority she needed. On the other hand, she failed to secure even a simple majority among her own coalition[6] as many parliamentarians were upset with the change in rules governing the ESM during the Brussels "summit."

On the Italian side there has been immense joy, at least among the government's negotiators. Headlines wrote of "Monti's delight." What essentially Monti obtained, with Van Rompuy's help, is that if the ESM were used to buy Italian bonds at auction, this would come with a lighter set of conditions than under current rules. That's hardly the big bazooka for the Italian economy. (That concession is subject to an ambiguity or misunderstanding as it was called into question on the second day of the summit.) In addition:

- German officials were adverse to Mario Monti's public claims of condition-free aid, and
- Finnish and Dutch officials expressed their dissatisfaction at the festivity, insisting there had been no changes whatsoever to Euroland's financial roadmap.

"It is absolutely clear that all the decisions taken last night were under the explicit understanding that the conditionality would remain unchanged," said a Dutch official. A senior Finnish official added: "They haven't been changed at all."[7] But Mario Monti cried "victory" in the (false?) hope of unloading trillions of debt, while the one who got the cash, to the tune of €100 billion to beef up his banks, was Mariano Rajoy.

Even this, however, is not sure[8] because it is subject to instituting a Euroland-wide bank supervision authority under ECB. It took two years to put in place the European Banking Authority (EBA) in Brussels, and it did not have to cross the charged wires of nationalism. Why will the new bank supervisory authority be put in place faster?

Diplomats said that the plot to trap Merkel was not engineered at the last minute. It saw the light a week earlier when Monti played host to a discordant "mini-summit" meeting in Rome with Merkel, Hollande, and Rajoy. Euroland watchers understood that Italy would arrive in Brussels prepared to play its hand.

The opportunity presented itself when the Brussels "summit" meeting reached an impasse late on Thursday evening (June 28, 2012). Then, in line with their plan, Monti and Rajoy insisted there could be no agreement on a growth pact (wanted by Hollande) without accord on a much broader range of issues. For evident reasons this included short-term measures to shore up the Italian and Spanish economies.

The trap worked, but analysts suggested that for Monti and Rajoy this was a Pyrrhic victory. Regardless of Monti's and Van Rompuy's interpretation, and in spite of the fact that in the early hours of June 29, 2012, they might have taken Merkel for a ride, without Dutch and Finnish acquiescence, if they choose to avail themselves of bond-buying aid they will still be faced with a full-scale monitoring program from:

- The European Commission, and
- The European Central Bank.

It is an illusion to think that some countries have the special horn and, after having asked for aid, this will come as manna from heaven not requiring the direct oversight of the "troika" that now monitors Greece and Portugal.[9] If anything, by making banks direct recipients of Euroland aid, the sophistication of the control mechanism should increase at least two notches. Short of that, the aid money will be wasted.

* * *

It did not take long for Germany, Holland, and Finland to establish that something went wrong with the late-night agreements at the end of June 2012. This led to the Helsinki meeting of September 25, 2012, between the finance ministers of the three countries, and plenty of people suddenly discovered to their horror that Germany will not allow Spain to dump the risk of its banks on to the European Stability Mechanism. The fact of the bottomless pit in the Spanish banks' finances is no more a secret and those who give the money would like to see a *sovereign guarantee* on the ESM's and ECB's bank recapitalizations.

Following this September 25, 2012, meeting in Helsinki, the German, Dutch, and Finnish finance ministers said in a common statement that a plan to move bad bank assets off the books of struggling eurozone governments would not apply to "legacy assets." This was a thinly veiled reference to the huge imbalances in the treasuries of the aforementioned banks. Two weeks later, on October 10, 2012, the IMF expressed the opinion that European banks may have to sell $4.5 trillion (euro 3.5 trillion) of assets.[10]

Although the Helsinki meeting did not clarify how the new principles of bank recapitalization would apply to current cases, the communiqué also called into question whether the scheme would apply to Spain's most troubled banks, which were scheduled to be bailed out with Euroland money. One of the thorny questions is how to distribute existing losses before moving toward a bailout of Spain's teetering domestic banking industry. When that deal was struck without anybody doing his or her homework at a high-stakes summit on June 28–29, 2012, it was hailed as a *game changer*, but it subsequently turned into a mare's nest.

3. Troubled Countries Relief Program

Established in the course of the Brussels "summit" of June 28–29, 2012, the Troubled Countries Relief Program (TCRP) is supposed to work on the basis of distributed responsibility among Euroland's governments. This has been the intention but no one really knows how it will be done.

The engineering still needs to be defined. No wonder, therefore, that economists, analysts, and journalists have asked themselves:

- Is the TCRP a breakthrough, or some old measure under a different name?

Asked for his opinion, one of the better-known Euroland observers answered that while it is still too early to say, he does not think that this distributed responsibility, *if* it is worked out, will be equitable or without frictions. What he could say till the details become known is that the result of that oral (and preliminary) TCRP agreement makes the summit's deliverables:

- More than most people expected, but
- Less than what the "troubled countries" need to get back on their feet.

Three things can be stated with a reasonable level of assurance: First, as far as financing is concerned, the European Central Bank will be kept out of the TCRP, and the same is true of the controversial Eurobonds. Neither is part of the deal, though the new European Bank Supervision authority (supposedly with wide cross-border powers) will be placed under the ECB's wings—which may or may not be a good idea.[11]

Second, the main mission of the TCRP is to stop the hemorrhage of the continental European banking industry and separate the banks from the state, breaking their unholy alliance (see section 5). This is easier said than done, not only because it demands plenty of money but also because the main handicap is the absence of a strong political will to go ahead with the trimming of sovereignty *if*:

- The self-wounded banks are recapitalized directly without their sovereign acting as intermediary, and
- The mechanism of bank supervision for all Euroland's banks is cross-border, centralized under the ECB and free of national pressures.[12]

Third, no new money has been authorized for Euroland, at least for the time being. The funds will come from the ESM, which is not yet fully funded and, in any case, ESM money will help the banks only after the Euroland-wide supervisory authority has been instituted and fine-tuned. Till the ESM stands on its own, the EFSF will fill in with financing the TCRP, but the funding rules of the EFSF and ESM are different (see chapter 4).

The fact that the EFSF and ESM don't have the same status does not make things easier. The ESM benefits from priority in the reimbursement of its loans.[13] One of the TCRP details to be worked out is what will happen to the money invested by the EFSF on the recapitalization of wounded banks if one or more of them go bankrupt after having taken the funds.

The funds in the EFSF, as well as in the ESM, are there to help the common cause but in reality they belong to the countries that advanced them. When in early June 2012 the issue was raised that the EFSF money might be used to recapitalize Spanish banks, Finland asked for collateral. The risk that bank recapitalization money will disappear in different deals is in no way minor, neither is it sure that there will be no Ponzi games and other scams.[14]

Since the loan made by the EFSF to, say, Spanish banks is not protected by seniority, the money may disappear through a dry hole. Moreover, who can guarantee that tomorrow there will not be a Spanish Private Sector Involvement (PSI) deal with a haircut of 75.3 percent or higher, as it happened early on in 2012 with Greece.

Already a day after the announcement of the Spanish banks deal made at the Brussels "summit," investors said the measures announced seem to offer more to bank investors than to sovereign bond investors. Private bondholders say they are tired of listening to political rhetoric,[15] pointing out this is only one step toward solving Euroland's woes.

A question raised on June 29, 2012, toward the end of the Brussels "summit," was whether Spain and Italy will benefit from "light controls," as compared to those imposed by the Troika on Greece, Portugal, and Ireland, because of being systemically important. There is no clear answer to this query, nor to the one begging to know the right level of supervision. The lack of appropriate controls essentially means that the EFSF and ESM kiss their money good-bye the very moment they loan it.

But there has been an unofficial answer that states: "Definitely not. There will be the same controls." This forgets that the situation is not so clear because Monti and Van Rompuy stated that Italy will not be subject to any controls. As for Spain, initially the TCRP will address the problem of its banks with the caveats outlined in the preceding paragraphs. Notice also that the IMF is not part of the deal.

Still another issue raised in the June 28–29, 2012, Brussels "summit" is using 1 percent of Euroland's GDP to relaunch the economy. François Hollande took credit for it, but this is not a new issue. Employing 1 percent of GDP to promote some sort of relaunching of the economy, and therefore employment, is relatively old stuff that has been around the corridors of Brussels since early 2011.

Critics say this "1 percent" fell victim to its own imprecision. If nothing was done about it, it is because the program, originally thought to be *the* roadmap, is both complex and lacks detail. The idea is not bad. The challenge is how to go about it, and the June 28–29, 2012, Brussels "summit" did not bring any clarification.

While the results of the late June 2012 Brussels "summit" have been unclear at best, German economists are alarmed by the commitments being made and the fact that these are ill-defined. Led by Professor Hans-Werner Sinn of Munich Institute for Economic Research IFO, in the second week of July 2012, 170 economists published an open letter denouncing the decisions of that "last chance summit."

What the economists said is that these decisions are a step toward a banking union, which means collective liability for the debts of all banks in Euroland. This would mean the citizens of countries that have stronger economies would end up paying the debt of banks in other countries. The gamblers and profligates were rewarded. This is indeed the message this book has brought to the reader's attention on several occasions.

Taxpayers, retirees, and savers in hardworking countries of Euroland will be made liable for backing the debts of other sovereigns, their banks, and their citizens. As the aforementioned letter by 170 economists puts it, this is unacceptable particularly since gigantic losses are foreseeable from financing the southern countries' inflationary economic bubbles.

Neither is the German economy the Rock of Gibraltar that it seemed to be in the course of the last half a dozen years. Its weaknesses have started showing. At 6.8 percent, unemployment has risen and business confidence fluctuates. Stated bluntly, Germany cannot carry the debts of Euroland's sovereigns. In fact when Moody's talks about downgrading Germany by chopping off one of the AAAs, it mentions two reasons:

1. Germany has loaned €350 billion ($425 billion) to Euroland's big spenders. For all practical purposes that money is as good as lost, whether Germany remains part of Euroland or decides that it is better to lick its wounds and get out.
2. The coming global crisis will hit the exporting countries.

The world economy is presently exposed to a synchronized storm which, most likely, will hit the European Union, United States, and China at the same time. This may well be an unprecedented event with great consequences, shaking the creditworthiness of every indebted sovereign and being unforgiving to those who are the most exposed.

In conclusion, what could be retained as the outcome of this June 28–29, 2012, "summit of last chance" is its lack of emphasis on issues that matter the most: money lost in bailouts and handouts. Also lost is the opportunity to learn how not to repeat the same mistake that, like it or not, leads to a financial tsunami. Instead, plenty of attention (and trickery) was directed at Euroland's banking union (section 5), and budgetary union, whose script is still to be written.

4. With Storm Clouds over Euroland, It's No Time for Miracle Weapons

As far as the markets are concerned, expectations have got ahead of themselves. What is done does not look like being enough. No matter how much money is thrown at the problems by Euroland's chiefs of state, the market is disappointed. And while the sovereigns wait for a miracle, a swarm of speculators wait for Euroland's disintegration to make a kill.

The therapy of "more integration" for Euroland has been practically rejected because of nationalism as well as the high costs it might bear—particularly for German taxpayers. And since the current uncertainty cannot continue forever, the alternative solution may well be disintegration of the euro, which would also bring big costs for taxpayers, who may unwillingly be paying for the losses hitting on the balance sheets of Euroland's banks.

Between the black and white alternatives of "more integration" and disintegration are other solutions characterized as tones of gray. The problem is that they require compromises that are hard to come by.

France has traditionally favored an intergovernmental EU, while jealously guarding its budgetary independence. "Today if you are going to give more power to Europe it means giving it to [the European Commission]. No one in France would accept that," said a European parliament deputy of the French Socialist party.[16] Other commentaries, too, about Euroland's future and more specifically the TCRP are worth recording.

- The June 28–29, 2012, summit has tried to address the deep debt challenges facing Spain and Italy, provided that they formally ask for help from the EU, the ECB and IMF. So far they have not.
- Getting the ESM to inject funds directly into the banks is only feasible once the single bank supervisor is in place under the ECB. This will take time and the touted solution of a supercontroller, while national supervisors are retained, will lead to trouble.
- The TCRP looks unlikely to do the trick. The markets continue to believe that both Spain and Italy remain odds-on to end up in full bailout programs.
- Italy cut through Germany's defenses, breaking German resistance to more far-reaching policy responses. But this match is not over yet and time works against Italy.

THE NINETEENTH "SUMMIT" 61

- "I am optimistic, but not optimistic enough to increase my exposure to the peripheral countries," said an investor. This response is gaining ground.
- "I don't think this is anywhere close to a permanent solution; it's a short-term fix," stated another investor. By mid-August 2012 he was proven right.
- The announced plans were the right first step, but there is a lack of detail that could start to worry the market. The market rally may last a day or a week, but would not be more permanent.

There has been a commentary saying that the June 28–29, 2012, Brussels "summit" was planned as fireworks, for the effect it will produce. At the end of the day the substance was missing, but there was intrigue. According to a published account, about a month prior to the Brussels meeting, François Hollande started to prepare an anti-Merkel front with the prime ministers of Spain and Italy. On June 5, 2012, he sent Laurent Fabius, his foreign minister, to Rome, on an exploratory mission.

Back from his meeting with Mario Monti, Fabius is said to have discovered a potential ally in the effort of modifying the power balance in Euroland. "I feel that the Italians are greatly interested in the French proposal on euroland's growth," Fabius stated to the council of ministers on June 6, 2012.[17]

Strengthened by these assurances, on June 14, 2012, Hollande went himself to Rome to meet with Monti. A common (but secret) plan was made: Monti and Rajoy will support Hollande's "growth plan" and the latter will give a hand to Spain and Italy who want Euroland money (read: German, Dutch, and Finish) to recapitalize:

- Their self-wounded banks, and
- Their treasuries as well as those of other profligate and bankrupt member states.

On the night of June 28, 2012, during the Brussels meeting, Monti put pressure saying that he was ready to negotiate till Sunday evening, if needed, in order to get confirmation that the machinery to spend Euroland money is approved. To confuse the countercurrent, he also stated that if he was not satisfied he would block the famous tax on financial transactions (which anyway has trouble seeing the light).[18]

Next morning, June 29, 2012, Hollande supported the Monti thesis and Rajoy joined in. With three "cavaliers" against a lady, Merkel gave in but she obtained an important concession: The European Central Bank will be in charge of controlling Euroland's banks of the banking union (which has been watered down to an ambiguous "supercontrol").

All told, the summit of June 28–29, 2012, solved nothing. Commentaries on its success were deeply misleading and media headlines were wrong. Edward Hugh, a Barcelona-based economist, said that Spain could be compelled to seek a formal rescue as:

- Foreign investors continue to head for the exits, and
- Spanish banks gradually become saturated with domestic government debt.

In Hugh's words: "The normal pattern of these summits is a period of euphoria, but we haven't had that this time."[19] Public differences over the details of the "last chance Brussels summit" have left investors unimpressed. "There seems to be disagreement on the agreement," said Philip Apel, head of interest rate strategy at Henderson Global Investors.[20]

The market's reaction did not wait for long. In less than a week after that "summit," Spanish ten-year composite bond yields were back to more than 7 percent and two-year yields to above 5 percent. The fact that gains quickly turned to losses is another reason why financial analysts think that Spain could be forced to turn to Brussels for help.

Many Euroland observers gave Monti, Hollande, and Rajoy the credit (or blame) for cutting through Merkel's defenses. In this, they were wrong. First, because this was a questionable "victory," and, second, because there were two not three protagonists who secretly worked to light the June 28–29, 2012, fireworks. Their names are Mario Monti and Herman Van Rompuy; the other two were stagehands.

It is not the first time that an Italian and a Belgian led the charge by working in unison. They did so three decades earlier in the famous case of the "avions renifleurs." Developed by geometra Bonassoli, a (supposedly) sophisticated instrument using high technology would have made it possible to pinpoint as yet undiscovered oil resources by flying at high altitude. All over Europe sovereigns and investors rushed to be part of that game which, when it ended, left them high and dry.

A much more colorful Italo-Belgian discovery—in this case of a miracle weapon—took place during World War II. Again an Italian and a Belgian had mastered the mechanism of a death ray that could detonate from a distance the enemy's ammunitions no matter where they were hidden. During the war, miracle weapons were supposed to be the holy grail, and the German high command listened carefully.

Initially, the demonstrations of the miracle weapon's might were successful and the Wehrmacht's top brass was not far from signing a contract. A last demonstration was held, attended by a swarm of German generals, but a young lieutenant spoiled the party by observing to his superior that prior to the explosion of stocked ammunitions, the two inventors had been horsing around in their proximity. This suggested that the death ray may not be so powerful, after all, or it might even be a scam—and it swiftly reached the commanding general's ears.

Subsequently, it was decided to repeat the demonstration while this time the Italian and the Belgian death ray designers were kept under guard, away from the ammunitions to be detonated. This time the miracle weapon acted like an unloaded gun. The invention was a gimmick based on intrigue and bluster, and the two inventors found out to their sorrow that joking with the Wehrmacht was reckless.

The moral of the story is that when a not-so-miraculous "currency union," or weapon, proves to be a lemon, you had better run to the other side of the house because you are going to get hit.

5. Euroland's Banking Union

Was the fire-brigade approach of any help in solving the crisis? Hardly. The triumphalist reaction of Monti and Rajoy after the late June 2012 Brussels "summit" was premature and the blah-blah about a European Banking Union is even more so. Nothing has been settled with this rush to judgment that took place in the early hours of June 29, 2012, when everyone was tired.

The most questionable notion of all has been that Euroland leaders finally embarked on a process to surrender sovereign control of banks to a powerful central supervisor. Theoretically, this was supposed to take place within six months, that is, before the end of 2012. But the political pledge to kick-start highly complex talks to forge the banking union was half-baked, and the statement itself was a contradiction:

- Given Euroland's well-documented bickering and inertia, six months passed by in no time, and
- Most of the time lost was spent on arguments on who is going to be allowed to inspect whom, and how far the ECB-based central regulator can go.

Transborder inspection of the banking industry as well as of individual banks has been both the prerequisite and the blocking factor. No expert who has contributed to my research questioned the statement that one of the most severe problems confronting a banking union is the transborder supervision of credit institutions.

To put it bluntly, this is a reversal of long-established conditions. While in the case of a common currency, the borders of member states are no more relevant in monetary and banking terms, bank supervision authorities in one country classically had very limited responsibilities for action in another country.[21] This reference includes the subsidiaries belonging to a financial intermediary whose parent company they fully control at home.

Trans-Euroland banking supervision would create a mare's nest of home-host problems. To it is added the fact that *if* banks are to be able to address themselves for their financing needs to each of the common currency's capital market(s), *then* their balance sheet should be totally transparent, which, inter alia, requires fully homogeneous accounting rules without favorable twists and exceptions—which today does not exist in spite of IFRS and GAAP.

The integration of banking supervision under one authority is a tall order because it means that both banking and accounting rules, now fragmented along national boundaries, must be rewritten in a comprehensive manner valid for all jurisdictions of member states. Without such streamlining it will be all but impossible to centralize responsibility in a common regulator and its supervisory agents. Even forgetting the language barriers, which can be as high as the Alps,

- The supervisors will simply not understand what they are reading in the banks' books,[22] and
- They will be even more ignorant about what is written in the footnotes of financial statements of the banks under inspection.

When a little over a decade ago, the then 94-year-old Dr. Enrico Cuccia—honorary president of Mediobanca, Italy's foremost investment bank, where he was the CEO since the end of World War II—was asked by the judge in Gemina's[23] trial if he knew that the financial holding firm had double books, he answered: "My son, in my long career I have not seen a company which did not have double books."

Neither is the transborder inspection of credit institutions a matter of only auditing the books. The carefully hidden cross-holding must be flashed out, loans to major shareholders must be identified, and legal issues properly looked up so that no ambiguity is left as to whether they have been properly handled. Examples include:

- Resolution entity,
- Deposit insurance, and other vital functions.

Complex as these problems are, above everything else the most difficult nut to crack is the game of personalities and of political influence that will be "on" all of the time. A Euroland agreement might stipulate that there are no more barriers, nationalistic or anything else, to transborder supervision within the common currency area. But wait until some scam is uncovered in one of the major banks and you tell me if its sovereign will allow that it is prosecuted by Euroland's supervisory authority.

The same "national politics-above-all" principle will be valid about the wish expressed by the June 28–29, 2012, summiteers to break the bank-sovereign feedback loop, thereby stopping shaky banks from laying low their sovereigns, and vice versa. Unless and until politicians get cracking, which they typically don't like to do, it could take until the end of this century to put that plan into practice. This is a different way of saying that Euroland's political union comes first and the rest of the jazz follows.

On June 27, 2012, Nick Clegg, the British deputy prime minister, published an article in the *Financial Times* that stated: "It makes sense for full banking union to be based on the euro," adding to this that the new arrangement could hold risks for Britain. Clegg's article was informing everyone that Britain would demand that the rules of the single market were not tilted to the benefit of Euroland members. The more positively inclined parties have been looking at a banking union as a platform for great cooperation on various aspects of an integrated financial system with:

- Shared principles on how to protect depositors,
- High minimum capital standards the banks should hold,
- Common rules on the restructuring of failed banks,
- A well-endowed and strong European banking authority, and more.

A fear prevailing among the pros is that such requirements will not be satisfied while proposals are hastily drawn up. Another concern is that a banking union's charter will include a host of unanswered questions such as exact lines of authority and responsibility, institutions the banking union will cover, and their relations with banks outside that framework.

The aforementioned issues provide food for thought about the foundations upon which a sustainable solution might be built and maintained. Still, according to the European Central Bank there is a need to go beyond these areas and conceive a *banking union* as an integral counterpart of a *monetary union*, predicated upon three main objectives:

- "First, strengthening the euro area-wide supervision of the banking sector in order to reinforce financial integration, mitigate macroeconomic imbalances and, therefore, improve the smooth conduct of the single monetary policy.

- "Second, breaking the link between banks and sovereigns—which significantly exacerbates the impact of any financial disturbance— also by establishing a European deposit guarantee scheme and EU-wide crisis resolution arrangements.
- "Last but not least, minimizing the risks for taxpayers through adequate contributions by the financial industry.[24]

The *Financial Stability Review* of the European Central Bank adds that these reforms will certainly take time to implement and may require substantive legal changes, including in primary legislation. A program for a full banking union should also focus heavily on addressing the challenges brought by the single currency, including the link between sovereign and bank debt, within the framework of a currency union.

Another vital element for a successful solution is that the Euroland or EU-wide bank supervisor is provided with powers to intervene in all European banks. Still another is the institution of a new deposit guarantee and bailout fund to be financed through a tax on the banking industry itself rather than through taxpayers' money. (This can be done in a way similar to the one chosen by President Roosevelt for deposit insurance.)

Adverse reactions to a banking union should also be paid due attention, given that most national bank supervision authorities are alarmed at having to give up power. Governments, too, are facing intense political pressure to maintain control of the politically powerful regulatory authorities.[25]

As the foregoing discussion documents, there is a long list of issues up for debate. Hence, it is not too much to ask that a serious plan about a banking union should do away with derogations and opt-outs that different Euroland member states are inclined to require and to support— which is also true for EU member states.

It needs no explaining that the foregoing demand plenty of time, not only to develop a serious, well-established control organization able to plan, direct, and carefully watch over developments in the banking union, but also to iron out differences of fact and opinion amongst Euroland's 17 EU member states—or the EU's 27 if the banking union expands all over the European Union. Rush will create an unstable system loved by nobody.

6. The Great EU Bank Robbery Started with PSI

The first Greek bailout took place in mid-2010. Greece, Ireland, and Portugal have been three Euroland member countries under economic stress and their governments waited too long before recognizing that they needed financial assistance. Their requests for support were submitted to the EU, ECB, and IMF—which in exchange required the implementation of a program of reforms to be monitored and controlled by representatives of the three agencies providing the funds—the "troika."

That first deal was between the sovereigns and the EU, ECB, and IMF. Orthodoxy prevailed in 2010 and in the early months of 2011. There was no thought of involving private lenders in sharing some of the money lost in imprudent loans to economically weak sovereigns, though in some banking circles there was discussion of securitization of nonperforming loans through special investment vehicles (SIVs)[26] and some hedge funds started flocking around looking for spoils.

By early 2011 it became evident that in Greece Bailout I was faltering. As a result, in the first months of 2011, negotiations began on how to lighten the public debt weighing on Greece, thus making the burden easier to carry for an economy that, for all practical purposes, was nearly bankrupt. Loans by the IMF, EU, and ECB were untouchable, but private loans (including those by banks) could be subject to a *haircut*—or, more precisely, to *confiscation*, as this was the endgame.

The process was christened Private Sector Involvement (PSI),[27] and it was projected that up to €213.7 billion ($277.8 billion)—out of a total Greek debt of €350 billion—could be subject to the haircut. The condition has been one of infantile simplicity, if one had a stomach for it. For the first time in its long history, Europe would be abandoning the sacrosanct guaranty of loans in an official way.

Suddenly under the weight of circumstances orthodoxy began to subside and certain intentional efforts pointed to a confiscation unheard of so far, intended to relieve sovereign financial distress without using taxpayers' money. There is nothing wrong with the PSI concept's principle—that lenders investors and creditors should:

- Fully bear the consequences of their decisions, and
- They should not rely on taxpayers' money to be backed out.

This is also a way for governments to get off the tax pedal. Moreover, saying that the private sector should contribute is good for public relations. It pleases the populace that (like François Hollande) "hates the rich," and also sends signals to investors, particularly the banks, that the Euroland sovereign debt should no longer be considered a "safe" asset. There is no more a guaranty that the capital will be repaid in full.

But there has been an obstacle. If Euroland adopted private sector involvement, it had to denounce the Lisbon Treaty's triple "No!": no bailout, no interest rate relief, no haircut. It helped that the "No bailout" rule had already been broken with the bailout programs for Greece, Ireland, and Portugal. All the while nobody in Brussels bothered about the Lisbon Treaty. The Brussels top brass just turned a blind eye to it.

Orthodoxy, however, is not dead. It has been carrying on a rearguard action. Under Jean-Claude Trichet, the ECB objected. It warned against private role in bailouts, though it stopped short of opposing outright private sector involvement in Bailout I for Greece.

The Bundesbank also criticized plans for private involvement as inconsistent, and warned that since they involve private sector banks that loaned money to Greece, this could add to Euroland's woes. They could undermine market confidence in Euroland's crisis-fighting tools—such as the rescue fund and the European financial stability facility.

By June 2011 the issue of private sector involvement had become political, with Nicolas Sarkozy, the French president, and Christine Lagarde, his minister of finance, pushing for PSI. At a meeting in Berlin on June 16, 2011, Angela Merkel, the German chancellor, and Nicolas Sarkozy said that the private sector should be involved but *only on a voluntary basis*. This they presented as a common position aiming to put an end to an ongoing public row between:

- The political will, and
- The European Central Bank, over the scale of private involvement.

There are worries that we want to cause a *credit event*,[28] Merkel told reporters alongside her French counterpart. They talked of this in their two-hour meeting. She added that a credit event was not what they want. The whole issue was about a voluntary participation. In practice, however, this position waned and, in the end, it proved to be a totally false premise.

Trying to find a midway solution between orthodoxy and PSI, and backed by the European Commission, the ECB argued for something akin to the so-called Vienna Initiative. This is a milder form of debt swap, in which bondholders rollover their debt but only when their existing bonds mature. Merkel reportedly said that the Vienna Initiative is a good foundation and it is possible to move forward on that basis. But there was no roadmap, just a four-point framework specifying that whatever is decided:

- Must be done quickly,
- Must involve agreement with the ECB,
- The private bondholder involvement must be voluntary, and
- A credit event, or default, must be definitely avoided.

Napoleon once said that it is not enough to give an order. The commander must ensure that his order is executed. Otherwise it will fail.[29] PSI failed in all four goals Merkel put forward. Nobody cared about them. Indeed, it is difficult to find a worse-managed project in finance and economics—that, over and above its failure, created a very bad precedent.

Neither did PSI deliver the safeguard for German and French government money connected to Greek loans that was, in all likelihood, the secret goal of the deal. The exposure of France to Greek debt was €19 billion in government bonds and €42.1 billion in private loans. Crédit Agricole, Société Générale, and BNP Paribas, the country's three biggest banks, shed blood and saw their credit rating placed on review for a downgrade by Moody's.

Germany, for its part, was owed €26.3 billion in government bonds and €10 billion in private loans. Rumor has it that it is Deutsche Bank that has gained by making huge profits out of PSI. There is no documented evidence that I know on this issue, except that on April 3, 2013, Bundesbank launched an inquiry into dealings in complex credit derivatives that can hide losses but also turn profits into losses, if necessary.[30] Some big banks are wizards in manipulating accounts through derivatives, and Deutsche Bank is said to be the best in this trade.

7. Private Involvement Might Be Good in Theory but Is a Huge Loophole in Practice

On June 6, 2011, Lorenzo Bini Smaghi, member of the executive board of the ECB, was part of a Reinventing Bretton Woods Committee conference in Berlin. In this, he brought to his audience's attention the fact that while the basic principles of private creditor participation in resolving the debtor's financial stress are uncontroversial, the application of these principles to sovereign debt is much more complex, particularly regarding debt in the public sector.

Assessing the solvency of a country is different from assessing the solvency of a company, said Bini Smaghi, if for no other reason than beyond the analysis of the cash flow, balance sheet, and assets and liabilities, it also calls for an evaluation of the political will to implement the measures needed to ensure that the country becomes solvent and remains so. In his opinion,

- Respect for contracts is one of the key principles of the market economy, and
- Imposing haircuts on private investors can seriously disrupt the financial and real economy of both the debtor and the creditor countries, ultimately damaging the taxpayers.

Bini Smaghi also drew his audience's attention to the fact that such unexpected consequences are particularly present in a region like Euroland, consisting of advanced economies and highly integrated financial markets, an integration promoted and encouraged for decades. He then went further to warn that: "If pursued imprudently, private sector involvement:

- Does not help save taxpayers' money; indeed, it may cost them more money,
- Favors short-term speculation over long-term investment, which is certainly undesirable, and
- Discourages, even delays new investments in a country implementing an adjustment program."[31]

This was an expert's conclusion, all negative for PSI. Did the politicians listen to it? Evidently not! It was too much for them and besides their mind was already made up (section 5); they would not be bothered by the facts. Typical politics.

Later on, when hell broke loose with PSI, all sorts of excuses came up, one of them was "It was asked by the lenders." It would be ridiculous to think that the lenders were eager to take part in a private involvement where they were sure to lose their shirt. In the spring of 2011, in Paris, rumor had it that Sarkozy, the then French president, was confronted with two options:

- Help in another bailout of Greece and never see his money again, or
- Refill the treasury of big French banks sure to be wounded by PSI, given their large exposure to Greek loans, and never see his money either.

But politics and the management of risk are two cultures as far apart as heaven and earth. In the end, PSI failed in a big way. After year-long negotiations, in which private lenders were represented by the Washington-based Institute of International Finance (IIF),[32] theoretically the Greek sovereign benefited from a hefty 73.5 percent confiscation on PSI loans. Practically, the Greek sovereign got nothing; while Sarkozy lost twice.

Greece saw no benefit from PSI. If anything, it made maters much worse, because the haircut negotiation revealed the fragility of its economy and market vultures circled around. The news was so bad that there has been, as well, talk of a third bailout.

One of the most curious aspects of this operation of forced private sector involvement is that it took a year to negotiate the debt haircut (read:

unwarranted confiscation), but no entity truly objected to the principle of it. It is *as if* everybody involved accepted the Great EU Bank Robbery steamrolling Euroland's financial landscape, without any questions being asked. Instead, all interest in the negotiations focused on the amount of the haircut, with the hilarious result that the more the IIF, IMF, ECB, EU, and the Greek government talked, the more the haircut increased since:

- The market watched the negotiations with interest, and
- It became evident that the Greek state was in a much worse economic and financial condition than the market had previously thought.

At no time was an ecosystem created ready to exploit profit opportunities even from a haircut imposed on banking loans and minor private investments. Vulture funds spread over the PSI scene almost overnight. The novelty of the event and the fact that it potentially involved a large cut of €213.7 billion has been a blessing in disguise for the most sinister operators of the runaway banking sector. The politicians who decided to go ahead with PSI against the advice of economists and financial experts were caught by surprise. But by then it was too late. There was no Plan B to fall back upon.

This is a very interesting case study on how fast the market gets into position. After the Greek PSI was announced in July 2011, hedge funds, special investment vehicles, structured product dealerships, and all other participants in shadow banking had their finest hour. They cherry-picked products that could be restructured at a profit and bought a large number of Greek government bonds at basement prices, with a view to swap them for fresh bonds of much greater value at the appropriate time.

The ineptness of PSI negotiations provided the shadow banking operators with a good deal of assistance. When the PSI negotiations started, the target was a 20 percent to 25 percent haircut. As they proceeded they passed over 30 percent (said to be a milestone) and reached 50 percent of the face value of Greek government bonds. The more the market heard of the negotiations, the higher the haircut became, ending at an unprecedented 73.5 percent.

In parallel to this, a really dangerous precedence has been created with politicians and EU authorities that got de facto free reign to confiscate a large part of other people's money. This has been a new and unwarranted policy that is on its way to becoming a "standard." A financial miracle weapon was born, invented by politicians and confirmed by the ECB, EU, and IMF whose private economic police constitutes the so-called troika.

After having disregarded all four conditions Angela Merkel imposed for PSI, the IIF-led negotiations got their own momentum and there exists

Table 3.1   Four classes of lenders in the Greek PSI

Lender	€ billion	Share
Greek and Cypriot banks	52.2	14.96
European banks and insurers	36.0	10.31
Domestic Greek creditors	35.5	10.17
Total by banks and Greek creditors	**123.7**	**35.44**
Other creditors (many unknown)	90.0	37.77
Total of all creditors subject to haircut	**213.7**	**73.21**

no evidence of any politicians standing in its way. To appreciate how far a bank robbery can go, the reader should look at Table 3.1, which identifies the four populations subject to the haircut:

- Greek and Cypriot banks, with the lion's share in exposure,
- Other European banks and insurers,
- Domestic Greek creditors, and
- Other creditors, many of them unknown.

Of the €52.2 billion of Greek and Cypriot bank money given as loans to the Greek sovereign, 73.5 percent went up in smoke with PSI. This amounts to an impressive €38.6 billion, which is evidently missing from the treasuries of the Greek and Cypriot banks. So the banks have to borrow from Euroland and the IMF and recapitalize, pay interest, and return the capital (if they manage to do so). For Euroland, the ECB, and IMF this is an internal (and infernal) money machine.

- Bank recapitalization money is a big chunk of the troika's loans to Greece and Cyprus, because their banks were badly wounded by PSI.
- Undercapitalization has also been the reason why Cyprus had to agree to humiliating conditions to get an EU loan that needs to be serviced and repaid, while the island state was also hit with a hammer (by Draghi, chapter 1).

The president of Laiki Trapeza (the island state's second largest bank that will be turned into a "bad bank") was right when he said that if it were not for the heavy haircut on Greek loans by PSI, all that would have been unnecessary.[33] Where he was wrong is in his failure to excuse himself to his clients, employees, shareholders, and the Cypriot public for having fallen in the catchment area of the Great EU Bank Robbery's infernal money machine by giving loans to Greece.

There is a last question to ask in connection with the Great EU Bank Robbery at PSI level. As Table 3.1 brings to the reader's attention, the total amount of private sector involvement has been €213.7. The haircut of 73.5 percent amounted to €157 billion ($194 billion). Where has *that* money gone?

It did not serve to lower the Greek public debt, since at the time of the first bailout it stood at €350 billion and now it is in excess of €400 billion. In fact, for the Greek sovereign the situation is worse than it ever was, since the majority of this €400 billion is in the ECB, EU, IMF loans (to be discharged only through plain bankruptcy).

Has the €157 billion been used to storm a fortress in Euroland that still held on to orthodoxy? Or some other fortress, for whatever reason?[34] In his letter of July 61 BC to his friend Atticus, Cicero, the great Roman senator, lawyer, author, and orator, writes that: "Philip (II of Macedon) said any fortress could be stormed provided there was a way up for a donkey with a load of gold on its back."[35]

With €157 billion from PSI, a whole army of donkeys can storm even the most impregnable fortresses. Which ones have been chosen? It is important to know what has happened to the €157 billion because, as Cicero emphasizes in this same letter to Atticus: "We should be judged arrant fools if we ignored it, and arrant cowards if we let it frighten us."[36]

4

ECB, EFSF, ESM, Eurobonds, and Political Horse Trading

1. The European Financial Stability Facility

The European Financial Stability Facility (EFSF) was established in 2010 to take care of relatively smaller financial problems confronting member states. The reason for its establishment lies in the fact that the EU's Lisbon Treaty prohibits bailouts. The EFSF has no such clause in its charter, so it can do things the European Central Bank cannot do without violating its statutes.[1]

Table 4.1 draws the reader's attention the vital statistics of Euroland's two financial support institutions. In contrast to the European Investment Bank (EIB) and the ESFM, which were financed by all the European Union countries, the funds of the EFSF and the ESM are provided only by Euroland's member states. Eventually the ESM will replace the EFSF.

The EFSF is that it grew out of the May 2010 Greece bailout, cobbled together by the European Union, the International Monetary Fund, and the European Central Bank—but with Euroland money. With the dramatic worsening of the European debt crisis, which enveloped not only smaller, peripheral countries but also larger sovereigns near insolvency, the EFSF evolved to fill a vacuum.

Critics say that the European Financial Stability Facility has morphed into a *transfer union,* with Berlin acting as guarantor of the debt of Club Med countries. As Kurt Lank, president of the CDU's economic council, had it, the danger is that Europe rushes "into an uncontrolled transfer union at high speed"[2]—which, indeed, is happening.

There are, of course, limits to the "Good Samaritan" act. Spain and Italy, for example, are too large to be covered by bailout mechanisms like the EFSF and ESM (section 3) though such vehicles may be used to keep peripheral banking systems solvent.[3] Politicians promoting this line of action point

Table 4.1   Euroland's financial support institutions, financed by 17 member states[1]

	European Financial Stability Facility (EFSF)	European Stability Mechanism (ESM)
Active from	June 2010	July 2012
Active until	July 2013	Open ended
Guaranty	In compliance with ECB capital key	In compliance with ECB capital key
Form of guaranty	Each country only liable for own share	Each country only liable for own share
Capital	€726 billion in guarantees, resulting in €440 billion total lending capacity due to cash buffers	Lending capacity €500 billion; Callable capital of €620 billion; contribution of €80 billion paid in five tranches[2]
Already committed	€192 billion committed to Portugal, Ireland, and Greece	–
Way of funding	Own bond issues	Own bond issues
Instruments used	Loans, lines of credit, bond purchases	Loans, lines of credit, bond purchases
Credit or status	Senior unsecured	Preferred creditor, junior to IMF

Note: [1]Based on an original concept by UBS, Chief Investment Office, June 11, 2012.
[2]With final payment in first semester of 2014.

out that banks and governments may be cut off from international bond markets for some time, but as long as the European Central Bank provides liquidity and support funds inject capital, a default could be avoided.

This argument is not espoused by everybody. Many people are against the principle of creating a nanny state for banks and sovereigns because at its core is a moral risk, costs money, and also violates previous EU accords. Others maintain that it is not doable till fiscal oversight is significantly strengthened and there is a Euroland-wide (even better EU-wide) bank regulator and supervisor Indeed, EFSF funding is finite with Germany being the major contributor as shown below:

Country	Commitment (in € billion)
Germany	119
France	90
Italy	79
Spain	52
Other countries	100
Total	**440**

There are economists, and also chiefs of state, who, while they like the aforementioned principle of sharing money contributed to a common fund, find that the war chest of the two funds, the EFSF and the ESM, is not up to the level of permitting major salvage missions. In their opinion, the financial resources of the two Euroland funds are scantier than they seem. Hence, according to this opinion, they always need to raise resources by issuing debt.

- While the EFSF backs its bonds with guarantees from the dwindling number of AAA-rated governments,
- The ESM has some paid-in capital. It is endowed with €500 billion (more on this later).
- But both could find it hard to raise the large sums that might be required for a recapitalization of Italy or Spain.

As for "swift action" in the fund's operations, this is a way of talking because long years of experience with EU-talk demonstrate that one must keep in mind Euroland's congenital need for laborious compromises. Finance ministers must meet time and again to decide how much money to make available in view of existing funds, commitments already made, and projected request for support.

As of mid-2012, there were €200 billion ($250 billion) in lending committed by the EFSF to Greece, Ireland, and Portugal, to be financed separately on top of the long-mooted €500 billion ($625 billion) firepower of the ESM. Eventually, the unused EFSF funds will top up the ESM's until the latter reaches full capacity, so that the full €500 billion uncommitted money is available from the start. Half a trillion looks like an impressive amount of money but it will fall way too short if Euroland decides on "swift action" to save Spain and Italy from bankruptcy at the same time.

Therefore, it is better to focus on *firm action* that does not involve fire-brigade approaches. Firm action would require as a fundamental prerequisite decisive fiscal stabilization of profligate countries (over which the EU has no authority), major reforms, and piecemeal provision of financial support through the EFSF/ESM and possibly the IMF.

It is nobody's secret that while plenty of authority and financial firewalls are necessary to contain a crisis, the no 1 ingredient is not money but discipline. Without discipline, a return to financial stability and healthy growth will remain elusive. This plainly means that not only outside assistance but also—in fact, mainly—radical national reforms are necessary to improve competitiveness in the long run. This is something that, with a few exceptions, Euroland's nations under stress have been reluctant (if not completely unwilling) to provide.

The result is a two-speed Euroland. Although it is nominally supported by all 17 member state governments, the EFSF's credibility and financial firepower have rested on its original triple A members—Germany, France, Finland, Austria, Luxembourg, and the Netherlands. Of its €440 billion guarantees, France accounted for €90 billion and Austria for €21.6 billion. Both have lost their triple A rating.[4]

This downgrading by Standard & Poor's has been bad news for the EFSF because it called into question the fund's leveraging based on credit guarantees (section 2) and it could leave it dangerously short of financial resources. To maintain an AAA rating the EFSF would either have to lower its maximum lending power or its guarantees would need to be raised until the ESM, the longer-term support facility, takes over.[5] According to analysts, however, given the link between the two funds:

- *If* the EFSF is downgraded to AA+,
- *Then* the way to bet is that this credit rating will be also carried by the ESM, unless either its maximum lending amount is reduced or it is endowed with a higher amount of callable capital.

Owing to prevailing uncertainties, the market thinks that both the EFSF and the ESM would find it difficult to raise funds at low rates if their credit quality lags behind that of other international agencies and development banks. A bailout fund wishing to be a credible borrower in international bond markets has to defend the AAA rating. On the contrary, large guarantee commitments may weigh on credit rating:

- Limiting the possible policy responses, and
- Increasing the pressure on the ECB to take an even more active role in handling the ongoing debt and credit crisis.

In a CNN interview on February 23, 2012, Bob Parker, a former senior executive at Crédit Suisse, said that the EFSF "fund has not been organized to deal with repetitive debt problems in euroland." Adding to the problems resulting from its thin capital base is the lack of a forward-looking policy. The EFSF has been used in a way similar to that of Fannie Mae and Freddie Mac in America (both now bankrupt) where when there was a major mortgage problem anywhere in the country it was thrown on them.

In conclusion, this section brought to the reader's attention that a hastily assembled EFSF has been a source of frustration, and this since its inception. Confidence that it can act decisively has been undermined by the fact that the fund has been left with only about €250 billion to build a financial firewall to protect Italy and Spain. It should as well be remembered that the EFSF has to provide a large portion of the second Greek bailout and help recapitalize European banks that find it difficult to tap the capital markets.

2. European Stability Mechanism

From the beginning of the sovereign debt crisis and most particularly Lehman's bankruptcy in early September 2008, it became evident that measures have to be taken to manage acute problems, present or expected, in Euroland's member states. Two issues stood out by way of a solution:

- A fund to provide short-term assistance, and
- Longer-term action to overhaul the fiscal framework of Euroland's member countries.

The necessity for structural changes did not come as a surprise. The Treaty on the Functioning of the European Union had identified national fiscal responsibilities, and the no-bailout rule reminded Euroland's members that they should not expect manna from heaven. There were, as well, guideposts aimed at enhancing crisis prevention.

For instance, the structural deficit of a country must not exceed 0.5 percent of GDP, but *if* its debt ratio is significantly below the 60 percent ceiling and the risks for long-term sustainability of public finances are considered to be low, *then* the structural deficit may amount to a maximum of 1 percent of GDP. Another milestone in the financial behavior of Euroland's member states that provided a fairly sound course, more or less free of problems, has been the *fiscal compact* agreed upon by the different governments at the beginning of December 2011 (chapter 6).

The aim has been to move toward a stronger economic union. This has been the objective of the intergovernmental Treaty on Stability, Coordination and Governance in the Economic and Monetary Union (finalized on January 30, 2012) that came into force on January 1, 2013.[6]

In parallel to the roadmap formal agreements provided, Euroland's member countries, confronted by debt problems, benefited from money from the EU, ECB, and IMF that allowed the recipients to ease their stress. The downside is that this money has also been used an excuse to put off tough economic measures and needed reforms. This proved counterproductive because it:

- Prolonged the problems of the countries under stress, and
- Made it likely they would seek more loans in the future.

With the aim of improving crisis resolution, the European Stability Mechanism (ESM), has been endowed with fresh capital beyond that already allocated to the EFSF. Taken together, the money spent on the LTRO and that endowing the EFSF and the ESM, Euroland put on the table nearly €2 trillion ($2.5 trillion). It is only normal to ask for something in return: That has been the fiscal compact.

Right after being elected president of France, François Hollande wanted to renegotiate and downsize the fiscal compact rules and discipline, not the money. A better way would have been to look at the EFSF/ESM and fiscal compact (see chapter 6) as two indivisible parts of the same system that stipulates that government budgets must be at least close to balance in structural terms, and this must be hardcoded into national legislation. Additionally, Berlin insisted on an automatic correction rule that is triggered if targets are missed by a significant margin.

There is as well the need to define the pace at which existing structural deficits will be effectively reduced, and set the deadline for achieving a disciplined budgetary objective. Brussels will oversee the so-called *debt brake*—the transposition of budgetary rules into national legislation—and if it finds fault with this transposition process, contracting parties will bring the case before the European Court of Justice (ECJ).

- Legal action and strict timetables for corrective action can be seen as the stick that inevitably accompanies the carrot.
- The carrot is the ESM that, like the IMF and the ECB, is a *preferred creditor*. Therefore any borrowing from them is first in line for repayment.

Germany, Holland, and Finland would like to see stronger sanctions in regard to excessive deficits. Stronger sanctions can only be effective if chiefs of state with voting rights pledge to follow the proposals or recommendations of the European Commission in an excessive deficit procedure. The loophole is that a qualified majority can oppose it through a process known as a "reverse qualified majority."

The consensus opinion is that at this point in time it is not at all sure that sanctions will prevail. It is more likely that this provision will become a paper tiger, as it has happened with the Stability and Growth Plan's sanctions. Budgetary discipline will only be promoted if each member state actually makes fiscal soundness a priority and carefully watches over compliance with the common budgetary rules. It would have been more effective if, by statute, wrongdoers were automatically deprived of access to EFSF and ESM funds. When, budget deficits or no budget deficits, the money is anyway paid by someone else, who cares about compliance?

As with the EFSF, the bigger contributor to the ESM is Germany. Critics said that putting so much of taxpayers' money on the line is a serious political gamble by Angela Merkel; at the same time it is a mixed bag in regard to its impact on Euroland's economy.[7] Neither is Euroland characterized by a spirit of solidarity that will justify going far out on one leg. M6, the French TV network, conducted a poll on "paying for Greece." The viewers were asked: "Are you ready to pay for Greece?" The answer was:

- 12 percent, *yes*
- 85 percent, *no*
- 3 percent, no opinion

The pros say that the EFSF and the ESM are themselves an evidence of solidarity. Is it so, or are they evidence of mismanagement of public money? During the June 28–29, 20,12 Brussels "summit," the ESM was suddenly downgraded. When it makes bailout loans to governments, starting with Spain, it will not automatically enjoy priority over other creditors. Though this has been presented as a "one off" case, it matters a lot. The money in the ESM's coffers can be depleted in no time as:

- Euroland's governments continue to run unsustainable deficits;
- Austerity policies have not delivered expected benefits till now; and
- Greece remains at risk of bankruptcy, and may be joined by Cyprus as well as other Euroland members.

Moves to pool borrowing and banking regulation among the Euroland members require a lot of preparatory steps as well as some ceding of sovereignty that could take years to negotiate. Beyond that, in several countries, electorates will probably not accept even a minor loss of sovereignty, turning all this talk about a fiscal union on its head.

The current race among Club Med countries to get the most in ready money brought up the risk that the ESM's endowment of €500 billion will not last long. This brought up the question on how to leverage the ESM alone or in unison with the EFSF (see also the discussion in section 3). Different ideas have been circulating:

- Make it a bank,
- Make it an SIV,
- Make it an insurance fund.

"There is a consensus that a eurozone break-up would cost more in the short-run or medium-run than managing the crisis," said Erkki Tuomioja,

Finland's foreign minister, in an interview to *The Daily Telegraph*. "But let me add that the break-up of the euro does not mean the end of the European Union. It could make the EU function better."[8]

Tuomioja further stated that Finland would block attempts to strip the European Stability Mechanism, the bailout fund, of its senior status at the top of the credit ladder. He voiced a deep suspicion of plans by a "gang of four" EU ministers—including the ECB's boss, Mario Draghi—to ensnare member states into some form of fiscal union, adding, "I don't trust these people."[9]

That's the climate prevailing in Euroland today: Lack of trust made worse by the profligates, who want that the ESM is given unlimited money by the ECB to buy government bonds (of Spain, Italy, and eventually France). That's nonsense. The big spenders[10] maintain that the ESM could provide better assistance if it were a leveraged bank. Germany does not want that, but Germany is becoming isolated in Euroland, where the big spenders who swim in a sea of red ink are the majority.

It is evident that the ESM cannot pay everything in bailouts (banks, sovereigns) with its current funds but leveraging has risks; it is not a free lunch. The IMF is not prepared to participate in such a venture because it is weary of investing its money in deals whose main objective is to consume plenty of money.[11] As for Britain, it simply does not like the idea.

Theoretically, this leaves open the Chinese connection, but practically it does not matter because the Chinese are only interested in contributing to the IMF, which has other advantages and where their money will be more secure. Since the late 2011 appeal to China by Nicolas Sarkozy, then president of France, nothing has happened. Moreover, French socialists have been revolting against the idea of the Chinese getting an economic and financial footing in the EU, and now they are in power.

The puzzle about which black hole will consume the ESM's capital looks unsolvable. Germany cannot pay for everything. Others don't have the money or don't care to contribute. Even gearing will not provide the miracle solution, because a beefed-up EFSF/ESM will be asked to:

- Pay for Greece,
- Pay for Cyprus,
- Pay for Slovenia,
- Pay for Ireland,
- Pay for Italy,
- Pay for Spain,
- Pay for Portugal,[12] and
- Eventually, also pay for France.

At the same time, it is asked to pay for restructuring the Spanish banks (and why not the Italian, French, and other mismanaged banks) "in need" contribute to the European banks' regulatory capital; and proceed with bond buying of sovereigns' debt as well as of banks' debt by investors while also holding up the dam of contagion. Looking at the total picture, one can easily see that it is ridiculous, *as if* it was made by five-year-olds.

In an article published in the *Financial Times*, Wolfgang Münchau spoke of "the effective collapse of the silly idea of leveraging the EFSF...A leveraged EFSF would have the worst kind of Eurobond: a tranche in a toxic debt security."[13] Münchau says that he hopes EU leaders "will come to their senses and stop pussyfooting with dubious financial instruments. The Eurozone needs a risk-free asset class, and this means something boring and simple."

I agree with this statement. Where I disagree is Münchau's love for Eurobonds (section 4). Whether we talk of gearing up a capital perceived to be insufficient, or using Eurobonds as a bottomless pit that swallows the savings of those who work to pay for the profligates, we make reference to irrational and unethical practices that can only be stopgap.

Despite the fact that the euro crisis reflects important structural deficiencies in several of Euroland's member states, the politicians concentrate on short-term issues like the debt of the Club Med countries. The longer-term perspective is being addressed only superficially and the necessary Lisbon Treaty changes are rarely talked about. This is a continued muddling through.

* * *

As of this writing, the future of the ESM, indeed its very existence, is still undecided. On October 23, 2012, the Luxembourg-based European Court of Justice started hearing arguments surrounding objections by Irish MP[14] Thomas Pringle to the European Stability Mechanism's ratification.[15] Pringle has good reason for his legal action. Cash-strapped Ireland is to pay its first installment of €500 million to the fund, after it came to life on October 8, 2012. If the ECJ judges rule against it, the ESM, its ratification, and any payments made to Luxembourg (where the ESM is based) will be deemed illegal.

"I do not think the terms of the ESM are in the interests of Ireland. The ESM is designed in a way that will divide the EU and result in its destruction," says Pringle. "The EU must make decisions which respect the rights of all the countries and their laws, as is enshrined in the EU Treaties." He adds that the ESM breaches EU treaties not just because the "no bail out" clause has been violated and because there is no legal protection against the ESM, but also because the ESM is a new instrument that exists beyond the reach of EU treaties.[16]

In the opinion of Mattias Kumm, law professor at the Social Sciences Research Center, Berlin, there exist Euroland decisions largely based on the will of member states without the involvement of European institutions, without discussion in parliaments, and without judicial review by the European Court of Justice. In other words, democracy has taken a leave and ethics went along with it. The March 25, 2013, strangling of Cyprus by Ecofin and its shameful conditions masquerading as a bailout, provides full evidence—if one is necessary (section 6).

3. Leveraging Euroland's Funds Is Wrong-Way Risk

One of the opinions that I heard time and again in the course of my research is that it is doubtful if European politicians really grasp the full implications of leveraging the EFSF and its successor the ESM. Funds being leveraged because they are viewed as being too small to do the job, do not really gain public confidence, and confidence is precisely what is missing.

Neither is the arm-twisting and attempts at intimidation practiced by some governments the way to find missing funds. Berlin is not alone in opposing silly spending. There has been opposition from Holland, Finland (which has asked for collateral), and Slovakia. Slovakia challenged Euroland's decision that it has to contribute to the Greek bailout, saying that per capita GDP in Greece is higher than in Slovakia. (At the end of the day, Slovakia paid its share, since the standard-of-living thesis was rejected by the other chiefs of state in Euroland.)

Neither is it the central bank's business to try to bypass these constraints by covert operations like the trillion dollars injection of liquidity in December 2011 and end of February 2012 (see chapter 5 on the LTRO). That the ECB found a way to bypass its Authentic Act and charter has been a shock, not an act deserving congratulations.

It was enough that since its beginning in June 2010, the European Financial Stability Facility was too small to appear sufficiently credible. What the gearing up of the EFSF aimed to do is to transform its existing capital into an equity of sorts, gearing its balance sheet up to €2 trillion. The idea was to use that money to buy European government bonds, saving the ECB from the embarrassment of purchasing government bonds directly. Again, the five-year-olds seemed to be at play, looking at leveraging as the way to make the EFSF fund bigger.

Those among the EU's bureaucrats and politicians who bet that way, thought of using financial engineering of the sort that caused the global crisis in the first place. Herman Van Rompuy, president of the European Council, sounded very much convinced that this is the right way. For centuries, he said, banks have taken deposits and used them to multiply money—implying that this is precisely what leverage does.

Conveniently forgetting about the risks, the favored option has been to get the EFSF to insure government bonds from countries known to be on the verge of bankruptcy, acting as the issuer of credit-default swaps (CDSs). This has been Plan A. Nobody seems to have explained to the chiefs of state that the guarantors of CDSs may go belly-up.

An alternative option, considered by otherwise serious people, has been to set up Special Purpose Vehicles (SPVs), the sort used with sub-primes that ushered in the present deep economic and banking crisis. Presumably, the SPVs' mission would be to seek to attract funds from private investors or sovereign-wealth funds in Asia and the Middle East by offering to take the first losses in sovereign defaults.

This Plan B of Euroland's fathers would have created a sort of collateralized-debt obligations (CDOs), another infamous instrument of the subprime crisis. Risks aside, none of the wise guys seems to have questioned why any investor would put money into such vehicles after the descent to the abyss of the banking policy of creating, through secu-ritization and fake credit rating, new classes of garbage debt. Whether with Plan A or with Plan B, speculators could have a ball at the expense of taxpayers.

- Leveraging the EFSF in order to make it worth around €1 trillion,
- Keeping the ECB out of the debt write-down or the leveraging of the EFSF, and
- Requiring all European Union banks to have a capital ratio of 9 per-cent, in case some financial shocks had to be absorbed.

Critics were quick to comment that rather than a "grand plan" prom-ised by European leaders, this was a "bland plan," given the risks that it involved, augmented by lack of detail. It was as well a documentation of the politicians' inability to produce a fully cohesive plan to contain Euroland's debt crisis.

Blind leveraging was judged as being by far worse than the other stu-pidity of asking China to participate in the EFSF. In the one as in the other case one-sided decisions were taken without counting the aftereffects on credibility and on the viability of an independent European currency.

Apart from the legal issues arising from a transformation of the EFSF (and eventually of the ESM) into a gambling vehicle, there have been economic issues associated to an inflated version of Euroland's support funds. This policy brought in perspective the fate of "*bonnes à tout faire*" in the US mortgage market known as Fannie Mae and Freddie Mac.

- Both were illusory real-estate recycling vehicles, and
- They were expected to solve all problems encountered with mortgages, from liquidity to solvency, till, in September 2008, they went virtually bankrupt.[17]

The reasons why a leveraged EFSF and/or ESM was attractive to politicians are the same as those for why those subprime mortgages were attractive to homeowners-to-be: The gearing disguises the absence of money. The price is that of holding a toxic product that has all the qualities to become the amplifier of a crisis.

All this makes an interesting case study on the analysis of behavior. After the banks and their clients deeply wounded themselves with structured products and needed lots of taxpayer money to be bailed out, sovereigns were prepared to commit the same absurdity, betting on a construction that has only one way to go: ultimate collapse.

- Leveraging massively increases the probability of a loss for those who look upon it as a savior, and by so doing allow themselves to be taken to the cleaners.
- Worse, they go for a leveraging absurdity knowing well that in a crisis of the profligates there can be no technical quick fix because this crisis is, at its heart, political.

There is as well another similarity worth recording. Like Fannie Mae and Freddie Mac in their advanced age, when they had overstretched themselves many times over, the newborn EFSF and ESM do not have the necessary clout. As we have already seen, the €280 billion ($350 billion) remaining in the EFSF and €500 billion in the ESM fall far short of the trillions that would be needed to shock and awe the markets in the face of further attacks on the finances of Spain or Italy.

There has also been talk of using leveraged EFSF and ESM funds to kill two birds with one stone: to manage secondary market purchases of government bonds and provide further financial assistance for governments and banks. (This leads to a much deeper question: Should Euroland concern itself with Spain and Italy as long as these countries fail to assure markets with decisive consolidation measures?)

It is moreover surprising that prior to talking of leveraging, Euroland's father did not pay enough attention to the fact that those assuring the debt of Euroland issuers would themselves be grievously weakened if a neighbor defaulted. Gearing might have enlarged the size of the EFSF but it could also have concentrated greater risk into the sovereigns that guarantee it.

If the EFSF aims simply at buying the debt of a vulnerable country such as Spain, it should expect to get back less than half of the money if there were a default because of a relatively high haircut. The PSI in Greece provides an example. But even a very conservative haircut of just 20 percent on the value of the insured bonds would wipe out all the money pledged by the EFSF as insurance. With gearing morphing into a mechanism that transmits panic in the market.

In conclusion, if asked for their opinion, people with independent minds and of independent means, and who, therefore, are not afraid of expressing their thoughts, would have advised that a leveraged stability fund simply makes no sense. Whether the EFSF alone or the EFSF with ESM, it would only be fighting the symptoms and not the cause of excessive government spending and ballooning debt-to-GDP levels.

By trying to make the EFSF money grow faster, the gearing will bring more a long-term risk than short-term relief, and taxpayers will be called to cover huge losses in the years to come. The true problem is one of fiscal spending. *If* spending remains on an unsustainable path, *then* everything else is alchemy.

4. Dead Cat Walking: Eurobonds

With the fuzzy notion of *eurobonds* loved by all profligates, Euroland governments, their central banks, the European Central Bank, and a long list of officials (including the three presidents of the EU) find themselves in unfamiliar surroundings. This is by no means a "one-off" case of economic solutions running off the track.

Hurling ever more liquidity and public debt at economies, thinking that what led us into trouble in the first place will also get us out of it, is plain and simply wrong, says Andreas Höfert, UBS chief economist. Eurobond is the *alter ego* of printing money, which is now the only weapon available for central banks to help governments mitigate the effects of the financial crisis. On May 23, 2012, Euronews quoted Wolfgang Schäuble, the German finance minister, as having said that eurobonds are "a bad solution at a bad moment for a bad purpose."

Several, but not all, economists suggest that the ongoing eurobond proposals do not make much sense unless a draconian form of European fiscal union is its *alter ego*. Short of this, eurobonds will be a waste of money, and an excuse for avoiding economic restructuring—as well as for redefining the difficult relationship between markets and politics, which has always existed but got magnified with the euro crisis.

Euroland governments that promote eurobonds—France, Italy, Spain—
say that they will become a force bringing nearer to reality a federated
Europe. No attention is paid to their downside or to the fact that, as the
interminable Euroland "summits" demonstrate, such a concept is a very
unlikely vision for the future.

- By what laws and regulations will a centrally administered Europe
  be governed?
- How well will it handle nationalisms increasingly featured by advo-
  cacy groups?
- Will a federated Europe be governed by those promoting fiscal discipline or by the profligates?
- *What if* people in the economically weaker countries vote for permanent eurobonds?

If eurobonds are used to collectivize past, present, and future high
public debt by the crisis-hit countries, *then* they will use the manna from
heaven to ask for reestablishing their entitlements even if they are unaffordable and unsustainable. The reader should notice that only governments of countries with difficult budget problems and a high cost of
debt are calling loudly for eurobonds. They also enjoy the backing of the
Brussels EU Executive, which would lose its authority, its salaries, and its
pensions should Euroland fall apart.

It does not come as a surprise that Holland, Finland, and Germany are
not willing to guarantee the united debts of Europe, which would put the
wealth of their economies at stake and hold them hostages in the future.
They also know quite well that the call for eurobonds is a trap. The result
will be a runaway train because the Club Med countries do not want
northern Europe to tell them how to manage their national budget.

It would have been much easier to handle economic and financial
problems if a group of countries that had similar budgetary policies and
debt levels, as well as economic strengths, were working together more
closely. This is not the case. Euroland expanded too rapidly in all directions. Saddled by their uncontrollable debts, chiefs of state of the weaker
economies adopted a new paradigm that can be expressed as

- My money is mine, and
- Your money is also mine, in the name of solidarity.

"Your money" is the one that sits in Euroland's rescue funds (sections 1
and 2) and as already stated, it is not enough to satisfy every profligate's
requests.

By the end of 2012, the debt level of Euroland exceeded €8.6 trillion or about 93 percent of the GDP of all 17 member states. The level of this debt is expected to increase in 2013 by 4 to 5 percent, as the new year will add more deficits. This means that the eurobond rating can be neither AAA nor AA+. High credit rating will be out of reach, an A+ is more likely, but far from being sure. Standard and Poor's said that the weakest economy in the deal will define the level of credit rating for eurobonds. In that case it will be a plain C.

Missed in all this commotion is the fact that sovereigns who try every trick to get money, because they suffocate under their public debt, are no more *risk-free state debtors*. Eurobonds may become a boomerang even if the national central banks of Euroland member states and the European Central Bank act as godfathers. They have already harmed themselves by accepting the sovereigns' toxic bonds as a security.

As for commercial banks, in lieu of providing the private sector with credit needed by their economies, the big banks have been trying to heal the wounds of Euroland states, turning the whole operation into a source of profits. German and French banks, for instance, built up risk clusters with the debt of European countries, and so did the ECB as creditor of last resort.

After having tested the euphoria of the nanny state and bet their future on it, private citizens are being burdened by all sorts of taxes, a policy that is already turning counterproductive. As Albert Einstein put it: The significant problems we face cannot be solved at the same level of thinking we were at when we created them. Along with a rising taxation, eurobonds are part of this lower level of thinking that says:

- Roll up the debt if you can through useless certificates, and
- *If* this is not feasible *then* tax, tax, and tax as far as you can reach.

The underlying idea is that of an old communist principle attributed to Lenin: "From each according to his abilities, to each according to his needs." Nothing has been learned from the 1970s, the years of stagflation that ultimately led to the fall of communism. No thought has been given to the discovery of a shocking truth that *if* the Leninist principle reigns, *then* nobody has any abilities anymore, but everybody has needs. This is, down to basics, the sense of:

- The nanny states, and
- The *mutualization* of Euroland's member states' debts.

Politics is the moving gear in assuming this wrong-way risk. Telling the electorate that it can keep its standard of living and "don't worry about austerity because this is not our problem" is the message that might assure reelection. But it's a lie. The gap is filled by taking over the neighbor's wealth while misinforming the electorate.

"I cannot accept the French demands because I have to count with the coalition and with the Constitutional Court in Karlsruhe," said Angela Merkel to François Hollande during their June 27, 2012, meeting at the Elysée. To this Hollande answered: "And I, too, have to count with my parliament."[18] Yes, but Hollande has a comfortable majority in the French parliament and senate while Merkel does not control the German Constitutional Court.

Moreover, Merkel has to ask her coalition partners and the German parliament for money (read: handouts) to give to other jurisdictions. By contrast, Hollande would find practically everybody in accord with the mutualization of France's debts. History books say that the Habsburg emperors who ruled Austria-Hungary for several centuries were always short of money. The same is true of French governments, particularly after 1973.

Europe and with it the French economy are stalling because economic and fiscal imbalances have put a lid on growth. But nothing will be gained by sinking deeper into debt. A sovereign cannot have growth on demand.

- *If* this were possible,
- *Then* the Soviet state would not have fallen to pieces.

The Soviet Union was rich in resources but these were mismanaged by bureaucrats who did not know how to choose and follow a growth course because their no 1 priority was "not to make mistakes"[19] and this set the tone of the economy. In the West, both bureaucracy and a huge, unsupportable debt—at state, company, and household levels—keep the economy hostage.

Promoted by those who don't want to put their economic and financial house in order, eurobonds will only help to reignite the governments' spending spree. The US has gone to great lengths to apply this silly policy, with the compliments of Federal Reserve, which has tripled its balance sheet, but its outcome has been questioned even by the pros.

The so-called *mutualization* of public debt pushed by Hollande, with Monti seconding, has been invented to unload the unaffordable public debt of France and Italy onto the other EU members—who see the plot and reject it. Following the "no" vote at the May 23, 2012, "summit," Hollande took the podium to say that the eurobonds would not have been used "for growth" (read: for throwing money at the unemployment problem).

This was precisely the opposite of what he had said prior to the "summit," which is another example of the politicians' inconsistencies.

Should eurobonds be launched without an effective and tightly controlled fiscal union in Euroland, the consequences would be devastating for its core countries and it may rapidly make the euro a weak currency. As the insolvency of Greece, Portugal, Spain, Italy (and eventually France) is well known in the market, if eurobonds were launched, investors would carefully look into the sort of guarantees provided by Germany, Holland, Luxembourg, and Finland: how binding are they? Those who think that they can hide under German cover have shown a combination of:

- Shortsightedness, and
- Financial illiteracy.

George Osborne, British chancellor of the exchequer, correctly emphasized the approach he feels his country must take to return to stronger economic growth: "This country borrowed its way into trouble and we're going to earn our way out."[20] With this, austerity measures remained in place and total borrowing is projected to fall largely in line with established limits. France, Italy, and Spain could learn from the British experience.

5. The French Connection

With the election of François Hollande as president of France, demands have arisen in Euroland for a growth compact to become the main engine for aggregate demand and business operations. Theoretically, the idea is not bad. Practically, its chances are minimal because it doesn't answer how this growth will be:

- Engineered, and
- Financed.

Eurobonds are debt and using additional debt is jeopardizing the path to stability. Hollande wants Euroland countries to pool new public debt. Is it acceptable, he asks, that Spain must borrow at 6 percent[21] while Germany can raise money almost for free? (In the last week of May 2012, when this statement was made, Germany sold two-year bonds with a 0-percent coupon.)

The answer is precisely the opposite of what Hollande expects: Yes, it is right that Spain pays so much more interest on its bonds because the sovereign's finances, that of the regions and those of its banks are in a shambles. Spain, Inc. should not have allowed itself to fall so low. Once it did, it became one of the market's "odd man out."

The situation in Germany, where eurobonds are widely judged to be the wrong prescription brought up at the wrong time and for the wrong reasons, is quite the opposite. They are as well a twisted case under existing EU treaties and do not contribute to market confidence. Speculators, of course, would love to see the eurobonds launched because they can increase their profits and bonuses for the year by so much.

Europe needs eurobonds, declared George Soros in mid-August 2011 as the subject started to be debated. But unlike politicians who specialize in blah-blah, as a financial person Soros knew that the money for eurobond guarantees, if at all, would come from Germany. Therefore he advised: Germany should establish the rules others can follow. Try to tell that to the profligates.

It is not surprising that Germany rejected the idea of being Euroland's paymaster. On the surface, eurobonds sounded as another tranquil debt instrument, but people who understand what lies behind even tranquil appearances see that they may mask a deep resentment. To understand it you have to study the underlying currents and conspiracies between politics and money. There are plenty, and time adds to the list.

From August 2011 to July 2012, the divisions over eurobonds among Euroland countries have deepened. Austria, Finland, and the Netherlands joined Germany in strongly opposing the introduction. Some critics said that as long as Germany can successfully oppose eurobonds, it will continue to benefit from the support of a dwindling group of countries with a stable AAA rating, which currently allows very low cost financing.

On the other side of this economic and financial divide in Euroland have been France, Spain, and Italy. Short of eurobond profligacy, François Hollande has called for the EFSF and the ESM to be used for purchasing Euroland government bonds, leaving Angela Merkel in the increasingly isolated position of having to say that this is not a subject for debate right now.

In a political sense that defines the French connection. Hollande is handicapped by his campaign promises. Politicians can scarcely admit that whatever they say on the campaign trail is contingent on events and circumstance in the world beyond. But the choices confronting the French government are now more limited than at any time since World War II.

A six and a half decade struggle to hold on to pre–World War II status and influence in the world has become much tougher to sustain, and on top of that come campaign promises. Populism during the campaign trail is one thing. Populism after being elected is another. The uncomfortable reality is that the social policies France has pursued have run off the road after having been overtaken by events:

- One of them is that what used to be affordable is no more so.
- In a globalized economy, high social costs make the French produce uncompetitive.

For example, in an effort to balance election promises with fears of impacting employment, on June 26, 2012, the Hollande government decreed the rise of the French minimum wage to 0.6 percentage points above inflation. Shortly thereafter, the professional association representing small and medium-sized enterprises said it was a "political decision that will have negative economic costs, risking investment and employment."[22]

- The other significant event that does not permit to proceed "as usual" is the unlikely but ongoing alliance between big banks and the state.

The French banking industry at large has a high level of total assets to GDP (and as compared to shareholders' equity). This is not sustainable over time, and analysts say that should lead to a deleveraging of big banks. Credit institutions also feature a very low level of loans to total assets; moreover, French banks have a relatively low profitability level compared to those of other countries.

Another negative is the level of nonperforming loans related to the current weak economic environment, and that of credit of coverage of the nonperforming loans. The latter, incidentally, is one of the main issues that other European banks are also facing and might lead to bailouts.

The fact that French banks have a low level of loans to total assets is an indication that they are largely involved in nondirect lending business, which means derivatives, trade finance, and securities. As for the very low level of risk-weighted assets (RWA) to total assets, it could be an indication that French banks don't have a lot of truly safe assets.

While the banking pattern that has just been described can be found in other European countries, it does not stop being a worry for the government, which is also faced with an acute lack of widespread public understanding of France's unfavorable economic trends. The share of manufacturing output in French GDP is below that of Britain and though the government controls the parliament, senate, and most of the regions, its space for maneuvering is limited.

One last thought to make the economic pattern of present-day Europe more explicit. Market tensions remain high as risk aversion continues to drive investors away from the common currency. In addition, financial market stress is impacting the real economy as companies are starting to hold back investment and employment. Under these conditions, business sentiment is affected and this makes it more difficult for governments to reach ambitious targets.

Higher wages and much higher entitlements aside, France has a problem of competitiveness affecting its industrial capacity, which has got worse over time. Therefore, rather than using the nanny state's excuse of social issues to justify inordinate expenses, the best policy is to admit that the current crisis ranges:

- From budgetary deficits
- To negative balances of payments.

That's not just my opinion. In early July 2012, the CEOs of three well-known companies—de Castries of AXA, Bernabe of Telecom Italia, and Löscher of Siemens—penned an open letter to *Le Monde*, the French newspaper, urging European politicians to revive growth by cutting public spending and encouraging private investment. Notice that this is precisely the opposite of what François Hollande and other chiefs of state are doing. No wonder that France, as well as Italy, Spain, and Greece are confronted with:

- Stalled growth,
- High debt,
- Growing unemployment, and
- Declining industrial prowess.[23]

In addition, there is spoilage. The Cour des Comptes, the statutory authority that audits the French governments' books, has reviewed the state of public finances and delivered its verdict. In practically every year it found gaps between receipts and expenditures. For 2012–2013, the result has been a €6–10 billion deficit and an even bigger one, of €33 billion, for 2013. That makes it very difficult for the French government to meet its deficit-reduction commitments.

Whatever has been said in this section converges with what the Bank for International Settlements' eighty-second Annual Report has advised: That by itself easy monetary policy cannot solve underlying solvency and structural problems. One of the illusions of this make-believe world of finance is that it makes comfortable both the politicians and the public. This comfort does not last as sooner rather than later it is discovered that the policies being followed have been a waste of time.

6. Too Big to Jail

Taboos, sacred cows, and the turning of a blind eye to malfeasance have reduced the options to solve the crisis and save the Western economies to practically one course: Doing the same thing over and over, but expecting different results even if these shine by their absence. This is of course insanity.

The Federal Reserve, Bank of England, Bank of Japan, and ECB made of this policy a new tradition; none is trying a "different" course unless it requires turning the central bank's printing presses at a still higher speed. "Do not fear to be eccentric in opinion, for every opinion now accepted was once eccentric," said Bertrand Russell, the British mathematician, who by obeying the laws of science looked for outliers that are at once novel and constructive, ways out of the beaten path. This text has followed Russell's advice all the way to bringing the wrongdoers to court and from there to jail.

The excuse that most jurisdictions don't have a law to punish the wrongdoers at the vertex of the state and big banks does not wash. Democracy has to protect itself. Ancient Romans had no law against patricide, because the lawgivers supposed no son would be so wicked. However, once this has happened, they made a law to severely punish the hideous crime as soon as it was committed. In our wicked and irrational society of the twenty-first century, the punishment for wrongdoers in:

- High finance, and
- Mismanaged government duties is unheard of.

There was a time when a person was held responsible for his or her doings, though occasionally punishment was not as severe as it should have been. This was the epoch of Enron, WorldCom, Global Crossing, Adelphia Communications, Banco Inter-Continental, and several others, as US justice was cleaning up more than two years of corporate scandals.

Executives, but not politicians, who covered the wrongdoers, were finally facing a judge or a jury. Samuel D. Waksal of ImClone Systems, the drug company, was fined and sentenced to over seven years in prison for his role in an insider-trading scandal. The US attorney Jim Comey said the sentence "shows that corporate crooks will serve real jail time."[24]

One of the bigger shots to a well-known chief executive's reputation came in the trial of former Tyco International CEO L. Dennis Kozlowski, followed by the trial of Tyco's CFO Mark H. Swartz. With his penchant for art collection, sales tax evasion, and extravagant parties Kozlowski had come to symbolize the excesses and greed of the late 1990s. Together, the CEO and the CFO were accused of stealing $600 million from the company and its shareholders and sentenced to prison.

The yearning for justice, however, suddenly dropped off the screen with the deep economic, financial, and banking crisis that started in Wall Street in July–August 2007.[25] Curiously this policy of turning a blind eye to economic crime arose, somehow, simultaneously in the US and in Europe (though in Europe the search for wrongdoers at high places has never been one of the priorities).

In the most curious way, as, quite unwisely, sovereigns moved in to save self-wounded big banks from bankruptcy, penalties turned to rewards. Hundreds of wrongdoers at the top in large financial institutions were not only allowed to go without prosecution but also allowed to define for themselves (with the support of rubber-stamp boards) bogus bonuses and golden parachutes for having destroyed their banks.

The sovereigns used taxpayers' money to refill the empty coffers of publicly quoted banks, and the CEOs had a ball over the wounded institution's body. An example from Europe has been the golden parachute of Lucas Mühlemann, chairman and CEO of the Crédit Suisse Group. After he failed as top executive he was showered with goodies, in spite of huge losses at Winterthur;[26] a torrent of red ink at the New York-based Crédit Suisse First Boston (CSFB); and $11.8 billion paid for the unnecessary acquisition of DLJ, a Wall Street investment bank. According to experts, DLJ was worth about two-thirds of what Mühlemann had paid for it in 2000.

The party of unjustified bonuses and parachutes is still continuing on the financial landscape. In the intervening years rare has been the case of banks that regretted their fat bonuses policy when they were confronted with huge losses. On March 23, 2009, ING, the big Dutch bankassurance, asked employees to "return" the 2008 bonuses pending review. But then Holland's huge financial entity had gone nearly bankrupt, was saved by Dutch public money, and needed to show that it had become virtuous.

Needless to add that the "bonuses" for having wrecked "this" and "the other" big bank were paid by the taxpayers. Worse yet, like so many other cases in Europe and in America, nobody from the bank's top brass was prosecuted as a wrongdoer. The crash of Lehman Brothers, fourth largest US investment bank, brought the global economy at the edge of depression, but Richard Fuld Jr., the CEO, retired nicely. No questions were asked by any federal prosecutor about liabilities and responsibilities.[27]

Kozlowski had done wrong and was sent to prison. Fair enough. But the damage he did to the American economy was 1,000,000,000 times smaller than that created by Lehman Brothers and its top brass. Kozlowski served real jail time (nothing wrong with that). But other CEOs who committed king-size economic crimes were not even sent to court.

The concept of untouchable wrongdoers at high places who mismanage the entities under their watch, and spoil or misuse their wealth, plays havoc with the nation's economy. Those responsible must be brought to justice, but this sane approach to democratic equality has disappeared from the radar screen. Wrongdoers are now welcome to continue their good act, or get the chance to leave with all the money they have collected—legally or illegally.

In the wake of the 2007–2013 deep economic, financial, and banking crisis and in a matter of a few months, togetherness in power and in profiteering has forged a strong sovereign-big bank alliance. It also created a new class of untouchables: people "too big to jail." Politicians gain from their association and in return they try to cover all sorts of financial scams by administering mild verbal reprimands or calls for moderate selfishness.

For example, on December 13, 2009, two and a half years into the deep economic recession, while unemployment zoomed but bonuses at big banks continued unabated, President Barack Obama and two of his economic advisors, Lawrence H. Summers and Cristina D. Romer, unleashed sharp criticism of what the president called "fat-cat bankers." This happened a day before he was to meet top American financial executives to urge them to:

- Free up lending practices, and
- Hold down executive bonuses.

"The people on Wall Street still don't get it," Obama said in an interview taped for CBS's *60 Minutes*. "They're still puzzled why it is that people are mad at the banks. Well, let's see: You guys are drawing down $10-, $20-million bonuses after America went through the worst economic year in decades, and you guys caused the problem."[28]

So the "you guys" caused the problem and to this there is general agreement. *If* the law condones that the few can profit by amassing millions on the back of the unemployed, *then* something is wrong with the law and it should be changed. Three and a half years passed since Obama's public relations announcement of December 13, 2009, and nothing really has happened toward changing the law.

If the law condemned such practice, as it condemned Kozlowski's, Swartz's, and Waksal's, *then* the "you guys" should have been brought to justice. They have not. Both in Europe and in America democracy has acquired double standards. The new oligarchy is characterized by people at the top in banks who are too big to fail, and who, therefore, hold the purse strings, and by political bosses on their way to acquiring the Noble Prize of being too big to jail.

5

Throwing Money to the Four-Letter Wind: LTRO

1. Long-Term Refinancing Operation: The Sarkozy Trade

By statute, the ECB cannot buy sovereign debt but behind the scenes it can authorize other institutions to do so. For instance, banks getting the €1.02 trillion ($1.36 trillion) the ECB put in the market in December 2011 and February 2012. Officially this has been known as the Long-Term Refinancing Operation (LTRO).[1] Market professionals say that it was Nicolas Sarkozy who, together with Mario Monti, convinced Angela Merkel that it will turn the market around. It did not.

The effect was only ephemeral while the cost was huge. Still, Sarkozy was proud of the LTRO's parenthood. On May 2, 2012, in a televised debate with François Hollande in the course of the French presidential election, Sarkozy said: "I have obtained it (the ECB's LTRO) together with Monti."

The LTROs are loans from the ECB to European banks for three years at a rate of just 1 percent. Theoretically, the scope of this lending program has been to stabilize the banking sector and induce the credit institutions to give loans. Instead, the money found its way into different European governments' coffers as the banks bought sovereign bonds while they continued not performing their role of intermediation.

The LTROs came in two installments: €529.5 billion was dispersed in December 2011, and in February 2012 another €489 billion was thrown to the four winds. Its effects have been ephemeral even if it allowed Spanish and Italian banks to get some €600 billion in fresh liquidity, which they used within no time to buy their government's bonds—a very bad investment. Apart from the first couple of days, the market did not turn around. The negative outlook continued.

Post-mortem, Sarkozy has been criticized for suggesting that Euroland's banks could make profits by using the ECB's funds to invest in government bonds. While at first this indeed seemed to work as it reduced the interest rates of Spanish and Italian bonds, the interest rates on the debt of the two wounded governments rose again and banks that had made such trades suffered losses.

The buying of Euroland government bonds by the ECB through intermediaries also lost much of its power when it became clear (in the wake of the Greek default)[2] that any bonds purchased by the ECB become senior compared with those already outstanding. If the ECB buys Spanish bonds now, the private investors still holding Spanish bonds are subordinated to the ECB. Hence these bonds lose value, and the loss of principal may go beyond 75 percent as it happened with the Greek PSI.

The pros say that all went well because the concept underpinning the official version of the decision that led to the three-year LTRO has been its ability to prevent a credit crunch in Euroland. This might have been true *if* in the Spanish and Italian jurisdictions the banks that vastly benefited from the LTRO did not rush to buy government bonds with a dual objective:

- To help the sovereign in reducing the interest rate for its bonds, and
- To benefit from the difference between the 1 percent they must pay the ECB and what the sovereign has to pay them (which at the time stood at 4.5–5 percent).

Part of the LTRO's official version has also been the goal of improving market confidence. In a first time, this was achieved up to a point, but its effect faded too fast. All counted, it has failed to remove the tail risk in the risk distribution characterizing the broader financial system. Positive confidence shocks are welcome provided that:

- The confidence persists over a period of time, and
- The cost associated with them is neither exorbitant nor has other negative aftereffects.

The effect of this over €1 trillion LTROs in recapitalizing Euroland's banks has been minimal, as demonstrated by the more recent need to recapitalize Spanish banks to the tune of €100 billion. Using that money to ease the life of profligate governments has been a great mistake when everyone knows that both in Europe and in America many banks remain highly leveraged and undercapitalized despite their statements that they are busy pruning their balance sheets.

Not only has the banking industry inflicted liquidity and solvency problems upon itself in the past, but it also continues doing so on a grand scale through gambles with derivative financial instruments and by lending to governments that are sinking in a sea of red ink. After a brief reduction in its volume, which was largely crisis-induced, derivatives trading again became:

- An illusory source of income for big banks,
- A way of (incorrectly) justifying big bonuses,
- An opportunity to break the law by manipulating trading statistics, as it has happened with Libor,[3] and
- A major source of risk and exposure that can once again turn the global economy on its head.

This does not mean that the interest rates paid by governments to find buyers for their bonds should not come down. But it is only the country's government that, by improving the country's creditworthiness, will end by paying less for its loans—not the ECB or another sovereign. Asking for *a global nanny state* is not only a totally wrong policy, it is unsustainable as well.

Higher creditworthiness is the key in appreciation of the fact that elevated bond yields are having a negative effect on the economy and on the country's accumulated debt. A sovereign's high borrowing costs have a knock-on effect on:

- Households,
- Corporate borrowers, and
- The sovereign itself, which is in the market for loans in competition with the private sectors of the economy.

A government that finds it difficult to attract the interest of capital markets for its debt can manage on high yields for a while, but the damage done to the real economy may be swift and severe all the way to hyperinflation.[4] Therefore, a sovereign has all interest in avoiding cornering itself into a debt trap. Nevertheless:

- *If* the government is unable to do so,
- *Then* it should not be pulled up from under through occult LTRO-type operations.

In essence, what has happened with the LTROs is that the ECB violated its statutory clause that it cannot buy sovereign debt, with the complicity of politicians and of banks. Still, a host of worries remained. Spain and Italy have to pay a high rate to sell their bonds and banks are required to meet the minimum capital ratios set by Basel III for which they should have used the LTRO money.

Since equity is hard to raise in the prevailing market environment, banks have to carefully marshal the capital they obtain. In addition, as intermediaries, they have the obligation to give loans to consumers and firms. Instead, on February 1, 2012, the ECB's quarterly bank-lending survey reported a substantial tightening of credit conditions.

With governments sinking in the sea of red ink they have created for themselves through unaffordable debt, sovereign bond purchases leave banks at greater risk of anxieties about public solvency. The more banks pledge collateral to draw on long-term ECB financing, the less attractive it is for investors to buy banks' unsecured bonds, as they will be further behind in the queue in the case of bankruptcy.

By now addiction to ECB funds is particularly acute. The European Central Bank's recycling of commercial banks loans has planted seeds of European Union's disintegration, said experts interviewed by *Bloomberg News*.[5] Critics commented that the fact that €1 trillion disappeared without leaving a trace did not come as a surprise. The commitment was poorly studied in terms of usage and results. According to one analyst, €3 trillion is the minimum needed to deal with Euroland's crisis—and even that will be characterized by uncertain deliverables.

The aftereffects of the negatives associated with the €1 trillion liquidity injected by the ECB were not studied. With a torrent of money from heaven, Euroland governments felt much less pressure to restructure labor laws and to take other painful initiatives to get their economies running again. Moreover, the banks too delayed action required to:

- Prune their balance sheet, and
- Rebuild their longer-term funding by the market, after having demonstrated their creditworthiness.

Euroland's banks that profited from the LTRO are more or less the same (on this side of North Atlantic) that brought upon the Western economy the deep economic and financial crisis that started in 2007. As for the ECB, because it knows that banks getting its money in ultra-cheap loans buy government debt—Italian and Spanish banks in particular—it took measures to avoid the least wanted bonds as collateral. For instance, it announced that it will not accept Greek government bonds (though later on this decision was reversed).

On the positive side, the LTRO mitigated funding concerns of self-wounded credit institutions. Italian banks, for example, were cut off from unsecured bond funding for several months in late 2011, essentially transferring their stress to the ECB.[6] Plenty of banks in Euroland created new ECB-eligible collateral of €60 billion in the form of new government-guaranteed bonds, which they pledged as collateral for three-year LTRO loans.

In his arguments on the LTRO advantages, Mario Draghi, the ECB's president, included a positive implication for the functioning of the banking system. Critics did not buy that argument. Instead, they pointed out that flooding the market with liquidity is not a monetary policy but an outlier that may well be hiding another big risk.

Theoretically, a large liquidity facility, backed up by cheap money, has the potential to solve the banks' capital needs. Practically, it can as well reduce their incentive to deleverage in the medium to long term, which is a negative. This and the losses suffered by banks by buying government bonds led many critics to consider the ECB's LTROs as reckless.

2. Euroland's Drift to Financial Mismanagement

The December 2011 Long-Term Refinancing Operation by the European Central Bank was made available to 500 credit institutions According to Mario Draghi, the purpose was to help banks refinance at medium-term maturities and support lending, especially to small- and medium-sized enterprises. Billions of euros in three-year loans provided ample liquidity, with the theoretical potential of changing the dynamics of Euroland's banking landscape. But in practice,

- *If* the expectation was a better functioning banking system offering its services to cash-starved enterprises,
- *Then*, as critics predicted, the outcome has been widespread deception.

Prior to the LTROs, the ECB had tried to ease pressure in the banking industry by offering one-year loans to banks. This, however, did little to encourage them to lend to companies and to people.[7] The failure of the LTROs is measured by the fact is that they changed nothing in this regard, while shortage of longer-term funding still contributes to the risks assumed by the financial system.

The flood of money being pumped into banks by the ECB should have gone a long way toward easing their funding pressures but for reasons explained in section 1 this is not the case. Analysts suggest that while the

ECB has essentially made an offer of unlimited funds, banks were still constrained by how much they could borrow by the quality of the collateral that they are able to hand over (collateral is subject to reduction in value through haircuts).

Right after the first LTRO, Spanish and Italian banks allegedly made government bond purchases of €20 billion and €5 billion respectively. This caused Italian and Spanish debt yields to fall from about 7 percent to under 5 percent but then, in quick succession, they moved again north as the government commitment to reforms waned in Italy and Spain. This covert strategy of pumping money into economies in deep red ink also explains why different politicians rushed to make a statement that Euroland is "better prepared" for the "next default" than it was two years ago.

The use of the ECB as a lender of last resort through the LTRO and similar operations has been designed for the larger Euroland countries. By contrast, Euroland's rescue fund for small countries has been the EFSF and its successor ESM (chapter 4). In a reversal of strategy, the EFSF is now used to recapitalize Spanish banks to the tune of €100 billion or more than 20 percent its original capacity, which suggests very shortsighted political decisions.

The principle with a fund whose size is limited by its goal and structure is that the more countries have to be bailed out, the fewer there are to take on the burden of rescuer. Neither the EFSF nor the ESM could credibly bail out Italy, if that was necessary. Jointly issued eurobonds (chapter 4) might have led to burden-sharing across Euroland members, but eurobonds are a free lunch that has been anathema to some Euroland members and for good reasons.

Neither is it conceivable that countries asking for help in the face of adversity impose their conditions. Yet, this is what Spain did on March 2, 2012, when it rejected any EU control over its galloping deficits. On the one hand, this rejection has shown how hard it would be to implement a spending discipline. On the other hand, lack of discipline speaks volumes about the failings of the euro as a currency, and of the fact that its shortcomings have barely been addressed.

- The absence of a coordinated fiscal policy,
- Ongoing loss of competitiveness, and
- Perpetual banking troubles

explain why Euroland has tipped into recession even if beyond the €1 trillion in early July 2012 the ECB also cut its deposit rate to zero (this is the rate paid by banks parking money overnight at the central bank).

That move aims to provide banks with a large deposit base and greater incentive to lend to other eurozone banks overnight. We shall see.

At the same time, by spending €1 billion to beef up banks and sovereigns, cutting its main policy interest rate a quarter of 1 percentage point on July 5, 2012, and bringing the rate it pays on overnight deposits to zero, the European Central Bank has used its ammunitions. It has moved close to the end of the road in terms of what a normal monetary policy can do to revive a stalling economy.

The financial markets have not been impressed by this course of events. Analysts said that they doubt that a 25-basis points (1/4 of 1 percent) seems to acknowledge that the cheap three-year loans provided to banks in December 2011 and February 2012 has not had the desired effect. "Several months have passed and we see that credit flows... remain weak," Draghi himself commented.[8]

The €1 trillion liquidity removed the problem of banks not having funds to lend, but left unchanged the associate problems of having insufficient capital or appetite for risk. By Draghi's admission, "The baseline has not changed... some of the risks to the baseline scenario are now materializing."[9]

In retrospect, two reasons may lie behind this lack of success. One, as other previous initiatives in different countries have demonstrated, jump-starting the economy is a hopeless enterprise. Two, management was not at its best. Based on the experience of LTRO 1, there should have been covenants attached to LTRO 2 that borrowed funds should be used by banks to:

- Encourage them to increase corporate and household lending, which has remained scarce, and
- Discourage them to lend to governments or buy sovereign bonds.

With the December 2011 LTRO, some banks abstained from borrowing because of a perceived stigma by the market. For instance, Deutsche Bank has risked a clash with the European Central Bank by indicating it sees a problem attached to lenders trying to ease the eurozone's funding crisis. Josef Ackermann, its chief executive, signaled that Deutsche might not take up the ECB's next offer of unlimited three-year loans because it might be seen as tantamount to government aid.

Unlike the Spanish and Italian banks that correspondingly financed the Spanish and Italian government by buying their depreciated bonds, Ackermann had no need of doing so. Correctly, he looked at the ECB's LTROs as an inverse and covert government aid, documented by the net increase in government bond purchases by French, Spanish, and Italian banks following the first three-year LTRO.

This sharp spike in purchasing government bonds of profligate econo-mies led analysts to the expectation that a big part of the new uptake will again flow into the government bond market. Here is how one of the major credit institutions looked at the aftereffects of LTRO 2.

Immediate market reactions in the aftermath have been muted at best…Considering the yield paths of shorter-term (2-year) and longer term (10-year) yields of safe haven bonds in the aftermath of the last LTRO, we have seen a volatile development nonetheless ending on a flattish note.

While we expect the tail risk of a European bank default to be reduced and the stress on the interbank market to decline further, we expect the LTRO's impact on safe-haven bonds in the near and medium term to be rather limited, since fiscal problems of the Eurozone remain the undis-puted driver of any possible flight to quality. Those issues are unlikely to be permanently solved through a double liquidity injection.[10]

The accuracy of this analysis is documented by the fact that for the most part there have been Club Med banks (Italian, Spanish, and French) who queued up for ECB's cheap money. The way an article in the *Financial Times* had it: "For sure, some banks were worthy recipients as funding dried up; for others it covers maturing debt. But for *many banks, it is a chance to print money.*[11] Intesa Sanpaolo, the Italian lender, may be doing a bit of both:[12] the EUR 24 billion it took amounts to just over half the EUR 45 billion of debt that Italy must refinance this month[13] and next."[14]

It is quite interesting to note that more than half of the 800 banks that took LTRO funds were German but among themselves they borrowed less than 6 percent of the total cash.[15] There are two ways of looking at this statistic. Either the German banking industry is dominated by small players, or, most likely, those who were liquidity hungry and got the lion's share of the LTRO cash were non-German banks, mainly Italian, Spanish, and French.

3. The Destination of LTRO Funds Is as Important as Their Amount

With the euro, Europe entered a world of chimeras and unrealizable dreams of well-being. As section 2 brought to the reader's attention, the more than €1 trillion LTROs by the European Central Bank have been manna from heaven but they were used quite unevenly by the banking industry of the different member states. Next to the nearly €580 billion taken by Italian and Spanish banks came the borrowing by French and Belgian banks—around €200 billion; banks in Greece, Ireland, and Portugal took about €160 billion; and banks in Germany, Finland, and Luxembourg took a mere €80 billion.[16]

Economists said that the best credit institutions could do with that money was to allocate most of it to increasing their cushions of capital to help restore confidence. This was a course also championed by the IMF and by the Brussels-based European Banking Authority (EBA). But as we have seen, the road to higher capital levels was not the LTRO funds' final destination.

Neither the pruning of the wounded banks' balance sheets nor loans to small and medium enterprises, which provide the best employment prospects, have benefited from this mountain of ECB money borrowed by the banks. The favored final destination of funds taken by banks were the Club Med government bonds—which means the ECB money was sterilized.

For the first time, the amount of cash deposited by the borrowing banks overnight with the European Central Bank hit a record. On March 1, 2012, credit institutions parked €776.9 billion overnight in the ECB deposit facility. Some bankers said joyfully that the Long-Term Refinancing Operation is *"money printed at low cost"*[17]—and they were right. Owing to its destination, it was downgraded to second-class funds.

Also as a first, central bankers tended to play down the significance of the rapid rise in ECB deposits, saying that it was an automatic opting for safety. But analysts commented that in reality it has been one of the frustrations resulting from the ECB's massive intervention that commercial banks were:

- Either hoarding the cash, or
- Using it to buy government bonds.

Mario Draghi himself stated that he was disappointed the banks were not extending loans to companies and families to get the economy moving again. Economists were not positively impressed by the fact that Italian and Spanish banks have been much more likely to use their LTRO cash to purchase government debt than banks from other countries, such as Germany. Critics added that the risk was LTRO money stayed in ECB coffers and did not roll out into the economy, thereby defeating its objective.

Some banks could not perform their classical mission as intermediaries because their balance sheets were in a shambles. Take as example

Banca Monte dei Paschi di Siena (BMPS), an institution that dates back to 1472, and is today the third biggest Italian bank. So to speak, BMPS is more self-wounded than all other Italian credit institutions, and it was given until the end of June 2012 by the European Banking Authority to detail how it will raise the €3.3 billion of extra capital required.

- Its 8.7 percent core Tier-1 capital ratio (excluding €1.9 billion of the so-called bailout bonds) is 30 basis points shy of even the EBA hurdle, and
- The usual tricks to bolster its capital ratio, raising more than €2 billion by converting hybrid bonds and weakening risk weightings did not work. It still needs at least €1.2 billion more to satisfy the EBA.

Classically, in times of trouble, Monte dei Paschi di Sienna was addressing itself to its shareholder foundation, which owns 35 percent of the equity. More recently, however, the Italian government is BMPS's sole capital source, as well as home to a big part of its liquidity. Still, while the bank is tittering, the nearly €30 billion BMPS took from the European Central Bank in December 2011 in connection with the LTRO was put into Italian government bonds, which is a shame. (See also in chapter 3 the cover-up of the scam involving BMPS, for which the former governor of the Bank of Italy, Mario Draghi, bears responsibility.)

Terms aside, the use of big banks as surrogates of the sovereign's doubts and misbehavior is irrational. As Edward Yardeni, a respected American economist, aptly remarked: "All this liquidity should lead to self-sustaining growth. If the global economy can't grow by itself now, then we really are in trouble."[18] Providing proof that the economy stagnates even with abundant liquidity was not the ECB's goal, but there was a great deal of risk in the mounting evidence that banks were not eager to function as intermediaries.

The bulk of LTRO money spent to buy the public debt of the Club Med countries ended up making weak economies even weaker because they found a way to delay urgently needed structural changes. The false sense of having found a sucker made it more difficult to implement them. In addition, sterile money augmented the risk of a confidence crisis spilling all over the European Union.

- Structural reforms are difficult and unpopular, otherwise governments would have undertaken them long ago, and
- If sovereigns find cheap money, they will continue to avoid hard choices, even if they know that this leads to deeper recession and unemployment.

Debt in the southern European countries became a burden because each enjoyed a decade of low interest rates. But instead of using the money to restructure and come up from under, they spend it on luxuries and consumer goods. In short, they eat it up. It was not long before both the government and the general public were hit by the financial crisis. In the "good times" there was a boom in cross-border lending. After the dip of September 2008, this dried up.

- Before the crisis investors thought that no Euroland government would default on its debt.
- Rare were the economists who stated that default could happen. Those who expressed such an opinion (including the author) were criticized as bad prophets.

Alert investors, however, asked to be rewarded for the extra risk created by weakening banks and slowing growth. Creditor governments (read: Germany) faced a dilemma. On the one hand, they wanted to save troubled governments to prevent contagion. On the other, they wanted to keep up market pressure for reforms. The destination of LTRO funds served the first objective, but it became an unmitigated disaster as far as the second objective is concerned.[19]

What has happened with the LTRO could have been foreseen using as reference the purchase of sovereign bonds by the ECB. Jens Weidmann, Bundesbank president, opposed that bond purchase scheme, reflecting the widespread bad feeling toward good money running after bad money, as well as the fact that the ECB was financing state spending by Italy and Spain by printing money. In Germany, the feeling was that if the European Central Bank continued to do this for too long, its credibility would seriously shrink.

The €1 trillion in LTRO money confirmed the spoilage. Still, the pros said that the ECB's action bolstered investor confidence in Euroland. Critics answered that the ECB had gone way beyond the bounds of its mandate, and what it was doing was legally questionable. The ECB, critics insisted, has tried to bypass its statutory limitation through the Long-Term Refinancing Operations. In other words,

- The LTRO was the tool, not the policy, and
- The ECB's policy was to provide support for Italy and Spain under favorable conditions.

The pros said that whether through the LTRO, direct purchases and government bonds, or other means, the ECB finds itself obliged to intervene to save the euro—because the euro has no father. It is a single currency with 17 national fiscal and economic policies, but it has:

- No common treasury, and
- No tax-raising powers.[20]

In conclusion, according to the pros, the ECB's Long-Term Refinancing Operation has reduced risk aversion in Europe, upgrading the growth forecasts and reducing short-term risks associated with the euro. According to the critics, the LTRO spent lots of money into the bottomless pit of government debt, failing to activate bank intermediation, and also failing to fulfill the urgent need to recapitalize mismanaged banks. Over and above everything else there has been a moral hazard.

4. LTROs Have Moral Hazard

On March 13, 2012, Jens Weidmann, Bundesbank president, said that the ECB governing council members agreed that the risks taken by the European Central Bank must be subject to continuous review. He also emphasized that while all crisis measures must not be immediately withdrawn, central bankers must study the ways and means they need to organize and implement an *exit strategy*.[21]

By asking Mario Draghi, ECB president, to develop and present to the board an exit strategy, Weidmann let it be known that he is watchful of the interplay between the unorthodox policies of the ECB and the more traditional monetary policy views of the Bundesbank, which believes in inflation-targeting. Therefore, he worries that the ECB's current policies are likely to create future distortions and imbalances.

The tensions between Weidmann and Draghi escalated when a Bundesbank letter voicing its concerns was leaked to the German press. There is no question that untested, unorthodox monetary policies create potentially dangerous effects for Euroland's financial system. Over and above that comes moral risk. Therefore, it is important to plan the withdrawal of exceptional help for eurozone banks in an orderly, properly studied manner.

Getting down to basics, the president of the Bundesbank is right when he says that the timing of an exit strategy should be studied now even if its implementation depends on the economic and financial environment. Sensible risk management, for example, requires that the ECB takes steps against the weakest banks that became dependent on its liquidity; and the same is true of sovereigns.

Both with the implementation of untested monetary policies and with exit strategies, particular attention must be paid to *moral risk*. Among other cases, moral risk is associated with easy central bank money and a policy of financing sovereign deficits in an occult way via commercial banks. *Moral risk is on the rise.* The LTRO has created a moral hazard and the resulting problems can be dangerous to financial stability. A way of looking at the ECB policy under current management is that:

- Banks have been given unlimited sources of funding to make what they want, including easy profits.
- The banks' incentives to restructure their balance sheets is no longer a priority, leading to another €100 billion being thrown to the Spanish banks.
- Sovereigns got the message that they can delay or simply put in the time closet reforms that would make them more resilient in the future.

The moral hazard is present in all three points above. By all evidence, the planned consequence of the LTRO program is to relieve the pressure in the sovereign debt markets of Euroland. This, however, is counterproductive, giving the impression that money grows on trees; at the same time the peripheral Euroland countries are pushed into a deep recession that:

- Exacerbates their fiscal problems,
- Creates renewed distrust in financial markets, and
- If it succeeds, conveys the message that there is deus ex machina who pulls the profligate out of the red ink sea

Italian banks profited widely from the liquidity expansion of the ECB's balance sheet, as evidenced by the fact they have been very active in using LTRO money for government bond purchases. In Spain, helped by the ECB's huge liquidity injections, the target fiscal deficit reduction for 2012 has been in a shambles and there are regional fiscal slippages as well.

The moral risk of the ECB's LTRO trillion euro operation did not take long to surface: The momentum of deficit reduction is fading. While the Spanish prime minister was the most outspoken against measures to bend the curve of his country's budget deficits, the other chiefs of state did precisely the same without much noise.

Spain is, reportedly, *only one of 12* Euroland countries reneging on agreed austerity programs. All 12 have asked the European Commission to change their jointly (and recently) agreed deficit-reduction targets.

Christine Lagarde, the IMF president, is right when she says that European debt problems are in no way behind us.

Interviewed on February 23, 2012, by Richard Quest of CNN, Bob Parker, a former senior executive of Crédit Suisse, presented his thoughts in these words: "It will be a long time before Italy and Spain start moving again. This is not the contagion of Greek crisis. These economies have internal weaknesses." In other terms, like the Greek situation, the one prevailing in Spain and Italy is a source of contagion.

Economists, analysts, and politicians who made public their concern about potentially damaging spillover effects from the €1 trillion in three-year loans the ECB provided to Euroland's banks proved to be right. While Mario Draghi somehow signaled that the three-year liquidity offers are unlikely to be repeated, the ECB continues meeting in full banks' demands for loans lasting up to three months—another moral hazard. Easy money leads both sovereigns and banks to adopt unsustainable business models.

- Governments slowing down the pace of fiscal and structural reforms are in for a new round of troubles.
- Banks foregoing their role as an intermediary to bet on risky trading, both forego their social duty and harm themselves.

They also engage in unlawful practices that cost their shareholders dearly in terms of king-sized penalties. The $450 million Barclays had to pay American and British regulators because of manipulating the Libor is an example; the nearly $1 billion penalty that confronted HSBC is another.[22]

Something is wrong with the banking culture and evidence has been accumulating since 2007 when the economic and financial crisis started. Some central banks contributed to it. As for sovereigns, the profligates tend to forget that Euroland's debt is directly associated with big budget deficits of its member countries. This has not been a random event, and each member country itself must find its way out of it.

In addition, as bad news never comes alone, while deficits are large, growth is minimal. Not only Greece, which is so often finger-pointed, but also Italy, Spain, Portugal, and, to a lesser extent, France, don't have enough growth to maintain themselves as competitive forces in the global market. Year-on-year, their economic development:

- Is not even enough to pay part of the debt they have accumulated, and
- Instead of deleveraging, they take on more debt.

The Greek sovereign debt drama has merely paused for an interval, says Mohamed El-Erian.[23] That is true not only for Greece but also for all Mediterranean member countries of Euroland, as well as for Britain and the United States. In three years, from 2008 to 2011 the government debt:

- Of the US increased by about 19 percent,
- Of Spain by 24 percent, and
- Of Britain by 28 percent.

Of the three, only Britain started a consistent (though rather timid) effort to pull itself out of the red ink sea. Sweden and Finland, both hit by big crises in the early 1990s, had a strategic plan that accepted a *temporary* rise in fiscal deficits to protect their economy from the forced retrenchment, but in subsequent years both countries concentrated on pruning their economy and restructuring their balance sheets. They worked hard on this plan and they succeeded.

Instead of asking somebody else to recapitalize its banks, like Spain is doing these days, the Swedish government took out of the banks' portfolio non-performing loans and all sorts of heterogeneous investments that should have never been there. Take the case of PK Banken (Nordea) as an example. Rather than doing a fire sale, the government set up Securûm, a new company.[24]

- Securum was given the mission to dispose these assets slowly, as the market recovers, and
- Securum managed to sell such holdings, on an average, at 80 cents to the dollar. They would have fetched less than 50 cents in a fire sale.

Sweden's and Finland's economic recovery is a textbook case study. It is also what Euroland governments and their banks should do today to come up from under rather than going, hat in hand, to the ECB, the EU, and the IMF. This self-adjustment path depends on the government's determination not to be a beggar and on institutions not to throw money to the four winds. As long as Euroland's profligates allow themselves to keep on asking for money, their creditworthiness will suffer and their rating will remain down in the credit rating scale—while unemployment zooms and the economy remains subdued.

5. The Powerful Became Powerless

Southern Europe's debt crisis and its aftereffects were by no means inevitable. Its father has been mismanagement and its mother the policy of spending beyond one's means. Even so, if Club Med governments had taken care to adopt the Swedish and the Finnish models of economic and financial recovery they would have been out of the tunnel by now. Instead, there has been lots of resistance and a vacuum in leadership whose roots can be traced back to:

- Bad policies, and
- Dubious economics.

The wrong assumption has been repeated twice: at the Treaty of Rome and at the birth of Euroland. This assumption has been that the economies of member states would converge and, sooner rather than later, they will operate at about the same levels of performance. It did not take long to find out that the safeguards set to protect the common currency were gamed, first and foremost by Jacques Chirac, then president of France.

Chirac insisted on and obtained the renegotiation of the Stability and Growth Pact, watering it down to nothing. This gave member countries the incentive to overstep the criteria on debt ceilings and budget deficits, without any penalty by the European Commission. As debt soared, it became clear that monetary union without fiscal union was risky at best. It proved to be disastrous.

The convergence of Europe's northern economies with the southern economies became a joke. Alarm bells rang all over but economists were hopeful that better days lay ahead and politicians took no notice of the alarms until it was too late. For nearly six years in the Western world, since 2007, when the global economic, financial, and banking crisis began with the subprimes:

- Government debt skyrocketed from a fraction of GDP to over 110 percent, and
- Government overspending fed the debt spiral, which went from 1.5 percent to 6.5 percent of gross domestic product.[25]

While taxation brought less money into the sovereigns' treasuries because of the economic crisis, the cost of the Western governments' social safety net ballooned. The crisis provided evidence that the management of the economy was, at best, wanting. In the chaos that has followed, the rich got richer while the Western middle class has been obliterated.

Even the governments of formerly powerful nations—the US, Britain, and France being examples—became powerless because they lost the sense of measure. With deficits becoming monstrous as politicians showed no interest in controlling them, red ink spilled all over. At the same time, the government-run State Supermarket, into which has grown the nanny state, was simultaneously confronted by rapidly:

- Rising health care costs,
- Unfunded pension obligations,
- Upward racing costs for university education that is "free for all," and
- A low productivity but sprawling, highly expensive large public sector.

Financial ills and challenges aside, a net result has been a decline in perceived sovereign authority, which reflected strongly upon the sovereigns' creditworthiness. By not being able to throw money around at will to satisfy the entitlements, powerful politicians and bureaucrats found themselves without power, and started to contract huge debts with the excuse that the economy needs them.

There have been, as well, other fallacies. The perceived links between nearly bankrupt sovereigns and the banking industry led to increases in the borrowing costs of credit institutions, while governments first borrowed money from banks then recapitalized them.

Investors were not pleased to see that in their portfolios government debt became a substitute for bank debt, crowding the latter out. The vicious cycle was completed by the sovereigns' loss of risk-free status. This undermined financial stability in the large, but the aftereffect is particularly acute in the case of governments that cannot provide a backstop for the financial system.

It is not the least surprising that governments obliged their taxpayers to contribute. That was the easier way to obtain ready cash. Tax-and-tax spend-and-spend, however, became increasingly complex as it started being practiced cross-border. Much more than the EFSF and the ESM, the ECB's LTRO confirmed that the common currency has been turned into the instrument of a *transfer union*, and this took place in the most undemocratic way possible.

Earlier on, the excuse for setting up agencies with nothing but initials was the need to build firewalls. The pros said that they should be so high that one does not need them. The big question has been who pays? Everyone looked at the IMF, but the IMF stated it will not move until everyone gets involved. This brought the bill to the taxpayers' doorsteps.

It did not take long for everyone to find out that German taxpayers will not pay the debts of the big spenders forever. Why should they? With the change in management at the ECB, the latter assumed the role of the profligates' godfather. Indeed, it would be very interesting to know what changed the ECB's reluctance to be a lender of last resort. Draghi could provide the answer.

Critics say that this has been an abdication of central bankers' duties and responsibilities as banks bought government bonds and beefed up their capital with the ECB funds but left the private sector dry of funds. Moreover, by offering banks access to cheap funding on a longer- term basis, the ECB slowed down the pace of deleveraging—which is precisely the opposite of a rational solution.

A criticism frequently heard these days is that the leaders of EU member states and the European Commission should not have left crisis management to the ECB. Crisis management is a political responsibility and by relegating their duties so as not to be bothered by them the different governments de facto turned Mario Draghi into a politician.

At stake now is not just the ability to solve Euroland's debt problem but also stamp out the perverse logic that "more red ink is good for you." It is a measure of European politicians' capacity for delusion that they cannot pull themselves together and stop telling the public only what it wants to hear. America and Europe are bankrupt and their citizens cannot continue living the way they did during the last two to three decades.

By failing to watch carefully over their fortunes and their future, the powerful have become powerless in economic terms. With this in mind, it comes as no surprise that one of the key themes of the 2012 World Economic Forum, in Davos, was how to address Euroland's debt crisis. A forecast made prior to the opening of the conference was that the situation being what it is:

- From being an asset currency,
- The euro will revert to a liability currency.

This is precisely what is happening, aided by the LTRO and other useless spending that only creates accounting entries—not wealth. In a conference she gave in Berlin prior to Davos 2012, Christine Lagarde said that the current situation reminds her of the situation in 1930, and it might turn out to be a 1930-type crisis. Lagarde is not alone in expressing this opinion. Here are other opinions by the panelists of one of Davos 2012 events, held on January 28, 2012.

Guillermo Ortiz, former governor of the central bank of Mexico:

"We must be questioning whether all financial innovation is useful.

Jean-Claude Trichet, former president of the European Central Bank:

"Central banks can only reduce the intensity of bank collapse."

Peter Sands, CEO, Standard Chartered Bank:

"We never really know which banks are really systemically important."

Adair Turner, president, Financial Services Authority (FSA):

"A fundamental problem is sovereign uncertainty which reflects in the banks' capital needs."

In Turner's opinion, we should be more cautious now than before the crisis in allowing processes like high frequency trading, which may have unexpected and unwanted consequences. FSA's president also stressed the point that "banks should have internal ring-fencing," adding that anybody who, after dividing commercial from investment banking, forgets about investment bank supervision, has forgotten Lehman.

I would add that every one of the aforementioned 12 Euroland member countries who returned to their profligate habits by getting €100 billion for their banks and whatever they can obtain for sovereign spending, has forgotten Greece. Coming up from under is not only a demanding and painful process but also a rewarding process. However, when Europe's and America's political programs are as barren as they are, the vacuum is filled with trivia and ephemera.

6

Fiscal Compact and Outright Monetary Transactions

1. The Fiscal Compact Is an Upgraded Stability and Growth Pact

An adjunct to the Treaty of the European Union that established the euro as common currency, allegedly its *alter ego*, has been the *Stability and Growth Pact* (SGP). Its rules, indeed its very existence, were engineered by François Mitterrand, the French president, and Guilio Andreotti, the Italian prime minister, to trap Helmut Kohl, the German chancellor, into abandoning the deutschmark in favor of the euro. What become known as the Maastricht Treaty[1] was signed in February 1992.

The Stability and Growth Pact proved to be hot air. Not only were its rules taken lightly by its signatories, but they were also most significantly downsized by Jacques Chirac (who succeeded Mitterrand as president of France) during the Dublin meeting that was supposed to look into the SGP's proper implementation. These changes left the pact as a shadow of its original version, not to say meaningless, as documented by the fact that no government of a Euroland member state:

- Bothered to observe even its waterered-down version, or
- Was required to pay a penalty when violating the SGP rules on budgetary deficits.

Critics say that rather than helping to integrate the old continent, the different treaties and pacts of the European Union turned the clock back to Europe's age of absolute monarchies. The EU's "added value" merely consisted of another layer of bureaucracy—a nearly useless overhead of 35,000 bureaucrats in Brussels and of about 17,000 lobbyists. *Euroland*, the countries tied to the common currency, has also been a story of deception.

While the first decade of the euro went more or less smoothly, the second decade started badly largely due to:

- The global economic, financial, and banking crisis that began in 2007;
- Deteriorating global economic conditions, which swamped growth and aggravated the debt problem;
- Mismanagement of Euroland finances as a whole, which saw to it that there is plenty of debt but no financial discipline;
- Profligacy accompanied by steady budgetary deficits, particularly among Euroland's southern member states;[2] and
- Flaws in the original design of euro and of Euroland, whose aftereffect increasingly began showing up as the common currency came under stress.

Two decades after the by-now irrelevant Stability and Growth Pact, the *Fiscal Compact* (FC) saw the light. Its signatories affirm their commitment to structural reforms, budgetary discipline, further dismantling of barriers to competition, and reduction of excessive bureaucratic procedures. The aim is that of hitting two birds with one well-placed stone: boosting potential growth while at the same time assuring monetary stability.

The main goal the Fiscal Compact set for itself is to bring a sense of responsibility into the making of sovereign budgets by Euroland's member states. The intention is good, but the question is: *How*?[3] This is a challenging query and it reveals that there are two views of the FC:

- A theoretical view, and
- A practical view.

The theoretical (in the sense that the probability of the Fiscal Compact being effectively applied is zero-point-zero) distinguishes between a *primary law*, at the national and intergovernmental levels within Euroland focusing on balanced budgets, and a *secondary law* (supposed to be EU-wide) targeting a resurrected, but not so much reinforced, Stability and Growth Pact.

An example will help to explain the difference between primary and secondary law. Under the SGP, the *medium-term objective* (MTO)[4] of budgetary discipline is "close to balance or surplus" (a vague statement) with a 1percent structural deficit of GDP for Euroland member states. The FC specifies "balanced budget or surplus" with the MTO maximal structuring deficit of 0.5 percent of GDP (more on this in section 2).

The practical view is documented and sustained by the fact that, given their past policies, sovereigns are not likely to abide by the rules of a system incorporating the balanced budget discipline—even if it is voted by their parliaments. As already stated, over the dozen years of the euro's existence, the SGP has never been really implemented; why will it be different this time around? Knowing how politicians interpret numbers and apply rules, it is not far-fetched to think that they would react by saying: "Make me laugh." Take the escape clauses as an example.

In the SGP, the escape clause for not applying the rules is severe economic downturn in Euroland or in the whole EU;[5] unusual events outside government control;[6] and implementation of structural or pension reforms. This means that under current conditions there is no need to apply budgetary discipline whatsoever. Budget deficits are welcome. That's a *very bad* rule and it has not really been improved under the FC, which "reinforces SGP"—another vague statement[7].

The SGP did not lack benchmarks in terms of convergence to budgetary objective. Its benchmark was the annual improvement of a structural balance of 0.5 percent of GDP, supposed to be higher in good economic periods. It was also a member country's public debt-to-GDP ratio at or below 60 percent (which is by now an impossible condition). Neither clause was taken seriously by Euroland's member states over the years of the SGP's existence.

The Fiscal Compact changes practically nothing in this approach, except an abstract addition of "evaluation of progress" and another general-type reference to "rapid convergence to medium term objective." This convergence is largely wishful thinking and it is even very poorly specified, as the details have been left to the European Commission— which is also supposed to take sustainability risks into consideration, a "make me laugh" clause.

Past experience is unconvincing. Fiscal consolidation in Euroland has not really taken off. Sizeable efforts are needed to restore fiscal sustainability, but the confidence for it is lacking. Uncertainty regarding future economic, fiscal, and financial developments remains high in many member countries and this uncertainty is further aggravated by adverse events and reform fatigue, even if little has been done so far to:

- Correct fiscal imbalances,
- Implement structural reforms, and
- Restore confidence in the stability of the common currency.

There is no viable alternative to rigorous fiscal adjustment in order to restore confidence in fiscal sustainability, particularly in countries receiving

EU/ECB/IMF financial support and those under financial market pressures. The negative consequences of a slow pace toward budgetary discipline hit hard. Relaxing already ambiguous consolidation efforts increases uncertainty and this affects private confidence and economic prospects.

The pros say that though the risk that Fiscal Compact rules may not be fully observed is real, the structure of it makes sense because a state budget's general provisions are clearly stated and are generally in accord with the European Union's regulations. In theory this may be true, but it is so often violated in practice that it makes no sense even to talk about it.

Euroland's and the EU's member states have demonstrated little inclination in complying with the torrent of laws, rules, and regulations coming out of Brussels and of useless "summits." For this they have two excuses:

- Sovereignty, and
- Costs associated with compliance.

The Fiscal Compact's balanced budget rule makes reference to the MTO of the SGP requiring the government budget to be close to balance or in surplus. In practical terms, however, that statement makes sense only when there is a supranational Euroland authority that:

- Controls each member country's budget, indeed all of its chapters, and
- Has veto power not only over the original budget but also over all subsequent excesses or even modifications to this budget in the course of its implementation.

As an example of modifications due to spending habits, on October 28, 2012, it was announced that the French government would guarantee €7 billion ($9.1 billion) of bonds by Peugeot, the auto manufacturer, which is confronted by financial trouble as it has lost 20 percent of its market. This clearly violated the balanced budget rule, as the French budget is already in deficit.[8] Peugeot's troubles started in mid-2012; hence no provision for the handout was made in late 2011 when the French budget for 2012 was elaborated.

In addition, prior to the €7 billion budget overrun, the French government had publicly said that it was searching for a new income of €11 billion to tie up the 2012 budget given current expenses. (It was also searching for an extra €32 billion needed for the 2013 budget.) That means the hole in the French government's budget for 2012 grew from €11 billion to €18 billion—a large sum. How does that fitt with the Fiscal Compact?

The pros say that the Fiscal Compact provides for an "automatically" triggered correction mechanism; however, how it will work is still unclear except for the statement that it will be based on common principles to be proposed by the European Commission. This is incomplete and unsatisfactory. What it practically means is that it is not the text voted by national parliaments but the Commission that must specify strict and binding requirements for the correction procedures, which subsequently may or may not be implemented in national law as some member countries will certainly object to them (as per their habit).

With regard to assessing compliance, the Stability and Growth Pact (which is now part of the FC) had provided a clause for estimating deviations for a member state that had not reached its MTO. Such deviations were defined as a simultaneous break of two criteria:

- Negative impact of expenditures development, and
- Structural deficit exceeding the limits mentioned earlier on.

The FC establishes as criterion for compliance evaluation "significant observed deviations from the MTO or adjustment path towards it," which is a vague definition bordering on a loophole. It also makes reference to two contradictory notions: common principles and independence of national monitoring. The common principles will be proposed by the European Commission—which has not yet been done and is another loose end.

Both the Stability and Growth Pact and the Fiscal Compact have a clause regarding the correction mechanism. That of the SGP rests on two legs: a warning by the European Commission (which in the past proved to be totally ineffectual) and European Council recommendations for needed policy measures (idem). The FC requires that the correction mechanism is:

- Triggered automatically,
- Implemented at national level, and
- Governed by debt dynamics that guide the course of correction.

The concept is nice, but how it will turn into reality is still to be seen. This will be probably done through enforcement, which is another open question. Under the SGP, the European Commission could propose financial sanctions with automatic implementation unless the European Council rejects it. No sanctions have been applied so far despite the budgetary chaos. What changes with the FC is that such sanctions can also be imposed by the European Court of Justice—which is an unlikely road to enforcement in the absence of political union.

2. What Might the Fiscal Compact Be Worth in the Longer Term?

The better way to answer the question posed by this section's title is to first examine the Fiscal Compact's heralded strengths. Its golden rule is that it fixes the limit of budgetary deficits at 0.5 percent of gross domestic product (GDP). However, this limit can be increased to up to 1 percent but only for countries with a government debt-to-GDP ratio significantly below 60 percent and with low risks to long-term fiscal sustainability.

In other words, such an upper limit of 0.5 percent is subject to different conditions. *If* the already accumulated public debt is more than 60 percent (which is the typical case in Euroland), *then* this greater level of public debt-to-GDP must be reduced at the rate of 1/20 per year. France, for instance, will have to reduce its nearly €1.9 trillion ($2.4 trillion) public debt by €600 billion (roughly $800 billion) over a period of 20 years, or €30 billion ($38.3 billion) per year.

To say that this will not be an easy thing to do, and it may never happen, is to state the obvious. No French sovereign budget has been deficit-free since 1974. The prevailing thinking that any remaining output gap after 2015 will gradually close at a rate of between 0.25 percent and 0.5 percent per annum, and that the rate of inflation will be at or below 2 percent, in line with the ECB's monetary policy,are ill-supported hypotheses made by people who enjoy being deceived.

In Paris, the government foresees the achievement of a structurally balanced budget by 2015, but the economic growth assumptions being made are too optimistic. Therefore, the case of this happening is rather remote. Much also depends on interest rates. The EU and the ECB assume that the pass-through of market interest rates to the average effective interest rate on government debt will not upset member state budgets. No two member countries, however, have the same profile. Whether or not a steady course proves to be the case, depends inter alia on:

- Existing and expected future maturity structure of government debt,
- Projected future financing needs of unbudgeted events,[9] and
- The exact definition of all factors involved in structural deficits, and indeed the definition of structural deficit itself (both are still missing).

As long as exact definitions are not available and rules are open to interpretations, each party feels free to make its own choices and calculations. The French Senate, for example, defines the structural deficit as one that will be observed *if* the GDP is not equal to its potential. But how would objective be the estimation of this "potential" and who would judge the "equity"?

The answer is far from being evident as the French ministry of finance has a different definition of what is meant by structural deficit: It suffices not to account for prevailing general conditions. And how are the "general conditions" going to be qualified and quantified? Will their evaluation be based on Euroland-wide criteria, or will each member country establish its own?

As if these discrepancies within the same country were not enough, supranational organizations have and use their own metrics of what is and what is not a structural deficit. For example, the French structural deficit, which was estimated at 3.7 percent in a measurement by the ministry of finance, stood at 3.4 percent by the IMF and 4.1 percent by the European Commission.

Another clause of the FC states that if observed deviations from the balanced budget target, or the convergence path toward it, are considered significant, they will be evaluated on the basis of an overall assessment. However, as long as the structural balance is used as a reference, including an analysis of expenditure net of discretionary revenue measures, France is in a better position than Italy, Spain, Portugal, and some other Euroland member countries. What applies to France should apply to them. In other words:

- In budgetary overruns, nearly one out of two Euroland member states will be in the sickbed, and
- There is no clause in the FC defining for how long they are allowed to stay under intensive care.

This intensive care will cost a fortune given Mario Draghi's decision to do "what it takes" to support the euro (evidently by printing paper money) and to buy an "unlimited" amount of sovereign bonds under certain conditions (see sections 5 and 6). Single-handedly, an appointed official (the president of the ECB) destroyed whatever might have been the impact of the Fiscal Compact on Euroland's governments. Socrates was right when he said that tragedy and comedy is the same thing, and should be written by the same person.

- If the ECB buys the member countries' bonds, provided they ask for ESM assistance, then profligate sovereigns can throw the FC, which has been voted by their parliaments, into the wastebasket.
- The lack of coordination between what the parliaments of Euroland's member states committed themselves to and the doings of appointed executives at the European Central Bank is so big that anything goes.

This most deep contradiction is no good news if you are living in Euroland. It is a flatfooted approach, unravelling economic and financial discipline. As if this was not enough, it happens at a time when austerity measures imposed on struggling countries contribute to social unrest Mediterranean style.

Appointed Euroland officials make small game of authority and once authority is lost it is nearly impossible to regain. Why should governments try to balance their budget when the ECB comes as deus ex machina? Lofty sermons about killing sovereign budget deficits weight very little if you have a friend ready to finance all your expenses and (may be) all your follies.

In fact, the timing of the Fiscal Compact itself is vague, leaving lots of freedom. François Hollande, the French president, has promised zero deficit for 2017 (that's the last year he is in office, if he does not get reelected). Hence the FC mechanism of doing away with the debt-to-GDP ratio of over 60 percent would not start getting in motion before 2018—and this, too, is overoptimistic. Even under that assumption, France will not conform to the Fiscal Compact's clauses prior to 2038. Other countries will comply even later.

Compliance at infinity and beyond is the way to bet if past performance in debt behavior among Western sovereigns is taken into account. Statistics published in late September 2012 by *Bloomberg Businessweek* and covering the period from 2002 to 2012, make small game of the Fiscal Compact's assumptions. The focal point of these statistics has been the *increase in debt per capita* over the aforementioned decade. In three-digit numbers this has been:

- 223 percent in Britain; hence, more than 22 percent per year,
- 151 percent in the United States; more than 15 percent per year,
- 142 percent in Portugal; more than 14 percent per year, and
- 105 percent in Greece; more than 10 percent per year.[10]

The important issue in these statistics is not *why* some countries have a three-digit number in terms of increasing per capita debt in the course of a decade (excuses will be always found), but the trend. This trend is very negative as far as budget discipline is concerned. The *Bloomberg Businessweek* statistics have six other countries with two-digit rise in debt per capita. These are:

- 94 percent in Spain, or 9.4 percent per year (Spain almost made it to a three-digit debt increase),
- 90 percent in France, or 9.0 percent per year,

- 63 percent in Germany, or 6.3 percent per year,
- 47 percent in Canada, or 4.7 percent per year, and
- 37 percent in Japan, or 3.7 percent per year.[11]

By focusing on just one variable, *increase in debt per capita*, one can work on the assumption that differences average out due to other factors. This is important inasmuch as Euroland's countries have different social and political structures, levels of industrialization, productivity, cost control policies, and export strategies.

The message coming from these references is that *if* disciplined countries have not been able to control their public debt, *then* the mandatory implementation of the balanced budget rule and automatically triggered correction mechanism at national level will remain highly theoretical issues. They will do little if anything to improve the national commitment to sound and sustainable public finances.

Whether we talk of economic projections, of postmortem evaluation of statistical evidence, debt-to-GDP scenarios, or change in debt per capita, these are nearly always based on assumptions. One of the most basic is that the governments concerned have the will and power to achieve structurally balanced budgets in the medium term. The debt-to-GDP ratio could stay in a downward trajectory only *if* Euroland governments:

- Live up to their commitments under the FC fiscal governance framework,
- Deliver the required progress toward structural balance, followed by surpluses, and
- Are able to enhance longer-term growth prospects by carrying out structural reforms, increasing the productivity of home industries, and gaining global competitiveness.

In conclusion, a general vulnerability of the FC and the SGP, as well as of their framework, is that they lack enforcement and correction mechanisms at the supranational level. Article 5 of the Fiscal Compact states that member countries who fail in their effort will be put under supervision. Who will have the authority to tell independent states what they must do? And what if all or nearly all of the member states fail to stop increases in their public debt, as it has happened in the past?

To make the puzzle more interesting, are the European Council and the European Commission to whom the Fiscal Compact makes reference, able to perform a really effective supervisory mission? Is their Authentic Act giving them the authority to do so? Do they have the skills? They may be happy to collect the 0.5 percent of GDP as a penalty from one or more countries failing to apply the rules, but having bureaucrats control other bureaucrats brings memories of the Soviet Union.

3. Economic Problems Mount as Sovereigns Lose Their Luster

As far as the Fiscal Compact is concerned, the argument of the pros is that its enhancements over the SGP should facilitate a more rapid convergence toward country-specific medium-term objectives (MTO), especially when due consideration is given to a country's idiosyncratic risks to fiscal sustainability. These are generally looked at as part of the aftermath of a financial crisis, but this is only partly true because they are as well the result of sovereign leadership. Nearly always, the absence of a strong leadership causes fiscal sustainability risks to rise substantially, as can be observed in many Euroland countries.

We enter 2012 in a very cautious and conservative mood, because a state of unfinished business is not a healthy environment for aggressive investing, said Andreas Höfert, chief economist of UBS, back in December 2011. A year later, we can say that we entered 2013 under deteriorating conditions because:

- The debt level of Euroland sovereigns has increased in absolute terms,
- Budget deficits of most Euroland member states are still high, even if they have been trimmed somewhat, and
- Under the weight of heavy debt, with the exception of the housing sector, the American economy still refuses to lift up.

The crisis of the euro will continue till the Euroland leaders fail to address the underlying problem of the crisis: the lack of political integration. Attempts to close the gap through half-baked measures lead nowhere. Ambitious steps toward improving Euroland's fiscal framework are necessary but not enough. Euroland's member countries must address a lot of loose ends by talking to one another, not in parochial, political languages, but in one everybody understands because all critical issues are put on the table.

In early eighteenth century, when Isaac Newton was Master of the Mint,[12] he answered a question about economic projections with the statement that he could not calculate the madness of people. We cannot do any better than that today. Nor are we able to calculate the aftereffect of resurgent nationalistic impulses in the old continent, which nowadays are financial rather than territorial.

Berlin's position is that both budget discipline and growth are necessary to stem the crisis in Euroland, with financial discipline being a precondition for sustainable growth. Officially, there is broad agreement between Angela Merkel and François Hollande on the need for fiscal discipline and growth. Privately, however, there is concern in the German government that Euroland's leaders "play politics" the old way. For example, Mario Monti, the Italian prime minister, is closer to the position of Hollande on the need for favoring economic stimulus by getting deeper into debt.

While the prime minister of Italy Monti backed the idea that government borrowing can be justified for investment, if not for current spending. This worried Berlin and led to a never-ending debate between fiscal responsibility and stimulus. If Paris did not fully see the need for fiscal discipline, Rome saw it—but it was haunted by another emergency: to protect itself from the Damocles sword of accumulated public debt of €2.1 trillion ($2.73 trillion).

Fairly similar challenges haunt Spain, another of Euroland's sovereigns who have lost their luster. The lack of a really comprehensive and fully agreed-upon strategic plan is the reason why 17 heads of government are unable to spell out concrete proposals that can cut debt and stimulate growth. One of the ideas that has been floated is to create the so-called "project bonds"—debt backed by all 17 Euroland countries—that would raise funds for infrastructure projects in depressed regions. It has been shot down because it looked too much like "eurobonds" (chapter 4).

A Plan B has been worked out by the profligates. It is archaic and supernationalistic, with very limited chance of success. Labeled "Second Versailles,"[13] it simply aims to eat up German euros for breakfast. Rumor has it that this Plan B still dominates French, Italian, and Spanish thinking. A practical example is the meeting of June 22, 2012, in Rome that preceded the Miracle Weapons "summit" of June 28—29, 2012, in Brussels (chapter 3).

During that Rome meeting, which followed back-to-back with the failed "summit" of G20 in Los Cabos, Mexico, Merkel declined to endorse affirmations by all three of her colleagues of the "need" to use Euroland's bailout funds (EFSF, ESM) to stabilize financial markets. "We need to use all existing mechanisms to stabilize markets, to give confidence, to fight speculation," said Hollande. Merkel answered that Europe, and most particularly Euroland, had to:

- Respect existing rules, and
- Work toward common structures to regulate the euro rather than have policies emanating from "17 parliaments each with national sovereignty."[14]

Like the Greeks and the Portuguese before them, the Spanish, Italians, and eventually French, are confronted with the triple whammy of rising labor costs, a generous social net (of their own making), and a strong currency (with which they lack experience). The Club Med countries never really put their economic and financial house in order. Their debt has never been written down sufficiently to give them a new start. Therefore,

- They look at the ECB, which they conquered,[15] as the savior, and
- Bet on pulling and pushing the central bank to receive relief.

It is no less true that nowadays several Western central banks no more resist the governments' appeal to come to their rescue or to keep interest rates near zero; but this is flawed. Looking back 20 years, the US tried a low interest rate policy in 1992–93 and this led to bond market speculation in 1993 and the market crash in 1994 when the Fed increased interest rates. The Japanese repeated the same wrong-way strategy in 1995 to salvage their overexposed banking system, and this led to more than two decades of economic hibernation.

While their income reduced because of the economic downturn, governments are fearful of tackling the very expensive entitlements to right the balance. With the socialist push for a "Put the People First" agenda, entitlement programs have been rising without paying attention to the economic consequences. In the United States, the Congressional Budget Office says that cash welfare—mainly aid to families with dependent children (AFDC)—accounts for 65 percent of legal income among single mothers in the bottom fifth of America's income ranks. The best solution would be family planning. But under current conditions, who has the political courage to propose it? AFDC is also a racial issue because the beneficiaries are mainly African Americans, with many standing at poverty line level.

- Pensions, food stamps, medical care, and so on cost the government money and are part of the current big deficit.
- Future pensions, negative income tax, handouts of food stamps, doctors' fees, and so on are not properly accounted ahead of time.

Offering a pension is like incurring a debt, since it involves the promise of a series of future payments. When the government, the employer, or pension funds calculate the value of their liabilities, they therefore use a bond yield to discount future payments. As bond yields fall,[16] the liabilities rise—something that central bankers probably did not properly consider when setting and keeping interest rates near zero.

What I wrote about pensions is equally valid of Medicare/Medicaid costs in the US and similar health care social programs in Europe. It is surprising that legislators fail to appreciate that, beyond a certain threshold, social benefits are a big drag on the country's economy and therefore creators of unemployment, over and above the big deficits that are counterproductive. Ironically, as most studies show, every 10 percent increase in compensation benefits results in a 5 percent increase in the number of workers who file claims. Think of this when you read the statistics on unemployment.

4. European Banking Industry and the Liikanen Committee

The taxpayer is asked to salvage not only teetering sovereigns, but also mismanaged banks, which are more interested in gambling with derivatives and distributing fat bonuses than in serving their community and the economy with loans. The shifting aims and finite resources of the European Stability Mechanism (ESM, chapter 4) are also supposed to take care of self-wounded financial institutions even if their losses date way back in the past.

In the 1950s, President Dwight Eisenhower had spoken of the *military-industrial complex* that was milking the American economy. Now we have the *sovereign-big banks complex* that is doing just the same in every Western country. With its largesse in using its printing presses the European Central Bank is ready to come to the self-wounded banks' rescue. The same policy is followed by the Euroland's ministers of finance.

Theoretically, but only theoretically, better economic governance and an improved financial stability framework could help to break this hazardous feedback between government and the financial industry. Practically, this is conditioned by two big *ifs*:

- *If* governments provide the example by living up to their responsibility to assure fiscal prudence, and
- *If* the banking industry returns to its original goal of acting as the economy's treasurer and developer.

The second *if* means that banks should act as trustees, and not as gamblers—whether this gambling is with derivatives, real estate, or anything else. In so doing they should both watch over their capital adequacy and restore sustainable profitability. With sound liquidity and capital profiles, they will be less vulnerable to changes in asset valuations, including those related to government debt holdings (which should be measured, not extreme).

This is indeed a desired scenario, but it does not reflect today's policies, and the time needed to achieve it will depend on proper decisions to that effect by legislators, chiefs of state, and central bankers. Results will, to a large extent, depend on how quickly new policies are adopted, how comprehensive they will be, and how well they are implemented.

A sound way to look at the prevailing banking crisis is as a consequence of structural economic weakness, proliferation of high stakes, and the unprecedented indebtedness of Western governments, to which banks are always ready to lend. Of course banks also suffer from other reasons like overexposure to one industry, like real estate, which led to the burst of the housing bubble. Not-so-prudent habits of the banks' management lead to investor skepticism and deteriorating asset quality.

The consequence is the banks' inability to build up reserves and to strengthen their capital base. While too-big-to fail banks got a permanent blank check, smaller institutions found it difficult to operate since they lack government support, central bank patronage, and the degree of diversification of larger peers. But the most common denominator of bank failures is disrespect for risks being assumed.

There are reasons to believe that this may be changing. The review of the structure of European Union banking by a committee chaired by Erkki Liikanen, governor of the central bank of Finland,[17] has come up with four important points for reorganization of the financial industry. The first is *ringfencing of trading*, not of retail activities, as the British Independent Commission on Banking (ICB) recommended. Ringfencing of trading is the central recommendation of the Liikanen Committee, whose members have been European policy makers and former banking industry executives.

Notice, however, that this is a recommendation—not the law. Already bank lobbyists are at work to demolish the Liikanen Committee recommendation as they did in the US with the downsizing of the Volcker rule. Neither is it clear whether a threshold will be set for the maximum volume of trading activities as a proportion of total assets, before a ringfence must be created. Politics have come into play to upset a sound proposal.

Another of the Liikanen Committee's recommendations focuses on capital requirements connected to trading assets and real estate loans. The committee also suggests an extra capital buffer for trading book assets. This is in line with Basel III capital requirements that enforce greater levels of loss-absorbent equity capital for the banks. Evidently, these will affect the return on equity (ROE).

The third recommendation by the Liikanen Committee demands a hierarchy of debt instruments that can be bailed-in. These instruments must also be part of senior management bonuses to align their interests with those of creditors, rather than with those of equity holders. The fourth recommendation is an extension of the third. The Liikanen Committee's report makes valuable suggestions for improved bank governance, beyond remuneration of executives and traders. The most important among them have to do with:

- Transparency,
- Risk control, and
- A more comprehensive, as well as greater, disclosure of risks.

A more comprehensive disclosure of risks must effectively include well-done and honest *stress tests*.[18] True enough, over the last three years there has been a certain reliance on stress tests, but these have not been dependable in terms of results.[19] They were done to prove a point—such as, there is no need for additional capital, or what is needed is limited.

Typically, though not always, this has been self-damaging. Look at the results of stress tests done time and again on Spanish banks, which have gone from needing a cumulative €25 billion to €65 billion, while the market thinks that what is really needed is €300 billion ($390 billion) or more.

Stress tests are most valuable when they are done right. Lies have short legs, because the market knows the tricks behind them. Consequently, the heralded results are unable to shore up confidence in banks. The market simply does not believe if wrongly done "stress tests" say that banks have enough capital to withstand a crisis. This brings back the need to recapitalize banks. The question is: Who pays?

The answer is a cocktail of Euroland's taxpayers' money and the output of the ECB's printing presses. These are practically handouts and, as such, they don't reassure depositors and investors that the banks are sound. Confidence also takes leave when "stress tests" are followed by revelations of deep capital holes in some banks.[20]

What self-wounded banks really need most of all is first-class governance and along with it more capital, which does not come from handouts but has to be obtained by the institution itself. For this, there exist three ways. The first is that practically all banks need to cut costs with a sharp knife to boost capital, keeping a close watch on requirements by both Basel III and the Liikanen Committee.[21] Costs matter.

The second solution is selling assets, provided the bank has any valuable assets left. For instance at the end of September 2012, Bank of America's Merrill Lynch division sold its non-US wealth management business[22] to Julius Baer. At about the same time, Citigroup sold Smith Barney to Morgan Stanley. Société Générale, meanwhile, has been selling its stake in TCW, a US manager, to the Carlyle Group. And at the end of October 2012, Crédit Agricole sold its loss-making Emporiki Bank in Greece for a symbolic €1 ($1.3)—absorbing heavy losses but at least stopping the river of red ink.

The third and better way to increase capital reserves is to get out in the market and issue bonds—or, preferably, equity. In September–October 2012, some European banks were able to issue bonds with relatively long maturities in currencies like dollars, that until recently were denied them. The lot includes France's BNP Paribas and Société Générale as well as Spain's BBVA. This issuance reopened a funding market that had been closed for about a year and a half.[23]

Late 2012 was a relatively good time to beef up capital because the banks' funding costs had fallen, reflecting a certain increase in market confidence. By contrast, bad news lay in the fact that recovery in bank-bond issuance was confined mainly to big banks and institutions in core European countries. In 2012, smaller banks cancelled planned bond sales after they were unable to attract enough interest from investors.

The fact that certain banks still face problems in addressing the capital markets in no way means that governments and the ECB should go ahead with the (wrong) policy of keeping on injecting capital. It is only normal that banks encountering financial problems go bust. Nor should the ESM take on the risk of bank investing, not least because it knows nearly nothing about the balance sheets of individual lenders—or, for that matter, those of sovereigns.

- If there is no firewall between taxpayers and banks, the habit of robbing the taxpayers will continue, and
- In the final analysis, the money the ECB manages and that of the ESM is taxpayers' money—it did not grow on trees.

The ECB's and ESM's creditworthiness are at stake. When Spain got downgraded in mid-October 2012, the market's reaction was that this reflected on the ESM's credit, even if the ESM was not yet fully functional. A similar statement can be made about the European Central Bank and its "unlimited" Outright Monetary Transactions (sections 5 and 6). Everything "unlimited" is suspect. Hitler, too, thought he had unlimited resources to conquer the world and you know how that ended.

5. Outright Monetary Transactions (OMT)

On September 6, 2012, Mario Draghi, president of the European Central Bank, announced a new policy of *outright monetary transactions* (OMT).

This consists of "unlimited" purchase by the ECB of sovereign bonds of Euroland's member countries provided certain conditions are fulfilled. Purchasing public debt issued by member states has been a violation of the EU's Lisbon Treaty[24] (Articles 123 and 125) as well as of the ECB's own statutes. Moreover, it has been a unilateral move contradicting other Euroland acts approved by parliament, such as the Fiscal Compact.

In Germany, Holland, and Finland, his proposed plan "to save the euro by buying the bonds of countries with distressed debt" has been poorly received, and for good reason. Large parts of German public opinion, and not only the Bundesbank president Jens Weidmann, consider the OMT a step that threatens to unleash hyperinflation by:

- Turning the ECB into a political plaything, and
- Putting taxpayers' money at high risk.

Draghi heard as much when on October 24, 2012, he acted as an experienced politician on a mission to win over deeply skeptical German legislators and public opinion. He spoke in a closed session to some 100 members of the Bundestag, defending his bond-buying program in an unprecedented appearance to convince them that the purchases would not lead to rampant inflation. The majority of those who listened remained unconvinced.

One German parliamentarian (on record) dubbed the Italian "a Prussian from southern Europe," but he was taken lightly by others. The majority were doubtful and dismissive. Frank Schäffler, a vocal critic of the ECB under its current management, said he doubts Draghi would combat inflation as had promised, adding that: "It's not enough to portray yourself as [an inflation] hawk when you're really just a dove under a hawk's feathers."[25]

Alexander Dobrindt, a leading Bavarian conservative (who did not attend the session), likened the ECB president to a "money-forger."[26] In its way this dramatizes the statement made by Alan Greenspan, the former chairman of the Federal Reserve, in an October 24, 2012, interview by CNBC: "We have substituted central bank credit for the fiscal deficit of countries."

Greenspan's and Dobrindt's views of the more recent central bank facts of monetary easing and busy paper money printing are two faces of the same coin. Both have been ringing alarm bells and rightly so. To understand the reasons, let's look in more detail at how this OMT metamorphosis of counterfeit money looks like.

For starters, the OMT has been Draghi's self-fulfilling prophecy. In July 2012, he publicly proclaimed that "within our mandate, the ECB is ready to do whatever it takes to preserve the euro."[27] A couple of months later, the ECB gave itself the right to engage in outright monetary transactions to address "severe distortions" in government bond markets, based on "unfounded fears" (whatever that might mean).

The pros says that the OMT has offered a backstop of support to politicians, helping them to press ahead with the difficult measures needed to restore competitiveness and growth in the region. Politicians have failed in this task for five years, why they will now go ahead with OMT is a mystery. In addition, the pros' claim is hanging on a fork. Though the OMT announcement did provide some comfort for investors, taking the pressure off the euro, this was a feat that only lasted a couple of weeks. Critics answer that the OMT is another unjustified handout.

- It does nothing to correct the economic weakness within the common currency area.
- No chief of state of a highly indebted country has used it since it was announced.
- Its effect on market psychology was quickly discounted by the markets.
- The further-out impact of the ECB's bond-buying plan remains highly uncertain.

According to the rules that accompanied the ECB's decision on the OMT, purchases of sovereign Euroland bonds will be conducted in the secondary market only, to comply with the monetary financing prohibition (Article 123 of the Lisbon Treaty). Jurists say that this is not a sufficient condition and therefore the Treaty of the Functioning of the European Union has been violated. In terms of its mechanics, the OMT:

1. Has as primary target future sovereign cases associated with EFSF/ ESM[28] macroeconomic adjustments (like those of Spain and Italy, as of early September 2012), being conditional upon a country asking for bailout.

Experts looked at the *conditionality* of the OMT as subjugating monetary policy, which is the ECB's prime business, to fiscal policy. However, like the Federal Reserve in America, the ECB has no right to enter into fiscal issues.

2. Addresses bond maturities of up to three years; hence, longer yields would stay elevated as bondholders remain concerned about countries' willingness and ability to implement necessary reforms.

The OMT may also be considered for Euroland's member states currently under a bailout program (Greece, Portugal, Ireland) when they regain bond market access—but not while they are still under the "Troika's" tutelage. Critics say that this is a discrimination suggesting that the OMT has been cut to fit Italy's and Spain's needs.

This may prove too optimistic because, in the opinion of securities analysts, the ECB's sovereign bond-buying program will not solve Euroland's problems, though it might buy peripheral member states time to improve a difficult situation. As for the choice of shorter maturities, these are closer to the focus of monetary policy as well as to short-term bank lending rates, but there is no guarantee that sometime in the future the ECB will not sell short maturities of public debt, and buy long maturities like the Fed did with "Twist." Nowadays, central banks have a cunning ability of copying one another.

In an article in the *Financial Times*, Wolfgang Münchau expressed the opinion that the dwindling chances of a banking union put Mario Draghi in a tight spot: "His OMT program needs a banking union to work. The ECB's liquidity backstops guarantees the banks, for now. The OMT guarantees the sovereign debt. As these programs run out—which they eventually will—the Eurozone needs an institutional framework in place to deal with the two intertwined risks of banks and sovereigns."[29] As chapter 3 brought to the reader's attention, however, the proposed banking union has been an ambush on Euroland's treasury, orchestrated by the Spanish and Italian prime ministers and joined by the French president. It is:

- A concept full of errors and omissions,
- Characterized by floppiness in planning, and
- With plenty of bad judgment regarding risks.

"Without the bond buying program, market volatility would put the future of the monetary union currency at risk," said Scott Thiel, deputy chief investment officer of fixed income at BlackRock. "You cannot eliminate massive budget deficits overnight. The deficits are the result of years of imbalances, which will take time to correct. The governments in question face a delicate balancing act, treading a fine line between austerity and regaining sovereignty."[30] Theoretically, this is right. Practically, it is characterized by a great omission: Profligate governments have no intention of balancing their budget.

Other arguments, too, are being heard. The pros say that the bigger worry is no longer how to promote and strengthen the Common Market and Euroland, but "how to save it." Critics answer that *if* this is the goal, *then* the impact of money printing destroys confidence in the ECB and its policies and, in the end, it kills Euroland.

Mario Monti, the Italian prime minister, is one of the pros. In mid-October 2012 he said that the single market was at risk of "rollback and even disintegration,"[31] as the euro crisis has produced highly varying borrowing costs and so on and so forth. Curiously, that statement made no mention of the fact that the euro crisis has been engineered by a tandem of profligate governments in countries like Italy. German, Dutch, and Finnish citizens should not be asked to pay the bill.

6. Why OMT May End Up in a Fiasco

The country that will benefit from the purchase of its sovereign bonds by the ECB must be attached to the appropriate EFSF/ESM program. The latter may take the form of macroeconomic adjustment, or of an "enhanced conditions credit line" (ECCL)—provided that they include the possibility of EFSF/ESM primary market purchases.

Program conditionality will terminate once its objective is achieved or when there is compliance with the macroeconomic adjustment or ECCL rules. The ECB said that it will seek the involvement of the IMF for the design of country-specific conditionality and for the program's monitoring. This, however, is far from sure. Some countries, like Spain, oppose it. Collateral must consist of acceptable marketable debt instruments that may be denominated not only in euros but also in US dollars, pounds, and yen provided:

- They are issued and held in Euroland, and
- Qualify as eligible collateral in Eurosystem credit operations.[32]

Draghi also announced that the sovereign bond-buying would be "sterilized." Theoretically, this means that instead of printing new money to buy government debt, the ECB will borrow money from the banking industry, at close to zero interest rates, to fund these purchases. *If* this were truly the case, it would suggest no major expansion of the ECB balance sheet, and no monetization of debt in the near term.

The sterilization statement, however, has an inherent contradiction as it is difficult to see that after having spent more than €1 trillion ($1.3 trillion) with the LTRO (chapter 5), at an interest rate of 1 percent, to support the banks of Euroland (read: Spanish, Italian, and French), the ECB will be borrowing money from these same wounded banks and pay them a zero interest rate. In other words, after having spent a trillion euros, we are back to square one.

The financial markets may like twisted deals as long as they provide them with hefty profits. But when things turn sour, or a crisis breaks out, twisted deals crash fast and market players run to the exit. The French and others talk of the "market's tyranny." This obscures the fact that the market, most particularly the global market, is a giant live poll of millions of people's views on the future state of the economy. Is it sure that in the case of a major crisis the OMT will not damage the economy of Euroland's member states and of Euroland as a whole?

The contradiction between the ECB's recent OMT, LTRO, and other (unfortunate) initiatives, as well as the Fed's quantitative easing (QE), Twist, and the rest of the lot, starts and ends at the same point. They are too much of a *printing press inflation* that greatly contributed to Germany's hyperinflation in the mid-1920s, China's hyperinflation in the late 1940s, Russia's bankruptcy in the late 1990s, and Zimbabwe's hyperinflation just a few years ago.

High inflation and hyperinflation, of course, are not the same thing. *High inflation* is a significantly greater level than that targeted by central banks, but still in high single or low double digits on an annual basis. It is typically triggered by too much money chasing too few goods, sharp rises in commodity prices, and other reasons. *Hyperinflation*, by contrast, is not just an escalation of high inflation. It is brought about by the *collapse of confidence* in a currency.

- This has been the common ground of the aforementioned hyperinflation examples, and
- The risk is increasing that it will develop into the common ground for the crash of the euro and of the dollar.

Carried to extremes, quantitative counterfeiting (or QE, if you like) can lead to hyperinflation. We are already at QE3.5. Central banks have chosen that policy supposedly to jump-start the economy—and frequently enough with the aim to correct a state of *credit inflation*. In our time, credit inflation started with the explosion of debt in the 1970s, the second half of the 1980s, the late 1990s, and in the first years of this century. But sometimes the medicine may be worse than the illness.

- Printing press inflation is created by the central bank, usually acting under government pressure.[33]
- By contrast, credit inflation takes place because the government's rules and regulations are lax, but this is condoned by the central bank.

Off-balance sheet financing, which started in the mid-1980s and has flourished from the 1990s till today, is a case of credit inflation. It rests on the premise that "debt is a blessing" and one should take full advantage of the resulting personal chance and business opportunity, as long as it lasts. But this "opportunity" also has it perils, which can be summarized as: credit risk, market risk, interest rate risk, currency exchange risk, and country risk.

Section 5 brought to the reader's attention how the OMT is intended to work and the reasons why it might end up as a fiasco. That was only a partial list. There exist as well a number of other factors that, to Draghi's misfortune, work precisely in the same direction:

- There is plenty of moral risk associated with the "unlimited" sovereign bond-buying by the ECB, resulting from the ability of smart, well-informed operators to capitalize on the volatility of Spanish and Italian bonds.
- The "unlimited" bond-buying policy reinforces German, Dutch, and Finnish concerns over excessive money printing to stabilize Italian and Spanish bond yields, while the depth of the abyss is unknown.
- The OMT could trip up on a number of implementation risks relating to the profligate countries benefiting from it. Hence the reserve expressed by those providing the funds.
- By acting as middleman, the European Central Bank finds itself obliged to draw up rules on the use of Euroland's funds, and it ends up being criticized even by its beneficiaries.
- Though the OMT's "conditionality" is a welcome clause, it cools down the already timid government efforts in highly indebted countries. The precedence of the Troika's demands in the case of Greece and Portugal is dissuading Spain and Italy from asking for "assistance."[34]
- In highly indebted countries and those in current disarray, there is no economic motor to get the economy moving again. Hence, countries benefiting from OMT/ESM funds cannot pay back the bonds they have issued and the ECB has purchased.

It would not be unreasonable to think that behind the decision to buy an "unlimited" amount of sovereign bonds, probably starting with Spain, lay a factual opinion that neither Spain nor Italy can avoid bankruptcy if left to their own devices. But can they repay their debts? Some economists say that, a priori, a "yes" hypothesis would be far-fetched, as illustrated by the precedence of the Confederate bonds issued during the American Civil War.

The Rothschilds refused to underwrite the Confederate bonds, but other bankers were happy to oblige. "Those who had invested in these bonds," says Niall Ferguson, "ended up losing everything, since the victorious North pledged not to honor the debts of the South. In the end, there has been no option but to finance the Southern war by printing money."[35] Sounds familiar? That's precisely what the European Central Bank is doing today:

- Buying sovereign bonds of a questionable creditworthiness, *and*
- Printing money to enable itself to keep on buying useless sovereign paper.

Take the "reforms" and "austerity measures" announced by the Spanish government as an example of going from nowhere to nowhere. These include some steps in the right direction, but altogether they are insufficient to reach the targeted budget deficit figures for 2012, 2013, and 2014 without further major cuts in entitlements and other expenses. These have to be made soon enough in socially sensitive areas that have so far been shielded from reforms like salaries and pensions—possibly resulting in a flare-up of social unrest.

When he unveiled his program in early September 2012, Mario Draghi outlined the possibility of triggering ECB bond-buying if an "enhanced conditions credit line" were requested from the ESM (whose legality is still being considered by the European Court of Justice). To do so, a loophole has been engineered by the friendly (to Spain) bureaucrats. The "aid" would be a "credit line."

As it should be expected, concern has arisen over the impact on Italy. While temporarily placating the markets, a "credit line" to Spain will shift the focus on to Rome, which has much higher debt levels. Mario Monti publicly backed Spanish aid, but nobody can tell this is a well-calculated reaction to open the door to an Italian request for similar or better money gift.

"There are two lines of thought," Monti said on October 12, 2012. "One says that speculators will, like a pack of wolves, move on other countries. But if the system is there and it works, I imagine that this would make market speculation less aggressive."[36] And what's the criterion that "the system works"? That it throws taxpayers' money to the four winds?

The decisive question is whether the ECB is conducting a monetary policy or a fiscal policy, said Carsten Schneider, a financial policy expert for the main opposition, Social Democrats. *If* this is financing state budgets, *then* the Bundestag and the European Parliament will have to decide on it. There is precisely the problem. Parliaments are being steamrolled by technocrats and bureaucrats.

To make matters worse than they might have been, the Spanish sovereign is not radiating confidence. Mariano Rajoy first negotiated the 2012 deficit with Brussels. Then he announced unilaterally that he would not stick to the numbers, answering critics by saying he does not need to ask Brussels's opinion on his negation. Has the Spanish government decided that bankruptcy may be the better way out?

In the late sixteenth and early to mid-seventeenth centuries, the Spanish Crown defaulted even if, at the time, the country benefited from interminable cargoes of gold and silver from the Americas. Partially or wholly, Spain suspended payments to creditors in 1557, 1560, 1575, 1596, 1607, 1627, 1647, 1652, and 1662.[37] Today the reasons that brought the Spanish Crown near default are:

- Excesses in real estate,
- Unaffordable entitlements, and
- Mismanagement associated with them and with the economy at large.

If the Spanish do it again, *then* many politicians and central bankers will end up with egg on their faces. It is not unlikely that Mario Draghi worries about his reputation as a central banker because of his decisions to go for bust with "unlimited" bond purchases, or at least he has some second thoughts. Asked when the ECB would buy bonds under the Outright Monetary Transactions program, he remained vague and said that the ECB looks at a variety of indicators and the "degree of disruption." (Whose "disruption" ?)

By omission or commission, no real safeguards have been associated with the ECB's OMT program. The only one that seems to exist is an early Draghi oral statement that the central bank would stop buying bonds "if countries backtrack on their pledges." No specifics have been given. No wonder therefore that these safeguards failed to win over the Bundesbank. Jens Weidmann has blasted the OMT as "being tantamount to financing governments by printing bank notes."

This reference to money printing tapped into a deep-rooted German aversion to Draghi's "unlimited sovereign bond purchases." It always should be recalled that economists widely believe the massive bond buying by Germany's central bank in the 1920s triggered hyperinflation under the Weimar Republic.

In conclusion, the OMT has been the wrong initiative. It is not good for the euro, Euroland, or its member states. It is expediency that in the months and years ahead can turn around and haunt its decision makers. A Machiavellian look at it would be "that much the better." As Thilo Sarrazin argues in his book *Europe Doesn't Need the Euro*, the common currency was never an economic project but a political one[38]—and it is now having unwanted consequences.

7

TARGET2: The Creeping Risk of a Financial Nuclear Bomb

1. TARGET2 Imbalances Are Still on the Rise

In his conference of October 4, 2012, Mario Draghi presented no new details in regard to the Outright Monetary Transactions (OMT) program, announced nearly a month earlier (chapter 6), though in a vague way he credited it with successes. He said that since the new ECB policy became public, the situation had already "relaxed a little," the yield-and-risk increases for member countries' sovereign bonds had ebbed, and capital flows within Euroland's important TARGET2 balance sheet—in which national reserve banks write their assets, liabilities, and obligations toward each other and the ECB—goes by majority "in the right direction."

TARGET is an acronym for Trans-European Automated Real-time Gross Settlement Express Transfer System. This is the settlements medium (network and balance sheet) used by Euroland's central banks, and the European Central Bank itself, to make payments to one another and post their credits and debits. Draghi repeatedly failed to explain what this balance really means, let alone the horror hiding between the lines of TARGET2:

- For some of its critics, this horror consists of *creeping transborder central bank runs.*
- In the opinion of others, the embedded danger is nothing short of a financial atomic bomb whose devastating effects increase with time.

As professors Hans-Werner Sinn[1] and Timo Wollmershäuser have pointed out,[2] exchanges (and changes) of cash flows, as well as imbalances within and among the member countries, carry a very important message regarding the behavior of Euroland's economy—and those of its member states. Prior to the euro crisis, which started in late 2009–early 2010, TARGET2 balances were ± zero. But as the euro crisis deepened, there has been disequilibrium within the system that worsened as time went on, with the result that:

- Central banks from northern Europe have become net creditors, and
- Central banks of crisis countries, in southern Europe, permanent net debtors.

Rooted in TARGET2 is another major exposure northern Euroland taxpayers have taken upon themselves, of which very little is being known even if so much is at stake. The debts the ECB has with the Deutsche Bundesbank aggregate to about €750 billion ($975 billion), and this exposure is on the increase: Only five years ago it was practically equal to zero and in early to mid-2011 it was estimated at around €500 billion.[3]

The argument by the pros (including Draghi) that an exposure of €750 billion the ECB has with the Bundesbank is something "normal" and "not at all risky" is unsound and in pure bad faith. To a large measure, this is money the central banks of Euroland's peripheral countries owe the ECB and the latter owes to the central banks of Germany, Holland, Finland, and Luxembourg, among others. If the euro system collapses, or the weaker economies go bust, that huge amount of money is lost to the creditors.

Stated in a different way, very large public deficits aside, southern European countries and their central banks have been big net debtors in the TARGET2 books. Part of the reason is that commercial banks in their jurisdiction are experiencing bank runs as the citizens fear that their governments might leave Euroland and reintroduce the national currency. When that happens, the latter would massively depreciate. Common citizens are also afraid that the socialist governments they (unwisely) elected will serve themselves with their deposits.[4]

In the wake of those fears, it is not surprising that common citizens withdraw their banking deposits and put the funds either under their mattresses or deposit them in banks in northern Europe, often in a safer currency than the euro. A massive transfer of deposits away from crisis countries—the way it has happened with Greece and more recently with Spain—dries up those countries' cash reserves, and their central banks replace it by means of negative balances in the TARGET2 system. As a result:

- Germany, Holland, and Finland are net creditors.
- Italy, Spain, and Greece are net debtors.

Though opaque, because it resides in the books of the European Central Bank, this is a hidden, king-size transfer of risk raising widespread alarm in Germany and other creditor countries. The size of the Bundesbank's TARGET2 claims are unprecedented for a system designed to settle payments between member states. The procedures of what to do with negative balances in TARGET2 has not been well thought-out on ECB's behalf.

Including the Bundesbank's claims of €750 billion, the total imbalance has soared well over €1 trillion ($1.3 trillion). While the German central bank has sought to allay worries about these hugely negative balances, focusing instead on the credit risk of lending so much to troubled banks against weak collateral, the market has started taking notice of it.

- The pros say that as long as Euroland remains a functional entity, TARGET2 claims are mere bookkeeping entries.
- Critics answer that if it were to disintegrate, the Bundesbank would take a hit, and the same is true of the Dutch, Finnish, and Luxembourg central banks.

This is not straight bookkeeping. It's creative accounting that adds its negative impact on the OMT's "unlimited" bond-buying. The pros say that at least the TARGET2 exposure is indirect, but this is not necessarily true because there is nothing between creditors and debtors. As a result, the former are in the frontline. The financial nuclear bomb residing in the ECB's books has three component parts:

- Serious TARGET2 imbalances,
- "Unlimited" sovereign bond-buying under the OMT, and
- Accumulated toxic waste from sovereign bond-buying under the Securities Market Program (SMP).[5]

It is wrong to think of bond-buying as being limited only to OMT operations (which had not yet started at the time of this writing because of problems with the ESM and Spain's reluctance to ask for a bailout).[6] In May 2010, under Jean-Claude Trichet, started the ECB's exercises in buying Greek government bonds through the then-new Securities Market Program. That led Axel Weber to resign as president of the Bundesbank (in early 2011).

In theory, the European Central Bank made some relatively small bond purchases of its own, but the large part is still done by Euroland's national central banks. The Bundesbank is buying around 25 percent of whatever the Eurosystem takes over in (garbage) sovereign bonds—exposing the

Bundesbank directly to the risk of losses from Spanish, Italian, and other sovereign bonds.

The Maastricht Treaty states nothing about liberties taken with deviations from monetary policy duties let alone about imbalances in the books of the ECB, for the simple reason that neither the ECB nor its clearance and settlement system existed in the early 1990s. Admittedly, however, there have been loopholes, exploited today to continue financing those member states of Euroland that don't care about making ends meet. But while Maastricht has no specifics about TARGET2, its rules are perfectly clear on sovereign debt. It permits the central bank of Euroland to buy public debt in the secondary market.

Financially squandering member states and their friendly economists say that there exists precedence, that of the US Federal Reserve, which has made purchases of sovereign debt on a grand scale as part of its quantitative easing (QE) policy. That argument is misplaced because though the Fed has purchased US Treasuries, hence federal debt,[7] both the Fed and the Treasury belong to the same jurisdiction: the US. By contrast, what Mario Draghi is doing by allowing imbalances to persist is to expose taxpayers in northern Euroland countries to risks of southern sovereigns.

Having said that, it is correct to give credit to Mario Monti, the prime minister of Italy, for having answered protesters against his austerity program the way he did. Early on in his tenure, when protesters to his austerity plan told him that the other members of Euroland should pay Italy's huge public deficit he responded: "No! because the others did not create these deficits. They were made in Italy." And he repeated that statement on October 27, 2012 (while demonstrations against him raged in the streets), adding, "The previous governments promised you things the nation cannot afford."[8]

In conclusion, as we saw with the example on exposure taken by the German taxpayer on TARGET2 alone, the amounts we are talking about are in no way trivial. In August 2012, four central banks from northern Europe made loans of roughly €1.05 trillion ($1.37 trillion) to the TARGET2 system. Ironically, this is the same amount of money that Draghi's Long-Term Refinancing Operation (LTRO, chapter 5) threw away to Euroland's banks—mainly Spanish, Italian, and French—who used it to buy government bonds.

2. Breaking through the Austerity Wall with TARGET2

The policy that has been followed by the European Central Bank under Mario Draghi[9] has taken monetary policy too close to fiscal policy. This is against the statutes of the ECB *and* it also compromises the ECB's independence. The critics are right when they say that Draghi should come clean about the fiscal consequences of a common currency rather than disguising them within the Eurosystem.[10]

Huge imbalances in the TARGET2 balance sheet make worse an already gloomy picture as they add to other deficits, indicators, and surveys pointing out that Club Med countries are confronted by a private citizens' money drain. Contrary to what Mario Draghi states, the ECB's actions have only a passing effect on markets. After that:

- Uncertainty prevails,
- Economic activity remains weak, and
- The psychology stays negative because of insecurity in financial terms.

A good question is who pays for these creeping transborder central bank runs? We already spoke in section 1 about the Deutsche Bundesbank's exposure. With over €750 billion in credit granted by Germany, every German lent to Euroland's peripheral countries over €9,200 ($12,000) through the TARGET2 system, probably money he or she will never see again. With €130 billion ($170 billion) "lent to" TARGET2, the Netherlands has made the second-largest occult contribution: €7,700 ($10,000) for every Dutch citizen. Most likely unaware of it, the citizens of tiny Luxembourg made an even more spectacular handout:

- With a population of just half a million inhabitants, the country has "loaned" TARGET2 over €124 billion ($161 billion).
- This corresponds to €244,000 ($317,000) for each Luxembourger, or nearly €1 million ($1.3 million) for a four-person family.

The bitter irony about these very significant and growing transborder central bank runs is that they are condoned in silence by the ECB president, Ecofin (the council of euroland finance ministers), European Commission, and chiefs of state. The common citizens of northern Europe don't know what is happening to them: Who put his hands in their pocket? As it is to be expected, the main beneficiaries from TARGET2 include:

- Spain, with €434 billion,[11] or €9,200 ($12,000) per capita,
- Italy, with €290 billion, or €4,700 ($6,100) per capita,
- Greece, with €110 billion, or €10,000 ($13,000) per capita, and
- Ireland, since its imbalance in TARGET2 stands at €100 billion ($130 billion), owes more than €21,000 ($27,000) per capita.[12]

Draghi evidently knows about the wrong-way account balance that has become a racket, but he does not fix it. This is discouraging, as TARGET2 was first of all supposed to be an emergency book balancing—just like the OMT was (also supposedly) planned as a brake in case financial markets speculate on a crack-up of the currency union. In both cases, the expectations of the profligates for "free lunch forever" seem to be self-fulfilling.

A Portuguese citizen to whom I was making this remark said that in the southern European countries people want to work at their own pace. They don't want to be pushed by the northern Europeans. To which I answered that then they should be living within the constraints of the more limited wealth they produce. They should not make it a policy to live on debt using the taxes paid by, and the life savings of, northern Europeans as a means to improve their own standard of living.

The big account imbalances in the Eurosystem's clearing mechanism have evolved into an unprecedented wealth transfer racket, a new "class of unpaid debt" within the common currency. The worst part of this bad deal is that Euroland's public has not been informed about it. Clearly, this violates the democratic principle of transparency, while on the technical side it distorts the sense of clearing. It allows cheap money transfers in favor of indebted governments without even a hope of:

• Leveling out these imbalances, or
• Helping Euroland countries become more competitive.

In the age of money, without backing by gold or some other real assets, persistent imbalances in the books of the ECB represent the ultimate beauty of *creative accounting*. They are creating money out of thin air. The pros answer criticisms of this occult tool of Euroland's *transfer union* by drawing attention to the political capital that has been invested in the euro. Political capital?

Europe's "leaders" have spent decades in creating a monster structure that feeds itself through money transfers, but this is by no means "political capital." Creative accounting and the occult transfer union are both matters of *ethics*. As a term, creative accounting was born to describe the manipulation of earnings by banks and other companies, including:

• Risks that they take,
• Their economic drivers,
• Loans with derivatives turned into profits, by magic, and
• Other financial results of their business.

Creative accounting manipulates annual and quarterly reports. In fact, the term is a misnomer because what takes place is neither "creative" nor is it "accounting" in the sense defined by Fra Luca Paciolo, who established the principles of accounting.[13] The practice of changing the numbers in the books to hide losses, beef up profits, misallocate funds, or otherwise manicure financial statements is:

- Corrupt,
- Quite often patchily done,
- Eventually leading to abysmal results, and
- Always demonstrating a disregard for business ethics.

This means lack of virtue and as Socrates once said, *virtue* is knowledge that cannot be taught. It is part of the ethical stance of the top management to ensure that within each reporting period, disclosure is consistent and comparable. Also, that between reporting periods, the books are always kept in accordance with rigorous accounting standards. It is also the top management's responsibility to see to it that financial information is presented in as simple a manner as possible, consistent with the readers' ability to understand the entity's performance.

This is a matter of core responsibility and accountability—which starts and ends with *ethical governance*. Unfortunately, as the facts show, the inventiveness of politicians and of (some recently) politicized central bankers has no bounds—which is indeed upsetting. Only a couple of decades ago, it used to be that the nanny state within a country transferred resources from its active citizens to those inactive by using its powers of taxation and patronage. Now this has become transborder.

The way the Eurosystem has come to work brings to mind what happens with pensions. Whether funded or unfunded, public or private, pensions are a claim by those who are no more active on those who still work. That's how the pension system was established in 1936 in the US by the Roosevelt administration and in France by the Popular Front—and that's how it continues operating.

It is *as if* with TARGET2 imbalances and sovereign bond-buying, the ECB has copied this pension system which is fraying at the seams. Theoretically, the absence of creditworthy collateral for the sovereign bonds and the existence of huge negative values in TARGET2 books is funded by means of a complex series of "voluntary" contractual arrangements. In reality, however, it is funded by coercive means because it is imposed by the ECB.

- There is no way the central banks of Euroland's member states can refuse paying other countries' bills, and

- The only alternative is that the member country to which the central bank belongs quits Euroland and the euro.

That much about Draghi's pledge, in late July 2011, to do "whatever it takes" to save the euro. Instead, what the ECB is now providing is a metamorphosis of welfare states' debts into a transnational dragon—which has been rather unexpected and can have very severe consequences. As a minimum, it adds a new dimension to the ongoing debate, in practically all Western countries, about pruning the sovereigns' balance sheets. That's an issue most societies are only now beginning to grapple with.

The occult export of financial imbalances and other transfers can be sizable, and, short of a control mechanism, they will keep on growing. In May 2012, for instance, the Greek central bank owed over €100 billion ($130 billion) to the other central banks that are members of Euroland. *If* Greece were to default on that debt, *then* the Bundesbank alone would probably take a hit of about €30 billion ($39 billion) based on its share of capital in the ECB, and much more than that in reality.

The ECB would also take losses on the €56 billion ($73 billion) of Greek government bonds that it, and other Euroland's central banks, have bought on the secondary market. Eurozone members and the International Monetary Fund would as well be on the hook if Greece defaulted on its bail-out loans. That much has been already stated. But so far no account has been taken of the unpublished extra €100 billion ($130 billion) that both weights on Greek public debt and can hit the creditor central banks of Euroland's member states like a hammer. What has been written about Greek accounting entries in TARGET2 is also valid for:

- Italian,
- Spanish, and
- Portuguese TARGET2 debts.

The associated risk could be avoided only if TARGET2 balances are netted every month, and countries with negative accounts are asked to pay for them immediately, albeit by increasing their public debt by so much. In this way, everyone becomes aware of the size of the Debt Hydra hidden in the books of the ECB's payments and settlements system.

In conclusion, a pragmatic way of looking at the TARGET2 netting procedure is that it operates without control at the supranational level. Even *if* prevailing imbalances are not really worrisome as long as the euro is limping along, *if* distressed countries start leaving Euroland or, even more likely, the euro collapses, *then* those large numbers of imbalances in central bank accounts would become net losses. The central banks of the countries advancing the money are going to lose a great lot, which is both:

- Scary for financial stability, and
- Totally unfair to the citizen of the countries who will be asked to pay the final bill.

The reader should as well note that some of the Debt Hydra's heads were promoted as a way to relaunch credit in Euroland, helping banks to become more stable credit institutions. The cost of the LTRO effort by the ECB has been more than €1 trillion ($1.3 trillion) and, as far as relaunching credit is concerned, the outcome is a total failure. As for the infamous Outright Monetary Transactions program, first outlined on September 6, 2012, it is still waiting to be used. *If* and *when* this happens it will further worsen the currently prevailing debt abyss. A fragmented common currency area would not allow a uniform monetary policy by the ECB. It is Draghi himself who said so and (at least on this issue) he is right.

3. The Creeping Risk of Financial Imbalances Can Destroy the Euro

Supposedly, all that silly business of TARGET2 imbalances and "unlimited" buying of the profligate sovereigns' bonds is "what it takes" to save the euro. Contrary to that claim about bond purchasing, however, what is now happening is the more effective policy to destroy the euro. It is *as if* double agents have come into the system and with them Orwell's nightmare of "double talk."

As always, there exist fellow travelers. That's the feeling I got on reading, on September 18, 2012, an article by Paul de Grauwe[14] and Yuemei Ji entitled: "What Germany Should Fear Most Is Its Own Fear." The first argument one reads in it is that "it is important to start from rock solid truths. If a country has net financial claims against the rest of the world, that nation must have had current account balances that were in surplus in the past. This means that Germany has accumulated current account surpluses against other Eurozone nations in the past."[15]

Indeed, it is so. Till recently, however, until Euroland's uneconomic member states decreed that it is virtuous to have debts, many debts, and ask others to pay for them, one was expected to pay his debts. Professors in economics don't need to have it explained to them. But neither do they need to justify delays in payments as de Grauwe and Ji are doing.

This minor miracle of being excused for not paying one's debts is done by (unwisely) equating severe TARGET2 imbalances with those in a country's current account. At best, this is sophistry. Persistent debts in TARGET2 and current account imbalances have little if anything to do with each other. Neither technically nor ethically are they the same thing.

- A current account imbalance is the remit of one country and its alone.[16]
- By contrast, TARGET2 imbalances are the concern, and the destabilizers, of the whole Eurosystem.

Mainly due to foreign trade (imports, exports), exported and imported tourism, and similar reasons, current account deficits and surpluses are two faces of the same coin. Cumulatively, and only cumulatively, the red ink of a bunch of countries is the black ink of other countries—those with a current account surplus.

Globally, current account deficits and surpluses balance out because creditworthy countries finance their (unhealthy) current account deficits by selling Treasury bonds that foreigners buy. Otherwise, a country accumulating current account deficits that it cannot finance is in trouble. It can finance what it imports only as long as the parties selling goods give it credit. Short of this it is in a hole.

A different way of looking at current account surpluses, albeit an unorthodox one, is that a country is saving and is spending less than it is earning. Also, it is consuming its own manufacturing produce rather than importing. Voluntarily, it is lending its current account surplus to a country that is spending more than it is earning and gets in exchange credit to the deficit country that may be in the form of:

- The aforementioned Treasury bonds,
- Another type of nominal debt contract,
- An equity stake,[17] or
- Payments made by the deficit country by way of loans it contracts with third countries or entities.

Japan, China, and Germany (in that order) have very important current account imbalances with the US. They are paid by taking equity in American bonds. This is, so to speak, an open market operation. They might as well choose not to buy US Treasuries. Washington would not send the Marines to force them to do so.

Quite to the contrary, as de Grauwe and Ji should have known, the exposure taken by "creditors" in the ECB's TARGET2 books is compulsory. If Germany, Holland, Finland, or Luxembourg say, "Stop! we give no more credit," the system will immediately collapse. Why each Luxembourg citizen should be €244,000 ($317,000) in the red so that retired Spaniards can enjoy fat pensions[18] in the sunshine, is a mystery. If anybody knows the reason, I am all ears.

Let's be clear on this issue. Current account deficits, and foreign debt arising from these deficits, are not necessarily bad as such *if* they are temporary, that is, *if* the deficit country does its damnedest to reverse the balances and eventually be a creditor. On the contrary, if this does not happen and the deficits are allowed to grow, they may become unsustainable.

- The borrower will struggle to service, roll over, and ultimately pay back its external debt,
- Or, alternatively, the lenders may have to write off part (or all) of their credits—which means their citizens' savings.

This worst-case scenario is precisely what is now happening with TARGET2 imbalances and the buying of profligate sovereign bonds by the ECB. De Grauwe and company should have known that, if they had done their homework. As economists they should have also appreciated that:

- Imprudent domestic lending and borrowing leads to a credit bubble and bust,
- Imprudent international lending and borrowing resulting from excessive current account surpluses and deficits becomes a global imbalance, and
- Sooner rather than later, such events, particularly major ones, end up in a balance-of- payment crisis, which can degenerate into a *currency crisis.*

For TARGET2, *that currency is the euro.* The two authors of the "What Germany Should Fear Most Is Its Own Fear" paper should have known that much. They should have also appreciated that the statement they make in the aforementioned article: "TARGET2 claims of Germany are not a good indicator of this risk since they are not a good indicator of German's net foreign claims" is patently false. The same is true of the statement: "TARGET2 liabilities have increased mainly as a result of speculative flows."[19]

While there are undoubtedly speculative funds in these huge deficits by Club Med Euroland countries—with speculators betting that in the end "Germany would pay"—not everything is speculation. The big and growing part is "I don't care" by those who believe in financial squandering, also based on the hope that "Germany would pay, if necessary by a second Versailles." All this is not only totally irrational, it is also unethical. Disgusting!

I don't care to spend more time with silly arguments but there is one more thing that caught my eye and should be brought to the reader's attention. The de Grauwe and Ji article states: "One could argue, however, that because of the higher Bundesbank TARGET2 claims it is the German taxpayer who now bears a higher risk. But this is also erroneous."[20] And why is it *erroneous*, please? Where do you think that the Bundesbank gets it money from? Has it planted the right trees which grow money like a fruit? That's taxpayers' money, and it is true of any other central bank.

It needs indeed no explaining that these eleventh-hour attempts to justify the unjustifiable make funny reading. The only sound way to examine how we have reached the state where we are in, is to return to the sources: how the euro was created, and try to find the original fault(s).

The euro's founding principle, and the initial euro mistake, has been to leave the responsibility for fiscal policy in the hands of each individual member state. Probably recognized, but not provided for, was the need to safeguard a joint monetary policy from individual member states' potentially unsound fiscal policies. Nothing was, however, cast in stone to guide Euroland's central bank inasmuch as:

- *If* fiscal policies were to be too expansionary,
- *Then* monetary policies should pursue a restrictive path to maintain price stability.

Instead, despite the Stability and Growth Pact, the road was left open for uneconomic member states to exert pressure on the Eurosystem to ease monetary policy, as well as to monetize sovereign debt. Temporarily, this may reduce the real burden of highly indebted countries[21] but it penalizes those countries that are working hard and their taxpayers, and eventually leads to a blow-up.

The euro was thought to be a grand scheme that pushed the boundaries of globalization by trying to integrate, single-handed, countries whose peoples have been enduring surpluses on the one hand and chronic deficits on the other. This was hoped for by politicians and technocrats against all logic—and without political union—in spite of the fact that in different nations peoples actually liked:

- Their national identities,
- Their way of living,

- Their devaluing currencies, and
- The control all this gave them over their economies.

Not everybody, of course, was in accord with Euroland's fathers' steam-rolling policy, or felt that his country was ready to join the euro.[22] An example is Dr. Antonio Fazio, then governor of Italy's central bank, who believed that Italy was not ready to enter the common currency. Fazio has been politically prosecuted for his resistance.[23]

In conclusion, contrary to what Paul de Grauwe, Yuemei Ji, and others are saying, Euroland is now paying a high price for having violated its own rules by those who govern. The result is disorganization, hence entropy at its best. As Ludwig Boltzmann, the Swiss physicist, demonstrated:

- Order is associated with low entropy, and
- Disorder results in, and is characterized by, high entropy.[24]

There are many different ways things can be thrown about to produce a disorderly, sloppy environment, hence high entropy. Financial squan-dering and disorder correlate and make a system proceed from low to high entropy—the economic and financial environment Euroland pres-ently has.

4. Without the German Economy, Euroland Is Off the Rails

Today's Germany is a nation of 81.5 million people and has a gross domes-tic product of €2.57 billion ($3,34 billion). These are 2011 statistics. That year the GDP growth stood at 3 percent, ahead of that of other Euroland countries but way below the growth rate of China and of other developing economies.

A characteristic of the German economy in the euro years is that wage inflation has risen more slowly than productivity, and significantly more slowly than that in other Euroland countries. These conditions, which provide evidence of sound governance, made Germany attractive as a manufacturing base. To it should be added the fact that the quality of German-made products excels that of comparable goods made in other parts of Europe.

Over the years, debt-to-GDP ratios have been rising in Germany as well as in other industrial countries. In the 1984 to 2009 timeframe, for which there exist comparative statistics, debt-to-GDP rose by 225 percent in Japan, a little over 100 percent in the US, some 90 percent in France, and 80 percent in Britain and in Germany. (In Germany the debt-to-GDP ratio currently stands at about 82 percent.[25]) What about the euro's impact on the German economy?

Angela Merkel, the German chancellor, is quoted as having said: "If the euro fails, Europe fails." But in his book *Europe Does Not Need the Euro*, Thilo Sarrazin replies that Europe did well for several decades before the introduction of a common currency. The euro is not a necessary condition for the European Union.

According to Sarrazin, Germany has not really profited from the euro because its exports to emerging markets rose more than those to the rest of Euroland. This is a debatable argument because emerging market growth was and still is significantly higher than that of European countries. But it is no less true that the growth of German exports to emerging markets has outpaced that of other Euroland industrial countries, for instance, France.

Capital goods are the main German exports (at 42.5 percent of the total, of which slightly less than 2/5 are motor vehicles). They are followed by intermediate goods (31.6 percent), consumer goods (16.3 percent), energy (1.8 percent), agricultural goods (0.8 percent), and diverse other goods (7 percent). Correspondingly, the larger import class is intermediate goods (29.7 percent). Then come capital goods (28.4 percent, of which less than half are autos), consumer goods (18.7 percent), energy (11.3 percent), agricultural goods (2.9 percent), and diverse other goods (8.9 percent).[26] The German economy is in no condition to carry the rest of Euroland on its shoulders. Still, with the value of exports exceeding that of imports, and therefore with a steadily positive current account (section 3), Germany:

- Is the envy of other Euroland countries, and
- Is seen as a sort of paymaster or, more precisely, Santa Claus.

In 2012, Euroland's inflation was about 2.6 percent and Germany's 2.1 percent. This is not much of a difference as both numbers are above the European Central Bank's target of close to but below 2 percent. More worrisome to the German government is its country's financial exposure to other Euroland member states.

Some experts say that Germany's share of guarantees for the EU bailout funds and the European Central Bank's securities market program would add more than 5 percent to its present 82 percent ratio of public debt-to-GDP. Worse yet, this 5 percent does not include the touted Spanish bailout package or any allowances for further state recapitalization of the German banking industry.

It comes as no surprise, therefore, that because of worrying about the aftereffect of unstoppable Euroland rescues on Germany's economy and financial condition, several citizens have gone to the country's Constitutional Court against that unstoppable give-away policy. The first important legal action concerned the government's decisions to boost German guarantees for the European Financial Stability Facility (EFSF, chapter 4).

In September 2011, the Constitutional Court rejected the citizens' appeal, but there has been a silver lining in its decision that brought happiness to the foes of jointly guaranteed eurobonds. The Court's ruling blocked their automatic introduction. Though rescue operations could proceed, the Court put parliamentary limits on throw-away money.

A year later, in mid-September 2012, came another German Constitutional Court decision, rejecting the claims for an interim injunction against the ratification of the ESM (chapter 4) and Fiscal Compact subject to a precondition and an adjunct condition:

- The Federal Republic has to assure, under international law, that its liability in the ESM is limited to the current amount of €190 billion ($247 billion), and
- The German parliament is to be informed on a timely basis about any upcoming decisions concerning the ESM. The Court stressed the budget right of elected representatives.

This decision clarified that there is no unlimited liability for Germany in the ESM and assigned the condition that the German government must assure it is not bound to the ESM in its entirety, if the outlined preconditions are not accepted or prove to be ineffective. This *"Jein"*[27] answer by the Court is quite significant given that the ESM cannot be established without Germany in light of its 27.2 percent share in its capital.

It should be noted that the citizens petitioning the Constitutional Court against the handouts ranged from the political Right to the Left. A record 37,000 Germans signed the petition, which added to a growing perception that the country is increasingly reluctant to be the major paymaster for the euro. Indeed, many Germans are against the European Central Bank's "unlimited" OMT plan to buy government bonds of crisis countries in tandem with the ESM.

The plaintiffs argued that the ESM, even though it cleared both houses of parliament with two-thirds majorities necessary to amend the constitution, cannot stand because it is fundamentally undemocratic and therefore violates the *eternity clause*.[28] Germany's constitution contains what lawyers have called an *eternity clause*, written in remembrance of the Weimar Republic that died because its parliament in effect voted itself out of existence under pressure from Hitler. Article 79 of the 1949 constitution states that certain changes, including anything that detracts from human dignity or democracy, are "inadmissible," even if willed by parliament.

One of the basic arguments on behalf of the plaintiffs has been that because of hidden liabilities, the ESM robs the German parliament of its control over the budget. Such a claim really hit the bull's-eye because the ESM will be awfully short of money without the German contribution and at the same time the ratification of the ESM is a precondition for the highly expensive ECB initiative like the outright monetary transactions (OMT, chapter 6).

Another way of looking at these comings and goings at the Constitutional Court in Karlsruhe is that German citizens have tried to protect themselves, their economy, and their pension from the voracious appetite for money of the uneconomic southern European members of Euroland. As for the latter's leaders, they give the impression that they are scared to institute needed structural reforms and are limping along simply by spending other peoples' money.

If they were wiser, they would have profited from Germany's expertise, not just its funds. That's what François Mitterrand, the president of France, did in the late 1980s when, after three devaluations of the French franc, he saw that the country's currency was still falling while the deutschmark was strong. With this, Mitterrand decided that the best policy is the Bundesbank approach. He defended the franc and made sure that the market took him seriously.

This has repeated itself with the euro. Member countries that have been disciplined and flexible enough achieved net benefits due to their membership in Euroland. An example is Finland. If one cannot devalue because of the common currency, then more fiscal and wage discipline is the way to go. Countries that lacked reform or did not pursue a sustainable fiscal policy like Italy, Spain, Greece, or Portugal, had to pay a price, even though they initially profited from the euro through lower interest rates.

Correctly, the German government did not throw public money down the drain. It dug its heels over some issues like eurobonds. Berlin resisted the idea of pooling together all sorts of sovereign debt unless there is, *first*, closer fiscal integration. "The pooling of debt is just one side of a coin where federalism is the other. Governments who are in favor (of Eurobonds) fail to point this out," said Bundesbank chief Jens Weidmann.[29]

Germany offered advice where this was needed. When the first Greek bailout came about, Merkel suggested restructuring employment laws to bring them in line with the German model, and setting up special economic zones to lure investors with tax incentives and less red tape. These proposals, however, proved controversial with the Greek electorate and the Papandreou government backtracked. Germany also offered Greece:

1. Training for its tax inspectors and help in restructuring tax collection.

Torn between what was needed to be done and preservation of the status quo, because of conflicts of interest, the Papandreou government did not even respond to this offer. Finally, in late October 2012, the Samaras government decided to go ahead with tax restructuring.

2. Help in building a bank like KfW for reconstruction of the Greek economy.

The Greek government entered in some early discussions on this issue but these led nowhere as, in government circles, the will to do what was needed for the country and its citizens was missing. Socialists find it difficult to appreciate that in every well-run enterprise there exist priorities that often require painful decisions. Anyone who does not care to respect his priorities should be prepared to pay a heavy price.

5. Aftereffect of Chronic Surpluses and Deficits in ECB Books

Who may be responsible for a German exit from Euroland, and what could be the consequence of it? These are themes discussed in the present and in the following section. A major factor in both of them is the way the European Commission and other Euroland member states are handling their liabilities in connection with the ongoing debt crisis.

It is nobody's secret that *if* it survives the present crisis, Euroland will face major challenges for the rest of the decade. Germany will not be a problem as such, provided that it is not being pushed around (as is currently happening) and that an ethical solution is found to TARGET2 imbalances.

Let's start with a reference to a recently published article. As an answer to Paul de Grauwe, Marco Buti had this to say on the assessment of imbalances (sections 1, 2, and 3 of this chapter):

> While there are links between surpluses and deficits within the euro area, the latter is not a closed economy. In other words a lower surplus in surplus countries does not necessarily imply the corresponding improvement in deficit countries. Depending on the place in the global value chain and export market and product composition, the effect may even be the opposite.[30]

That's true, and it means it is wrong to accuse Germany of collecting big trade surpluses that translate into outsized imbalances in the TARGET2 books. And as we saw in the preceding sections, it is also wrong to confuse inter-central bank accounts in Euroland with current account practices in the wider global economy. The compulsory debt in TARGET2 is a major problem on its own merit, with the result that if Germany and Holland pull out of Euroland, the whole TARGET2 system will head for collapse.

The other side of the coin, however, is that this being the case, the Club Med countries and France should be much more careful than they have so far been in pushing Germany toward the exit. By accusing Germany and by trying to make it pay for everybody, the policy Italy, Spain, Greece, and France follow resembles that of somebody who cuts the branch on which he is sitting. As Marco Buti points out:

> Surpluses may be the result of the competitiveness of enterprises and the productive structure, or they might reflect savings needs linked to the ageing of population. In this sense, a country like Germany is bound to remain in surplus though its size may have to come down, as is already happening.[31]

Neither are trade surpluses for some countries synonymous with building up of large debt balances by other countries of Euroland. Annual debt balances are the result of wrong-way policies, predominant among them being that of living beyond one's means. This is true not only of the national economy of the same country, as a whole, but also of sectors of the economy, even the least likely. The way an American sports expert put it in an interview he gave to *Bloomberg News*: "Debt is the greatest threat to the sports business."[32]

If debt can end by damaging the sports business, think about its effects on a brittle framework characterizing the common currency of 17 European member states. An economic area's fragility is hardly an academic issue, one that can be resolved through theoretical arguments. It's a hard fact demonstrated by the existence of an institutional system comprising:

- A single monetary policy, and
- Several incompatible fiscal policies.

With regard to monetary policy, the Treaty on the Functioning of the European Union (Lisbon Treaty), tasks the Eurosystem with the primary objective of maintaining price stability in Euroland as a whole. Quite to the contrary, as it has already been brought to the reader's attention, fiscal policy has been left as the unique responsibility of national authorities. They, and only they, are responsible for assuring a commitment to sound public finances under the vague notion of coordinating and laying down fiscal policy "requirements." This is an issue of long-term habits and the Fiscal Compact (chapter 6) is not going to change it.

If the Germans have been maintaining price stability, lower labor costs, and higher productivity against all odds, *then* they should be congratulated rather than cursed. *If* they balance their budget that much better for them, but the wasters who cannot keep their public debt from growing have no right to press the Germans to give them money. That's by no means solidarity; it is spoilage of a friendship.

At the same time, however, while surplus (like riches) provides a positive message to some, it creates envy in others. It is hard to explain to them that in a common currency area, growing deficits and resulting imbalances destroy the system, because they have a septic effect. Payments and settlements imbalances have to be corrected when they are still short term. In the longer term, they are not sustainable, leaving only two opt-outs:

- A fiscal transfer union, which is anathema to the hardworking, and
- The termination of TARGET2,[33] which is practically synonymous with ending the monetary union.

Since the likelihood of a transfer union is not on the cards but chronic deficits are here to stay, the euro is heading for the same fate that befell previous currency unions. It makes no sense to keep on accumulating net claims on the Eurosystem. Imbalances cannot be dismissed as a mere accounting phenomenon, or something akin to current account deficits as de Grauwe wants to have it.

It is wrong to justify the actions of wasters. Ironically, the European Executive itself (in Brussels) is an example of a big spender—not of cost control and thriftiness. In October 2012, Brussels demanded a hefty increase in its budget that Britain rightfully opposed. When the EU's member countries practise austerity, the fat cats in Brussels cannot continue with big spending and spoilage. An auditors' report:

- Flagged more than €5 billion ($6.5 billion) worth of misspending from the EU's 2011 budget, and
- Urged policy makers to tighten rules on how taxpayers' money is doled out.

The findings by the European Court of Auditors in the first week of November 2012 came amid growing tensions between member states over how much they should contribute to the 2014–2020 EU budget. The European Union heads of government have been meeting in Brussels in a bid to reach a deal on the longer-term spending plans, at a time when many of them continue to focus on austerity measures at home.

The auditors found an estimated 3.9 percent of 2011 budget payments were directed at projects that did not comply with the EU or national funding rules. For instance, researchers claiming costs not linked to their specific project, farmers not honoring environmental commitments, as well as misspending in rural development, fisheries, and health.

In one year there has been a 5 percent increase from similar misallocations in 2010, way above the auditor's target of 2 percent. The European Court of Auditors also found too many cases of EU money not hitting the target as well as systems and procedures aimed at detecting and correcting errors and misappropriations put in the time closet or half-baked.

We found the member states aren't doing their job as fully as they should. There needs to be a greater degree of commitment on the part of national authorities to the management and control of EU money, said the Court's president. He also pointed out that EU governments had enough information to detect and rectify some of the errors, which they apparently had not done, and corrective action was lacking.

The findings on spoilage and waste by the European Court of Auditors are significant inasmuch as they identify laxism with spending other peoples' money—a fact economic theorists typically fail to address. No surprise, therefore, that some of the EU's member states don't want to hear about "give me more money."

The argument of Britain, Germany, and Holland is that Brussels should focus on improving efficiency and swamping waste rather than asking for a hefty increase of the EU budget. This, however, is by no means a general opinion because other member states, and the Brussels bureaucracy itself, argue that increased spending is vital "to spur economic growth." This sort of controversy can also be found in the background of the imbalances of TARGET2.

Economic growth is a culture and a spirit. Money is only one of its components. *If* the others are missing, *then* a situation that is already fragile will further deteriorate. The "competitiveness shock," and higher standard of living that comes with it, will remain a chimera when the dominant factors are:

- Budgetary deficits,
- Weak tax regimes,

- Piling up of public debt,
- Demand-side effects,
- Current account deficits, and
- Payments and settlements deficits (TARGET2).

Euroland's built-in adverse financial-fiscal feedback loop poses severe challenges to monetary policy, led to a struggling banking system, and generated illiquid bond markets for sovereigns accustomed to living in debt. All this made it difficult to contain cross-border contagion and led to navigating in uncharted waters.

Euroland's crisis made small game of the thesis that all by itself a monetary union will be able to integrate the old continent's highly diverse economies. This idea was weak and its implementation led to a fiasco. A United Europe is a vast project that could have been materialized in the late 1940s, shortly after the end of World War II, or, in extremis, at the time of the Treaty of Rome.

- European integration was a project that had caught the imagination of the then young generation, and
- All those who had experienced the horrors of World War II (the author included)looked at it favorably.

By contrast, the second decade of this century is a time of rampant nationalism, unaffordable entitlements, and the quest for more and more easy living by consuming whatever remains of the wealth accumulated since the fifteenth century—Western wealth that by now has been nearly depleted. Both between and within countries exist the hardworking and the profligates; those who create and accumulate wealth and those who spend it, without much thought on how debts and bills they are accumulating will be paid.

The increase in standard of living is welcome, but *if* it is not commensurate with creation of wealth and significant improvements in competitiveness (as well as in productivity), *then* families, companies, and sovereigns drive themselves into bankruptcy. Marco Buti is right when he states: "The crisis is fundamentally a balance sheet recession... Therefore, it is of the essence that the credit of the government, on which any plan of successful crisis resolution ultimately rests, is preserved."[34]

The question is who pays to preserve it, because Euroland's hardworking countries that came up in the earlier days offering plenty of money are now suffering from *bailout fatigue*. Neither are Euroland's northern countries free of public debt, even if they are better off than the profligates. This raises a most critical question: Will Germany and perhaps Holland and Finland throw in the towel and opt out of the common currency?

6. Exit Germany?

Two diametrically opposed opinions exist on what might be the next act in the drama of surpluses and deficits in TARGET2 as well as all other sorts of red ink in the accounts of Euroland and its common currency. The one school says that Germany's respect for treaties won't permit euro exit. This looks rather far-fetched; after all, it was none else than General Charles de Gaulle who quipped: "Treaties are like roses and virgins: they last while they last." The other school states that Germany, like any other member state, can opt out (more on this later).

In the opinion of those who maintain the "no way out" for Germany (or for any other country wishing to exit the euro) without prior change to EU treaties, the "Second Versailles" is the next act in the euro's drama. That school bases its thesis on the assumption that the German government and the German parliament would have to make a deliberate decision "to violate" Germany's obligations under the treaties. That's plain wishful thinking because *if* we talk of violations *then* there is a long list of them:

1. They start in the 1960s when the French government "reinterpreted" the Common Market treaties in the interest of "national sovereignty," doing so without objection by other members and without really violating the terms of these treaties.

Historians have suggested that the unraveling of the Treaty of Rome started there and then, because the French "reinterpretation" provided the evidence that every member country can do as it pleases without being called to task. The theoretical, and only theoretical, "primary" European law proved to be nothing more than a rather vague principle member states might fulfill as a sort of agreement made in the normal exercise of community life.[35]

2. Violations of EU treaties and agreements have become common currency with the profligate Euroland member states who have been observing none of their obligations under the Stability and Growth Pact they had signed.

This is sure to continue under the Fiscal Compact and the "banking union,"[36] as it did under the EFSF, ESM, LTRO, and other abbreviations invented to confuse the issue. Cutting short a long list of violations, it is enough to mention the more recent (and more glaring) example of the European Central Bank that violated its own statutes and Articles 123 and 125 of the Lisbon Treaty with its OMT policy of buying "unlimited" amounts of Euroland's sovereign bonds.

While the attention of the public is deviated to magic abbreviations, useless "summits," and hefty handouts, real issues go unattended. This is the case of private capital flight from southern to northern Europe that enriches the coffers of northern banks, but creates a real and present danger for northern taxpayers. The amounts are huge.

- In a base scenario, they stand at €2.2 trillion ($2.86 trillion), and
- In a worst-case scenario, they reach €3.5 trillion ($4.55 trillion).[37]

Club Med governments have both the right and the obligation to stop this torrent of money, just like the German government has the right and the obligation to protect the well-being of German people. Under Article 20 of the German Constitution (Grundgesetz), the German people are sovereign and exercise that sovereignty through the institutions of the German state. The position that EU law is paramount has never been accepted by the German federal Constitutional Court that stated, on a number of occasions, that ultimate sovereignty resides in Germany.

Precisely because political union has been left in the time closet by the fathers of the Common Market (the EU's first incarnation), all major decisions by Brussels have to be confirmed by the parliaments of member countries, or through referendums. There is no doubt that a decision of the German parliament to withdraw from the euro would be recognized as legally effective by the German courts—which is the thesis of the second school of thought.

The same is true in regard to all other European members states. As sovereign nations they have in both international public law and constitutional reality, the power to unilaterally break treaty obligations. The silver lining of this is that there is no clause in the Lisbon Treaty, or in any other document of EU officialdom, that allows a group of countries to throw one of its members out of the union.

Germany, like France, Italy, Spain, Greece, and any other EU or Euroland member state, has an *exit option*, which it might wish to exercise. The reader should as well appreciate that even if Germany exits *now*, it would have to lick its wounds, though its financial wounds will get much worse by delaying a decision on exit and letting time pass by in inaction.

Let's not forget that Spaniards, Italians, and Mario Draghi have been pushing for (an ill-defined) "banking union"[38] because it would have triggered a shift in the burden of recapitalization of the self-wounded Spanish banking from the sovereign Spain to the multinational ESM. By all evidence, in a first time, both Angela Merkel and Wolfgang Schäuble, the German finance minister, misunderstood the deal. Then, when they got the message of what lies behind it, they did not really want a banking union at all—or, as a compromise, they would like to contain it as well as limit the remit of the pan-European banking supervisor.[39]

As Martin Wolf, the economist, wrote in an article in the *Financial Times*:

> The necessary cure for the ills of the Eurozone will impose higher inflation in Germany, which the Germans will detest; prolonged deflationary recessions in important Eurozone markets; and ongoing transfers of official resources to its partners. All this ensures that neither the economic nor the political gains of Eurozone membership are what German policy makers would have wanted. Worse, years of conflict over "bailouts", debt restructurings, structural reforms and unpopular adjustments in competitiveness now lie ahead.[40]

Charles Dumas, of Lombard Street Research, argues that going back to an appreciating deutschmark would squeeze profits, raise productivity, and increase real consumer incomes. Germans could enjoy higher living standards at home, rather than bailing out profligate foreigners (read: southern European) by compromising their savings and their pensions. In Dumas's opinion, a German exit from Euroland would also generate swift adjustment in the competitiveness of other Euroland members which, otherwise, occur too slowly.

The alternative, as Wolf has suggested, is the "transfer union" the Germans hate—but in reality, the transfer union is not the only swindle feared by the German electorate. As we will see, there are others, and at long last the German electorate wakes up to them. One, but only one, example is the fraud that has been going on for nearly a decade with *counterfeit money* by Western central banks through their so-called unconventional monetary policy—whether this is called quantitative easing (QE), outright monetary transactions (OMT), Twist, LTRO, or some other silly name.

The way some recent commentaries had it, the Fed will continue to counterfeit money until there is "a substantial decline" in the US unemployment rate.[41] No targets have been given about when the printing presses may stop working overtime. The way a *Bloomberg News* commentary put it, Bernanke will continue to target unemployment till the end of his term. Indeed on September 13, 2012, the Fed announced QE3 and the purchase of billions of dollars of mortgage-backed securities (MBS) every month—including US agency (read: defunct Fanny Mae and Freddie Mac) MBSs. Then in December 2012 the Fed came forward with QE3.5 throwing $85 billion per month to the market by buying dubious assets (mainly mortgages).

It looks like an ongoing, interminable competition between the US Federal Reserve and the European Central Bank on who will contribute more to inflation. The Fed under Ben Bernanke and the ECB under Mario Draghi have become jacks of all trades. The one buys whatever he finds in the bottomless pits of the US MBS, the other states that he will recapitalize Euroland's banks and empty coffers of sovereigns all in one go. Of this the Bundesbank does not want to be a part.

Just as a hint of what this means, the IMF recently stated that European banks may have to sell $4.5 trillion (€3.5 trillion) of assets to improve their financial staying power.[42] The IMF did not mention that Draghi is ready to come as deus ex machina with plenty of ESM and ECB money, but that's probably what will happen. If the ESM does not have enough capital, what remains will be leveraged, setting a (bad) example to others who are short of funds on how to beat the system.

A *Der Spiegel* report put it in this way: "Eurozone states are preparing to allow the bloc's permanent bailout fund to leverage its capital in the same way as its predecessor, so it can reach a capacity of more than 2 trillion euros and rescue big countries if necessary."[43] The EFSF is already leveraged, why not the ESM? It matters little that the leverage means debt and that the mountains of debt see to it that big parts of Euroland's economy are and remain flat like a pancake. Joined by speculators, the debt freaks are ecstatic:

> If the ESM gets approval to use the same leverage techniques as the EFSF, it would have a lending power of around 2 trillion euros without countries having to contribute any more capital to the fund.

Debt, debt, and more debt. But as Wolfgang Münchau writes in the *Financial Times*: "Have you noticed that the half-life of eurozone optimism is getting shorter."[44] Interpreting what is in the mind of Euroland's policy makers I would put it a little differently: If a given policy proves to be a disaster, let's repeat it—particularly so if one can also say a big lie—and it does not matter if the half-life of optimism gets shorter. It is always possible to find another cock-and-bull story or financial abbreviation[45] to bring the spirits up.

8

Redenomination Risk Following a Euro Breakup

1. The Euro Could Destroy the EU

When in the 1990s the decision was made about a common currency among qualifying member states of the European Union, no particular attention was paid to the need for longer-term fiscal discipline. The Stability and Growth Pact was, from the start, a "nice chaps" document, weighting about 1 percent when compared to the 100 percent of rules necessary for fiscal union and common currency stability requirements. In the 1990s, Euroland's member states rejected a biting fiscal discipline because they were afraid that it would:

- Take discretion away from them,
- Precommit them to austerity measures during tough times, and
- Expose the malfunctions in their fiscal, economic, and financial systems.

The first years of the euro tended to prove that the doubters of the need for a fiscal union based on hard rules were right. Fiscal discipline was wanting, but 2001–2007 were the years of the fat cows. Things radically changed with the deep economic and banking crisis that started in mid-2007 in America, with the subprimes. Western economies went through the first deep trough in September 2008 with the eleventh-hour salvage (with taxpayers' money) of AIG, Fannie Mae, Freddie Mac, and the bankruptcy of Lehman Brothers:

- The economic and financial landscape darkened, and
- The absence of a true fiscal discipline became Euroland's Achilles heel.

Not only did the lack of coordination and convergence on fiscal issues make itself felt, but also the rather chaotic administrative arrangements in Euroland and the EU hamstrung attempts to react to the crisis early enough. Each member state took a defensive position, though the means by which Euroland's member countries got themselves into trouble varied from one jurisdiction to the next.

Ireland was not profligate, but the Irish government foolishly offered blanket coverage of the liabilities amassed by the country's banks when the latter got into trouble. In the aftermath, Ireland suffered a collapse in sovereign creditworthiness because its mismanaged banks had engaged in high stakes and their losses affected their obligations to both their domestic clients and those abroad.

The case of Greece, Italy, Spain, Portugal, and eventually France has been different. Some, like Italy and Greece, were not ready to join the common currency and to qualify for it they cooked their books (particularly their economic statistics). Others, like Spain, had superleveraged themselves through a real estate boom and their economy depended on it *as if* it would last forever. What all these member states, the *Club Med*, have in common is that they capitalized on easy credit to finance unaffordable government spending. In parallel to this there was:

- Endemic tax fraud,
- Unaffordable entitlements,
- Highly expensive and abused health care, and
- A fair amount of nepotism and corruption.

The problem of the so-called peripheral countries was not only that they used their membership to the common currency to borrow at low German-like rates, but also that their economies were sclerotic, inflexible, and old-fashioned. To make matters worse, there has been no political will to restructure labor laws and get the economy moving again.

This highly defensive policy did away with common currency benefits, exposing each country's weak points. After the crisis broke out, investors demanded higher interest rates by several percentage points to hold Club Med's bonds compared to German ones. Whether or not the ECB and different chiefs of state like it, there has been a de facto *bifurcation* in the value of the euro.

George Soros was right when he said that the euro could destroy the EU.[1] *If* the currency union were just a fixed exchange rate arrangement, it would have had already collapsed; the fact that it is a monetary union will delay that outcome, but the euro is far from being out of the tunnel. Economists do not doubt that:

- A euro breakup would cause a global bust because Euroland is the world's most financially integrated region of independent states, and
- A breakup will be followed by defaults, bank failures, imposition of capital controls,[2] and litigation.

Not one but a number of reasons may lead to the breakup: a weak economy leaving the euro; a strong economy becoming independent of the euro; the creation of a large block in the north and another one in the south; or a chaotic breaking away with each party going its own way. Major currency swings will follow:

- Between the so-called neuro, the euro in the north, and seuro, the euro in the south, and
- Between the member countries in the core that might stick together and those on the periphery.

George Soros has said that the survival of the EU itself would be in doubt. It is not sure that the euro's breakup will mean the end of the EU, though it might. There is only one way to avoid judgment day: having a rich parent who would underwrite all debts and would continue doing so in the future. Who could be that "rich parent"?

When this question is asked, all eyes turn toward Germany, and there is already talk about a *Second Versailles*. The reference is to Germany's capitulation to the victorious allies with conditions that were unaffordable and unsustainable for a defeated nation. Signed in Versailles in 1919, the Treaty led straight to World War II less than two decades down the line.

It is quite interesting to bring into perspective a fact that has escaped the neo-Keynesians' attention. John Maynard Keynes was outraged by the folly of the Treaty of Versailles, which could not possibly be implemented. Germany would have had to generate an extraordinary trade surplus to meet its obligations derived from the Treaty, provided that food and materials could be imported first.

Without food imports the population would have been hungry, as it was in the last years of World War I; it would produce too little; and it had to satisfy internal demand before considering exporting to gain hard currency for reparations payments. There was as well a second absurdity. Those exports would have competed on world markets with Britain, in spite of the fact that German-British competition in the world market was one of the reasons for World War I.

After having lost two world wars, Germany is no more the debtor, it is the creditor. But the idea that Euroland can come into economic balance while Germany underwrites all of the profligates' debts is just as silly as the Treaty of Versailles ever was—and it is only causing bad blood.

In fact, Versailles was not only the incubator of another war but also of hyperinflation, years of financial instability, labor strikes, and social upheaval all over Europe. Today's Germany may be in a little better condition than Britain and France but it is singularly unable to carry on its shoulders the debt weight of Euroland.

- One indebted donor does not have enough power to sort out Euroland's messy finances, and
- An ideological defense of solidarity has no political legitimacy no matter how one looks at this issue.

A major question is whether or not there will be contagion outside Euroland, affecting the rest of the EU and may be the United States. Economic prospects are poor, and this breeds contagion. In the absence of a common fiscal discipline and therefore of the ability of weaker economies to stand on their feet, over-indebted governments have no room for maneuver, which make Hollande's claims of a swift return to growth total nonsense.

Greece has simply been the first of the peripheral countries to fall, but the plight of Portugal, Spain, Italy, and (to a certain degree) France is no better. Already in late November 2011 financial analysts projected that in spite of the EU/ECB/IMF loans, or because of them, default by Greece could only be delayed; it cannot be avoided.

Neither is the cloud of adverse economic conditions lifting. The IMF forecast that Euroland's economy will shrink in 2012 in real terms. For Greece, Italy, Portugal, and Spain, there is a negative growth forecast. For other European countries growth is (optimistically) projected, at close to zero and it will stay there in early 2013. This is politically perilous for the whole EU. Projections made in America about 2013 are roughly the same.

Seen from the perspective of the current economic climate, Soros's dictum makes sense. The euro's breakup will create a financial tsunami that will hit the shores of both North America and Europe. At the same time, however, the idea of having good money run after bad money in order to preserve the integrity of Euroland under all circumstances and at any cost, is a severe error.

Jens Weidmann, Bundesbank president, has argued that monetary policy has reached, if not exceeded, its limits. He is not alone in this conclusion. The more clear-eyed political leaders have started looking at a breakup as a more attractive way out than laboring under a common currency that they do not control.

A breakup will evidently create a host of problems, one of the more complex being that of *redenominations* (section 3). A country opting out of the unique currency it shared with other countries for a dozen years, will have to redenominate nearly all its assets and liabilities in the new currency it chooses. If not, the market will do so by default and the way to bet is that this will be asymmetric.

• Whether the redenomination is done in an organized way or by default there will be risks associated with it.
• Redenomination(s) transfer a sizable part of risks to the countries leaving the current common currency and their taxpayers, particularly risks that correlate with unsound public finances and misguided macroeconomic policies.

These are precisely the reasons that weakened the foundations of the monetary union. Whether or not they are perceived a priori as a constraint, redenominations largely reflect the principles of national fiscal responsibility and how the capital markets judge the stability of the new currency. In an indirect way markets will continue to exercise influence over individual national fiscal policies, the market's disapproval being expressed through a rapid devaluation of the new currency.

• Redenomination risk is negatively correlated to the risk of default, and this increases the complexity of a solution.
• But if a debt issuer from a weaker Euroland country is able to keep its obligations denominated in euros, the redenomination risk for investors will be reduced.

"Reduced" means a smaller risk that investment(s) would go down in value because of being redenominated into the new and weaker currency. Ironically, this would increase the risk that the issuer may default, as after opting out of the euro it will have to use its weaker new national currency to pay off its euro-denominated liabilities.

In addition, the resulting risks and burdens will no more be assisted by the other member countries in the common currency, those considered to be more financially sound. Hence there is a danger that the departing country's propensity to incur debt may increase even further, rather than being replaced by an accommodating stance. This is a risk to be weighted against a revised fiscal compact regime involving an extensive surrender of national fiscal sovereignty.

2. *Lex Monetae*: The Legality of Abandoning the Euro

If deglobalization and deregionalization become the new norm, *then* future "summits" must rethink and revise the rules written for a European Union and for a common currency to make them more flexible and to project the aftereffect of options that have been left open. In all likelihood, a breakup of Euroland will bring along a collapse in business and consumer confidence, leading to a vicious feedback loop that:

- Widens budget deficits,
- Inflates government debts, and
- Promotes popular opposition to reform that could have softened the switch.

The history of monetary unions does not offer much comfort. The euro has been the fourth, not the first, monetary union in the old continent. Its three predecessors date back to the nineteenth century. The first on record was the German Monetary Union (GMU), which lasted for 78 years. GMU was formed in 1838 when the currencies of the North German Confederation, Kingdom of Bavaria, and Austro-Hungarian empire were linked together; and it collapsed during World War I.

The next was the so-called Latin Monetary Union (LMU), formed by (in alphabetical order) Belgium, France, Greece, Italy, and Switzerland in 1865. It lasted for 61 years. Only gold and silver coins were included with the LMU. Each country maintained its own currency but with a fixed 1-to-1 exchange rate. Discipline, however, was not at its best. Italy issued an excessive number of coins with content in precious metal below the agreed-upon standard. The LMU broke down in 1926.

The third was the Scandinavian Monetary Union (SMU), which lasted for 42 years. It was formed in 1872 on the basis of 1-to-1 exchange rates between the currencies of Denmark, Sweden, and Norway. The SMU had a relatively shorter history than its predecessors to the euro. It collapsed in 1914 at the start of World War I.

In two out of three cases the reason for a monetary union's collapse was war but in one case it was cheating by one of the member states, and this may well be the reason why the euro comes down in flames. Article 50 of the Treaty of the Functioning of the European Union (the Lisbon Treaty) allows a member state to withdraw from the EU at the time of its choosing, provided it can secure an agreement approved by 72 percent of the members of the European Council.[3]

- *If* no agreement is reached,
- *Then* the member state has the right to exit the EU unilaterally after two years, such exit implying as well withdrawal from Euroland.

Moreover, according to Article 140(3) of the Treaty of the Functioning of the European Union, the rate at which the currencies of member states are fixed to the euro is irrevocable. Many people look at this as a questionable limit because, in the absence of political union, a sovereign country is bound by the clauses of a treaty that is deemed to contravene its national interest.

Other constraints have a deeper legal base, and some are not necessarily homogeneous. The courts of a country abandoning the monetary union will probably rule with reference to the domestic monetary or currency law: *Lex Monetae*. By contrast, courts outside the exiting country's jurisdiction may or may not recognize the currency law of the country that withdrew from the common currency. However,

- *If* a country were to leave the monetary union in breach of its obligations to the other member states,
- *Then* foreign courts may not recognize a monetary law passed with no regard for the country's Treaty obligations.

Lex monetae is the legal principle that allows countries to redenominate their currency without defaulting. In this regard there is precious little investors and lenders can do to limit risks on existing bonds and loans. The fact is that there may be disparities or even contradictions between a country's monetary laws and its other obligations assumed in a currency union.

At least theoretically, a member state would choose to leave the monetary union if the costs of staying exceed the costs of departure. Practically, this statement is fuzzy because the cost of staying may vary according to the then prevailing conditions, which are not cast in iron.

The better way for a member state to leave the common currency in a legal manner is to negotiate an amendment of the treaty that creates an opt-out clause. Negotiating an exit, however, is bound to take an extended period of time. The exiting country will not be negotiating with Euroland but with the entire European Union. All of the legislation and treaties governing the euro are European Union treaties and they are part of the European Union's constitution.

In addition, several of the 27 states that make up the European Union require that referendums be held on treaty changes, while others may choose to hold a referendum even if this is not mandated. As these references demonstrate, secession is a complex undertaking.

Under current law expulsion from the EU is not an option. To expel a member country requires an amendment of the Maastricht Treaty, which in turn calls for unanimous consent from all 27 countries of the EU. But there are a number of potential sanctions that can be imposed on an errant member country. According to Articles 7§2 and 7§3, for a serious and persistent breach by a member state of the basic principles of the EU Treaty, the Council can suspend some of a member country's rights, including its voting rights in the Council.

The often-heard argument that a seceding state would immediately have a competitive advantage through devaluing its new currency against the euro is not likely to materialize because of technical and political reasons. The devaluation of the new currency by the market will take some time, and on the political side it is unlikely that the other member states will regard secession with indifference. They might even impose a high tariff against the exports of the seceding country.

While a country has the right to have its own currency, the options of Euroland's member states must be examined within the context of economic realities. Since the initial Greek rescue package of May 2010, the European debt problem has spiraled into a perpetual crisis and a threat for the major economies, with financial interventions reaching unprecedented heights.

The member countries of Euroland have guaranteed direct loans and credit guarantees, while the European Central Bank has purchased bonds issued by the weaker Euroland countries often based on rather dubious collateral. These loans have seniority and they are due by the country that withdraws from Euroland, payable in hard currency. Hence, the breaking of relations with the other countries in Euroland and with the ECB can have aftereffects that go beyond the fact that secession or exclusion are complex and costly.

Critics of the way Euroland has been structured and operates are of the opinion that opting out of the Maastricht and Lisbon treaties should pose no problem because their rules have already been broken with the ECB buying government bonds, and by the majority of Euroland member states breaching budgetary deficit limits. The pros answer that at least the Lisbon Treaty has not been broken, because the ECB is allowed to buy bonds, and governments have been permitted to run higher deficits.

In the opinion of the pros, the problem lies with the politicians who, as policymakers, seem unable or unwilling to be bold enough. According to this school of thought, EU leaders have become adept at talking up grand long-term plans, like new treaties to advance political integration, but they offer almost no concepts for containing the current crisis, and even less for bringing Europe up from under.

The situation may be different in case a strong economy opts out of Euroland. Contrary to the case of a weak country, there is no need for a strong economy's government to default. Quite to the contrary, its fiscal position potentially improves if the new currency appreciates against the euro, because the euro-denominated debt falls relative to tax revenues in the new currency.

Legal experts have raised the question whether a government could repay domestic holders of its bonds in euros after having exited the euro. While *legally* there seems to be no problem with doing so, politically bondholders may revolt because of receiving an income in euros while their obligations, including taxes, are in the new currency.

As these two alternatives suggest, there will be options on which the strong economy's government will have to decide way ahead of secession so as not to be obliged to run like a fire brigade later on. The choice of options will also tell whether or not disruption ensues when a strong country has left. Beyond doubt, such move would raise questions about economic and political problems in the remaining Euroland, all the way to exercising pressure on other member countries to leave the euro.

While what is written in this text reflects a choice of events with greater likelihood, the cases of conflict being described will have to be tested in court. When this happens, the scope as well as nature of a withdrawal would, quite likely, be an important factor in deciding whether financial obligations assumed by the exiting country stay denominated in the common currency or are switched to the new one.

A thorny issue will probably be the legality of the exit from Euroland but not from the EU. If a member country were to withdraw in violation of existing treaties, this is sure to impact on whether or not its new currency receives international recognition. Such recognition is important inasmuch as monetary law is a well-established principle in international law:

- It stipulates that a sovereign state has the exclusive right to regulate its currency, and
- Therefore, in principle, the initial creation and subsequent substitution of currency is in the realm of the departing sovereign.

Such a principle however is only of limited help in case Euroland does not disintegrate because the lex monetae of the remaining member states will continue identifying the euro as the currency in which existing contracts have to be fulfilled. The other countries' courts and official bodies may not accept the departing country's decision, creating a contradiction in currency law applied on a regional basis, which will also have to be tested in court.

3. Redenomination Risk by Classes of Assets and Liabilities

The way Steven Leuthold, investment advisor, had it in an August 8, 2011, interview by CNBC, the debt debacle in the European Union has sealed the euro's fate. Leuthold gave the euro another three to four years till it fails and fades. He also projected that the new reserve currency will be the reinstated deutschmark. If this materializes, and the chances that it will happen are high enough to take them seriously, redenomination risk will be all over the place.

In a modern economy, in the realm of exit from the current currency, *redenomination risk* is a first-time event. Therefore, according to expert opinions, no one really knows which of the euro-denominated contracts found all over the world would or should be redenominated into the new currency, as well as whether:

- This is a case of one member country exiting the common currency, or
- The financial world is confronted with the slow but irreversible collapse of the euro.

In the latter case the problem's complexity is much higher as different currencies will show up at the same time leading to wide-ranging redenomination risks.

There exists as well a third possibility: A core of countries decides to restructure the euro by upping its requirements and conditions. In this scenario some of the current members of Euroland will not be able to meet the tougher demands of a reformed euro and they will have to opt out. There is a chance that this can be done in an orderly manner by renationalizing exposure, but the redenomination risk will be present.

Those are the main cases. No one knows which will prevail. What is known at this point in time is that sovereign treasurers and bank risk managers will be foregoing their duties if they do not make contingency plans for each scenario—starting right now. In fact, as anecdotal evidence has it, American banks are tweaking derivatives contracts to protect their claims in case of a euro breakup.[4]

Analysts, like economists, rarely agree fully on anything but in this case the general opinion is that movements in exchange rates would trigger a reweighting of assets and liabilities. The way to bet is that countries seeking a weaker currency would be faced with high inflation, and the danger of social unrest. Countries with a very strong currency will confront export problems in an environment of political uncertainty.

Redenomination risk will increase in the case of frequent exchange rate adjustments that would follow a collapse of the euro. Assets like real estate and equities would reflect these adjustments immediately. Nominal assets like deposits, loans, and bonds will confront a significant risk of redistribution as Euroland's financial market is unraveling.

Choosing the best approach to convertibility is a crucial issue that is at the heart of the current crisis. Its resolution involves a great deal of trial and error through simulation, while some uncertainty will persist including the probability of surprise events or moves. At any time during redenomination, the government of a former Euroland country could announce that all contracts and bank accounts within its jurisdiction will be redenominated in a new currency by:

- Invoking emergency laws, and
- Declaring a bank holiday until nearly all bank account changes are completed.

One of the crucial challenges is to pass the exchange rate devaluation to domestic prices without favoring some sectors of the economy at the expense of others. If this is done without favoritism and with appropriate controls—and provided that it is done at a fast pace—rising domestic inflation will most likely be kept within reasonable limits. Otherwise domestic inflation will reduce the real value of cash balances as well as of wages, and push up the costs of producers, canceling most of the expected favorable effects of the new currency's devaluation.

Legal problems will be legion, the majority of them being complex. Legal and economic considerations will lead to future regulations and specific contractual provisions. Retrospective clauses will be challenged in court. Plenty of important questions still await a definition. For instance, whether redenomination will be on the basis of nationality, or residence, or intended place of settlement. Still other crucial questions are:

- Which law of jurisdiction would decide?
- Which courts could enforce whatever was decided?
- How far and with what chances would an attempt to enforce a court decision be disputed?

There is nothing unusual with uncertainty surrounding critical questions. Every time dramatic changes occur—and a currency union breaking apart is such a case—no one can predict what will happen. There are too many *what ifs,* and a priori answers are making absolutely no sense.

Some countries may well try to force the redenomination of bank deposits in euros through legal decisions, while banks outside Euroland could only offer to redenominate euro deposits in a new currency at market rate. Most likely the central bank for the new currency will require that foreign banks exchange euros on the same terms as domestic credit institutions, but there is no assurance money center banks will accept that condition.

It can as well happen that in a weak currency country opting out of the euro, depositors and investors will exercise political pressures to allow them to hang on to their euro account (in case the euro remains the currency of a few stronger economies). The likelihood of such an event will increase *if* the national currency rapidly devalues. Eventually, however, contractually made obligations such as issued bonds and other loans will need to be redenominated into the new currency. The same is true of cash, deposits in banks of the exiting country as well as savings, time deposits, and insurance contracts.[5] Depending on the new currency's worth, this may potentially lead to a redistribution of wealth. For speculators:

- Nominal assets subject to redenomination in an appreciating currency will be attractive.
- By contrast, they will keep out of nominal assets subject to redenomination in a weaker currency, and even sell them short.

In the case of a euro breakup, not only will bond prices of troubled countries fall but bond spreads will also rise. The decision on which assets would be redenominated in a new currency and which would remain denominated in the current currency over a transitional period is a complex legal issue leading to wealth redistribution. The way to bet is that no decision will be widely satisfactory and therefore it will be tested in court.

Certain to be redenominated in the new currency are all tangible assets such as real estate and equities issued by companies of the exiting country that may be traded on both domestic and foreign stock exchanges. The way to bet is that in all of the aforementioned cases the redenominations may not be a simple arithmetic exercise—particularly so as in a number of cases lawyers have inserted into current contracts clauses governing payouts in the event of a Euroland breakup.

- The simpler clauses resemble the *gold clauses* during the gold standard, which fixed liabilities at a conversion rate to gold, or the dollar.
- The risk of litigation will be much higher with sophisticated clauses meant to protect the investor and/or accounting for dollar and gold volatility.

Somewhat less likely to present complex legal issues in redenominations are most government bonds and mutual funds specific to the exiting country. The level of complexity increases with deposits and savings in foreign subsidiaries of banks of the exiting country, and with corporate bonds and mutual funds with holdings outside the exiting country.

A complex issue will most likely be presented by euro deposits held in banks outside Euroland. Their conversion will probably depend on the convertibility of the new currency. Rather unlikely to be redenominated are contracts outside the exiting country that have no substantial connection with the country abandoning the common currency. For instance, loan agreements arranged by a non-Euroland bank for a client who resides in the exiting country, but for which the place of payment is outside that country.

An example of the organizational effort that is needed to untangle the complexity of these cases are the intricate preparations made over many years to introduce the euro. This is stated in the dual sense of planning for the exiting and of planning for growth and competitiveness under the new currency. It is conceivable that, after the passage of years, an exiting country will not be able to restore competitiveness even after:

- The write-down of much of its debt,
- The implementation of draconian austerity, and
- An effort to relaunch the economy that produces no tangible results.

That being said, a country that properly plans the gains and losses of currency transition will have significant advantages over those that lack the foresight and determination to take care of redenomination challenges. Countries that have failed to do their homework will be losers no matter which strategy they subsequently use to get out of the tunnel. At least for some time the situation will continue to deteriorate as a result of failure to implement early the proper political, fiscal, economic, financial, and psychological measures.

The greater risk may well be a political paralysis that grips the country in the absence of leadership. In case this happens, it will not be able to enact meaningful measures, cutting swaths of public spending and pushing through tax rises. In the past, political paralysis has been a major factor behind a tumble in sovereign bond prices, as investors demand higher yield to hold a country's debts as compensation for a higher risk of default.

Another failure that may cost dearly is that while political leaders are trying to paper over their differences, they fail to address the issue that concerns investors the most: how to regain market confidence. Discords typically arise amid tensions over how to deal with the crisis, forgetting the old dictum that success in any enterprise is largely a question of preparation.

4. Can a Fiscal Union Be the Solution?

Anyone who has had a ride on the San Francisco tramway knows that when the conductor presses the brakes, the system blocks all four wheels. Short of simultaneous action, the wagon going downhill will derail. Something similar can be said about managing the economy in a prudential way with growth as the ultimate objective. A modern economy's four wheels are:

- Monetary policy,
- Fiscal policy,
- Balanced budget,[6] and
- Balanced or positive current account.[7]

If one applies the brakes on only one wheel, for instance, on the monetary policy, then like the San Francisco tramway the economy will go off the tracks. This has happened in Euroland with the common currency's one wheel, monetary policy. Pressing the brakes of another wheel, that of fiscal policy, would not give the tramway stability. Let's however briefly examine what a *fiscal union* might provide since this is a term discussed daily at the vertex of the European Union as the savior of the euro. Can such a claim be substantiated?

By definition, a *fiscal union* is a grouping of different sovereign states that run a shared public spending and tax policy after giving up part of their sovereignty. In theory, Euroland's fiscal union would be able to even out regional economic imbalances through proper planning and control of national finances for the whole community of member states in terms of:

- Taxes,
- Public expenditures, and
- Transfer payments.

The task would be immense and one is permitted to doubt if there are persons able to fulfill it around. There are many types of taxes, quite heterogeneous from one country to the next. The chapters of taxation and of public expenditures vary widely among countries, and harmonization will be a difficult, controversial, and time-consuming process. Still, the more ambiguous is the third bullet of the aforementioned short list. What comes under "transfer of payments"?

- The classical notion of a two-way flow of goods and money with payment of interest and repayment of capital?
- Or, a one-way transfer because the woes of the troubled member states have no end?

What if several member states of the fiscal union time and again need immediate assistance, complaining that simultaneous spending cuts and tax increases led them to a *fiscal cliff*?[8] If the intention is to simply rename the status quo by calling it a fiscal union, this will be dishonest and it will not work.

According to Dr. Heinrich Steinmann, a fiscal union is like a contract between countries, which, to be honored by everybody, requires a supervisory board with full authority to decide on taxation and on expenditures. The competence of this body must include items that so far were part of a country's sovereignty. In terms of taxation these would include:

- Direct taxes,
- Indirect taxes,
- Hidden taxes,[9] and
- Tax exceptions and subsidies.[10]

Taxes are the backbone of fiscal policy. They are also the domain where politicians make special favors to their electorate, like the alignment of VAT in France to include luxury restaurants to the lowest common denominator of VAT for fast food. You cannot take these special electoral favors away from politicians, unless there is *political union* (section 5).

Closely associated with the authority of taxation is the planning and control of expenditures to be exercised by the supervisory board (more on this later), which should resist the tendency to increase taxes to pay for new expenditures. An integral part of the board's authority is not to condone the spend-and-spend policies of some governments.

Taxes are already too high in practically every country. One cannot continue increasing the taxes without negative aftereffects. "Too much taxation kills the tax," Jacques Chirac used to say prior to becoming the president of France, but after being elected he forgot his credo.

For all of the aforementioned reasons, the supervisory board's authority must be strong enough to overrule country-level decisions on taxes and expenditures. This requires a corresponding loss of authority not only by the member countries' ministries of finance but also by their parliaments. Decision on expenditures include, but are not limited to:

- Salaries of public servants,
- Pensions paid by the government,
- Health care expenditures,
- Educational expenditures, and
- Hidden expense chapters.

Taking all this together at the level of Euroland-wide taxation and expenditures will make the supervisory board a substitute for the member country's government. It does not take a genius to understand that the superminister of finance for the whole Euroland, an idea promoted by some countries, is an illusion. It cannot be a working solution because no state will willingly give up the fiscal side of its sovereignty.

Another important function of the supervisory board should be to call to order member states that are not facing up to their responsibilities. This is the better way to discover how many of Euroland's member states are fiscally lost. The way Dr. Heinrich Steinmann put it in the case of brainstorming on the theme of this section: "The reality is that euroland's governments cannot pay back their debts."

For all of the aforementioned reasons, a serious case for fiscal union cannot be made unless each member state's economic and financial history is examined in detail and a common roadmap is created with very few outliers for specific cases. Anything short of this will be half-baked because, fundamentally speaking, the key features of a fiscal union will not be honored. For instance:

- A common financial stability policy that is not only endowed with the right to infringe on sovereignty but also with that of making the final decision.
- Strict control on sharing of financial resources because in a multi-speed Euroland a free transfer of payments will favor the profligate, and
- Steady plan-versus-actual comparisons with reviews of performance and of competitiveness of member states made at frequencies defined by their deliverables in a way similar to quality control in engineering and manufacturing.[11]

The thesis of this section is that a fiscal union without harmonization of taxes and of government expenses, and characterized by a focused control of costs and expenditures, is bound to be something between a joke and an unrealizable vague idea. *If* cross- border fiscal supervision by a supranational authority, the suggested supervisory board, is not feasible or encounters significant resistance, *then* the only other option available is *political union* (section 5).

In conclusion, to be effective, the planning of taxes and control of expenditures by a supranational authority should engulf the whole spectrum of incomes and expenses of every one of the member states. In this case, the supervisory board becomes "the minister of finance" of every member country, with all that this means in terms of political, financial and a political impact. Therefore, it requires the full accord of each member country's government and parliament, in full knowledge that this might necessitate endless negotiations.

5. What a Fiscal Union Cannot Do, a Political Union Might

On August 8, 2012, the German socialist party (SPD) made the fiscal union a prerequisite to the issuance of eurobonds. This announcement, however, failed to define what is meant by a fiscal union, or to delineate responsibilities and rights of sovereigns entering into it. Therefore, it is a fair prediction that the vagueness of the term *fiscal union* (explained in section 4) will see to it that *if* it comes to pass it will deceive both the party itself and its voters—particularly those who believe that a fiscal union provides a good enough guaranty for eurobonds.

Cautious about endorsing solutions like the mutualization of Euroland's debt that risks alienating many voters, the SPD put this imprecise concept of fiscal union as a prerequisite for wild sharing of debts, and also mentioned the need for changes in the German constitution. The latter is a piece of good news for Germany and the EU. Adopting a common fiscal policy requires a change in the German constitution to be ratified through a referendum, which will not pass easily as:

- The public is aware of the risk to the stability of the currency, and
- It would like to secure its savings and its pensions, rather than throw them in the fire lit by politicians.

Beyond the constitutional issues a fiscal union worth its salt, the way section 4 defined it, could see the light only *if* it has the voters' full backing.

Practically, such a majority is most unlikely in any of Euroland's member countries (including the most profligate) and not only in Germany[12] where the hurdles are greater because of the so-called eternity clause in its constitution.

Pundits say that if and when a referendum is held, the SPD will be taking a political risk because voters are weary of pressures toward closer integration. The example of the hugely costly and ineffectual European Commission in Brussels persuades them not to want another featherbedded bureaucracy. Notice that this reaction exists not only in Germany but also in France and in many other member states of Euroland.

If a fiscal union is a nonstarter, what about a political union? The time for a political union were the years right after the Treaty of Rome, but this opportunity was lost. In these days, the chances for a political union in Euroland, and even more so in the EU, are slim. In addition, changes of the magnitude we are discussing have a much better chance to succeed when the economy runs like a clock. This is not the case today as the EU has entered a phase of institutional stagnation.

Let's not forget that voters in France, Holland, and Ireland rejected the Lisbon Treaty in public referendums. The Treaty was only passed once references to closer political union had been removed, which is another way of saying that countries are not going to give up their sovereignty for the sake of a "union."

A political union would have made a solution to Euroland's debt problems easier and more straightforward. But there is no reason to believe that this is going to pass 17 referendums. Optimists say: "Yes, it will come some time in the future"; time, however, is not on the political union's side. Neither is the political union helped by the fact that fiscal adjustments have stalled and structural reforms are strongly opposed by entrenched interests and by an electorate that is a misinformed electorate.

The bait of "one Europe" at an undefined time in the future is not enough to change deeply rooted attitudes. The talk about fiscal union or political union is, to some extent, an expression of the refusal to understand and appreciate the reasons for the debt mountain in sovereigns and banks—that has reduced Euroland's member states to competing with each other for who will take more money from the common purse.

It has been a serious error to start them in the first place as everybody knew that the current no-bailout clause of the Lisbon Treaty means that under no circumstances will a central fiscal authority be a lender of last resort. *If* the United States is taken as an example, as it often happens these days, *then* the no-bailout clause is fully applicable. The Federal government has rescued banks, but no states[13] or municipalities.

In the EU, the no-bailout clause will be credible only when there is precedence of sanctions. Sanctioning a negative behavior is important in the sense that it forces the misbehaving member states of a political union to adopt binding fiscal rules. Sanctions that are believable, and are not a paper tiger like the Stability and Growth Pact, prevent the tendency to game the system, or commit other acts of imprudence.

A precedent for believable sanctions within a political union exists in America, but not in Europe. Some years prior to the Civil War, eight states of the union learned their lesson when, following years of expansion and of rising land values, came a depression that left state governments insolvent. The Federal government *refused* to assume their debts and the states found out the hard way the need for balanced budgets. (Notice as well that the Federal government took a similar stand with the economic and financial crisis that started in 2007 in what regards the states. On the contrary, Washington bent over to save the self-wounded big banks from self-destruction, using taxpayers' money.)

In Euroland, different regions refuse to follow the national plan of austerity when this is necessary. We think the preparation of budgets is the essence of self-government, said the political leaders of Catalonia when in the first days of January 2012 the Spanish region rejected plans by the new central government to impose strict controls on budgets. The Catalans accused Madrid of trying to usurp the powers of the 17 autonomous regions, but a few months later they turned to Madrid for help with their deficit. This is one of the inconsistencies found in a political union.

"We would consider as a red line anything looking like previous line-by-line approval of our budget proposals," Andreu Mas-Colell, finance minister in the Catalan government, told the *Financial Times* on January 5, 2012. "It's something we will resist with all our political and legal resources." A spokesman for the Catalan nationalist government called the central Spanish government's proposals "inadmissible and unacceptable"[14] till Barcelona asked Madrid to give it billions of euros.

This is a real-life example of the attitude member countries in a political union may adopt versus a central authority. It is precisely the sort of problems that should be recognized and dealt with well before a fiscal union or political union takes place. It would have been even better to establish ironclad rules before Euroland was created. They were not, because they have been set aside in the hope that all by itself a common currency would create the convergence necessary for a real the monetary and budgetary union. The problem now is that instead of creating this convergence,

- The euro actually promoted further divergence among members states, and
- Easy money at low cost left in the dust the need for price competitiveness.

Little or no attention has been paid to the fact that both developed and emerging economies face structural challenges that continue to hold growth as a hostage. The same is true of misallocations that built up between the early 1990s and the middle of this century's first decade. Damaged balance sheets at the level of sovereigns, regions, municipalities, banking industry, and households create vicious cycles that:

- Distort the normal functioning of the economy, and
- Create odd situations like that of sovereigns under fiscal pressure who are losing their risk-free status.

Among profligate entities everyone seems to be living on debt. In addition, monetary and fiscal policies lack a comprehensive approach that is able to integrate short-term needs and longer-term requirements, with due attention to dangers developing in the economy. Concern about these issues is "a must" because a "union"—whether fiscal or political—cannot stand without financial stability. The safeguarding of financial stability requires identifying the main sources of:

- Risks and
- Vulnerabilities,

for a variety of underlying reasons. These may be inefficiencies in the allocation of financial resources, poor identification and mispricing of financial risks, defective monitoring of stability factors, shortcomings in the management of exposures, and plain misbehavior.

In all likelihood the most serious problem with a fiscal union without political integration is that its rules will not be obeyed; even worse, they will be gamed as has been the case with the monetary union. Even if politicians try to weed out these differences and incompatibilities, behavioral reasons will most likely prohibit a change in the psychology of taxation, endowments, expenditures, and debt.

Let's not forget that a light type of fiscal union has been proposed by the so-called *fiscal compact*, and the negative reaction to it is an indication that member states are unwilling to enter into a real fiscal union. Adding to the uncertainty is the fact that Euroland countries operate with different definitions when they talk about fiscal union—and, over and above everything else, they have second thoughts.

For France a fiscal union seems to include clauses like fiscal equalization and the socialization of fiscal liabilities, which are unacceptable to other member countries. Neither do all Euroland member states agree on fiscal discipline, nor would they submit to sanctions such as the temporary loss of fiscal sovereignty, which is the policy the so-called *troika* tried to follow in Greece. The carrot and the stick have lost their biblical importance.

6. Conclusion

While Euroland's breakup may not be a deliberate option, it might well come by default, with all that this means in terms of the legality of abandoning the euro (section 2) and of redenomination risk (section 3). The risk associated with this course of events could be significantly reduced *if*, rather than spending time in talks against an exit, the exit from the current currency is properly studied against three scenarios: single opt-out, multiple opt-out, and meltdown. While this three-way classification does not exhaust all possibilities, the more likely courses are:

1. One country abandons the euro, but Euroland and hence the euro continue to exist.

In this case the question of redenomination will be treated as devaluation, or revaluation, depending on the exiting member state, against a currency that is still legal tender (though it may also lose part of its value).

2. A small group of countries (the way to bet is the stronger) abandon the euro because of bailout fatigue.

This, for instance, might be the case of "neuro" and "seuro." Those opting out adopt a new strong currency while the euro continues to exist but depreciates versus the new currency. The countries opting out confront a relatively simpler mode of redenomination risk.

3. The domain and structure of Euroland completely disintegrates, hence the euro ceases to exist.

Theoretically, such a scenario could play out as a reversal of the process that established the euro. Practically, this will not be possible because, as it should be expected, there will be a lot of divergence in moves taken by member states as each tries to establish a new monetary equilibrium. Moreover, the economically weaker in the former common currency risk suffering a triple whammy:

- Sovereign default,
- Bank failures, and
- A continuing struggle with their new currency.

This triple risk significantly increases if the global economic outlook worsens. Therefore, the better option for any country that cannot meet its financial obligations is to default early, after having already established a well-rounded plan on how to use its new and devalued currency as an instrument to spur growth.

Without the ability to *come up from under* and provide a documented hope to the population as well as to investors to be attracted by favorable growth opportunities, a currency crash and devaluation will be accompanied by a severe economic recession. The bottomline is full of uncertainty, which has its own dynamics because it kills business confidence.

A real-life example of a situation that escapes government control is Japan. It is unfortunate but true that the current European economic landscape increasingly resembles what has followed the 1990–1991 real estate, lending, and stock market bubbles in Japan. Since then, the country has hovered in a state of deflationary stagnation exacerbated by demographics and its mounting public debt.

- Interest rates are stuck at zero, and
- At 245 percent the public debt-to-GDP ratio is the highest in the developed world.

Until recently, Japan had been benefiting from a current account surplus that partly helped in confronting the other negatives. This is no more the case. The Japanese trade balance is now showing consecutive negative monthly readings as if the former Asian dynamo were another member state of Euroland. Analysts say that Japan's trade figures are bearish in spite of Abe's (the new Japanese prime minister's) effort to kick-start the economy by accepting a higher inflation target (2 percent instead of 1 percent).

Abe did, however, succeed in lowering the yen exchange rate from 80 yen to the dollar to 95. Anecdotal evidence suggests that George Soros made a cool $1 billion profit betting on the yen's fall.

"Since Japan is prototypical of what is now happening to many developed economies including the US, its trade deficit could also herald what we can expect as the end game of the financial crisis of 2007: debt monetization followed by massive inflation," says Andreas Höfert, chief economist of UBS.[15]

In an article in the *Financial Times* Jamil Baz expressed a concurrent opinion: "First, because deleveraging has not even started yet, the crisis of the world economy has not begun either. All the perceived unpleasantness of the past few years is merely a warm-up act for a greater crisis still to come. The need to get debt levels down is as pronounced as ever in the Eurozone, particularly in southern Europe, but also in the US and Japan."[16]

This is the ideal situation for leadership to lurch toward an "out-of-the-box" solution, which means to think for ourselves and come to our own conclusions. Countries in three continents are suffering from the same virus, specifically: North America, Western Europe, and East Asia. The problems have been caused by the laxness of sovereigns, the lust of bankers, and easier life of households. All piled up debt and lost competitiveness.

The urgently needed leadership should not only resolve the current crisis but ensure it does not recur because of incompetence, mismanagement, and greed. As Saint Paul wrote in his first epistle to the Corinthians: "If the trumpet shall give an uncertain sound, who shall prepare himself to the battle?" Today there exist not one or two but seven major drags on growth in the Western world:

- The policy of spending more than one earns at sovereign and household level, waiting for someone else to pick up the bill.
- Public indebtedness that will not go away just by hoping that it will do so.
- Massive devaluation of currencies due to aggressive monetary easing, which will lead to inflation.
- Delays in painful structural reforms that are not being undertaken because of entrenched interests.
- Increasing illiteracy, and with it unemployment, in spite of university studies because the subjects the young generation chooses are not in demand.
- Lack of business confidence. Credit and maturity extensions are based on trust and trust has taken a leave.
- A radical change in demographics that deprives Western countries of an acceptable level of renewal, while the majority of people live in countries where the gap between the rich and the poor is bigger than it was a generation ago.

Only some of these points have been part of this book's theme. The reason for bringing them together in the Conclusion is to focus the reader's attention on the substantial need for rebalancing the economic forces while in parallel a consistent effort is made to increase the West's competitiveness by reducing labor costs, reindustrializing, boosting productivity, and bringing back confidence to promote entrepreneurial initiative.

We have to leave behind us the time when the longer-term consequences of current imbalances are consciously downplayed, and get back quickly to strong economic growth—one that is not financed by rising public and private debt. In this effort we should definitely remember that we have reached a limit on what a debt policy can do.

The political fight over the nature and extent of a grand political solution will surely be epochal. The eleventh hour is not the time to make everyone feel good. Sovereigns are struggling with colossal debt. Finding out how much money highly indebted banks owe is like unscrambling scrambled eggs. (Spain's Bankia is an example out of many.) The difference between *genius* and *stupidity* is that genius has limits, Winston Churchill once said. For more than a decade EU sovereigns, the ECB, and IMF have acted *as if* there exist no limits.

Appendix

1. The Pains of the Italian Economy

Following the so-called Italian miracle of the 1960s, the Italian economy recovered to the point that the country was one of the richer nations in Europe. The 1970s and 1980s, however, saw two decades of strikes along with rapidly growing entitlements. Fragile and unstable Italian governments overspent in all directions appearing to do everything they could to bring the economy to its knees.

The demographics did not help. The speed with which an aging Italian society ran toward a demographic and economic impasse is seen by the fact that on an average there are 1.4 kids per family. With receipts trailing the rising expenditures, the state became overindebted while no politician wanted, or even dared, to face the fact that Italy's economic model—like that of France, Spain, Portugal, and Greece, among others—is out of joint with the requirements for competitiveness in a globalized economy.

It comes as no surprise, therefore, that Italy's economy is currently feeling the full brunt of its fiscal maladjustment over more than four decades, but redressing the economy involves pain, and the public does not like austerity. With dismal economic data still the order of the day, the Italian economy contracted and in the elections of late February 2013, the electorate rejected Monti's wild austerity.

Not only does the central government find it difficult to balance its budget but also the regions are in dire straits and they are asking Rome for money to cover their deficits. Sicily has a deficit of €5.3 billion. Monti gave it €400 million as aid and fired the president of the region.

On the positive side lie Italy's advantages due to a strong private sector with relatively clean balance sheet, and low bank loan-to-deposit ratios. This provides a distinction between the likely fortunes of Italy and Spain, despite contagion risk. The Spanish economy has been highly mismanaged in the years the socialists were in power led by the blue-eyed Zapatero. It can, however, be argued that both countries have been wounded by successive weak governments.

Indeed, it is easy to forget how close to the edge Italy reached in summer 2011 under the erratic premiership of Silvio Berlusconi. Monti came at the eleventh hour with a fire brigade, but his year-long mandate ended in November 2012. It is not sure if the Monti administration will leave its stamp on Italian economic history, because of a split parliament.

In the post–World War II years, successive governments found a way to bow to labor unions' requests and provide entitlements by successively devaluing the lira. This is not doable with the euro. Like its neighbor Mediterranean countries, Italy cannot print money or devalue; its governments can no more depend on increasing the public debt. It is however no less true that:

- The Italian economy is too big to bail out. Euroland does not have such a king-size fund available, and
- An eventual collapse of the Italian economy, the third largest in Euroland, can have important systemic aftereffects.

Here precisely comes the challenge. Italy's demise could spell the end of the euro. In addition to what has been written in sections 1–4 of chapter 3 about the June 28–29, 2012, Brussels "summit," Mario Monti's problem has not only been that of convincing Germany that it should permit the EFSF and ESM to buy Italian bonds (to limit the spread) but also of convincing his parliament, senate, labor unions and the public to approve the measures he proposes.

The reader should as well notice that even the use of EFSF and ESM funds will be a gamble, since Italian bonds have fallen from grace in the capital market, and the country's debt stands at €2.1 trillion.[1] Nothing will be served by throwing more money to the market's wolves, because these Euroland funds are limited and, as we have seen, their effect is short-lived. A first-class demonstration of the limits of throwing money at the problem has been the €1 trillion of LTRO money used by the Italian and Spanish banking industry to buy government bonds.

- Interest rates in Italian and Spanish bonds temporarily fell,
- But, after a short time, they recovered.

Still, the majority of economists do not expect Italy to default on its debt within the next five years. However, should the reform process and austerity measures initiated by the Monti government be abandoned, the debt may grow to unsustainable levels, radically changing the preceding statement and bringing "bankruptcy day" closer. Worrisome is also the situation in Italy's financial industry, even if it is not as bad as Spain's. This contrasts to 2008 when Italian banks were seen as relatively sound because of not being exposed to toxic subprimes. Today, Italian banks depend on central bank liquidity as well as on eased repo agreements. Still:

- Capital positions remain stretched, and
- Asset quality deteriorates as banks suffer from low growth in the Italian economy.

The economy itself is in poor shape because the labor market reform—including easing layoffs and welcoming part-time jobs—has been incomplete. Mario Monti had a better restructuring plan to start with, but politicians trimmed it. Privatizations have been postponed. Measures to stabilize public finances and to simplify tax and assessment procedures have been watered down because of fierce resistance by labor unions. The parliament made them even less effective rather than restoring their cutting edge.

Inflation is also a problem. There is no real reason why it reached over 3 percent in 2012 in Italy, while in Germany it is 1.7 percent. Worse yet, the 2013 projection of inflation for Italy is nearly 4 percent; by contrast in Germany it is expected to drop to 1.5 percent.[2]

In conclusion, after the short-lived market upswing that followed the Brussels June 28–29, 2012, discovery of an "economic miracle weapon," it looks as if nothing can truly revive the Italian economy. Hopes are fading and this further underlines the fact that at home Mario Monti had a more difficult mandate than the one with Angela Merkel.

Rather than being thankful for the fact that somebody has the guts to try and right the balance, Italians are upset that Monti's government raised taxes, especially property taxes, and increased the retirement age.[3] If the Italian government is not able to come up with billions more in spending cuts, then what Mario Monti might have gained in late June 2012 in the Brussels "summit" will be of no consequence.

With all these background reasons acting in unison, economists believe that Italy sinks deeper into a double-dip recession. As long as uncertainty reigns and the deficits continue, the market is not going to look kindly at the Italian (and Spanish) debt. The "summits" can do nothing to establish market confidence for Italy. Only Italy itself can do it.

2. The Pains of the Spanish Economy,
Its Regions, and Its Banking Industry

As should have been expected, the agreement reached on June 28–29, 2012, at the Brussels "summit" did little to lift investors' sentiment on Spanish assets. The rally of Spanish government bonds was timid and its uncertain course ended after three days. On July 5, 2012, Spanish ten-year yields rose 41 basis points to 6.77 percent in secondary markets, which meant gains from the rally following Euroland's summit deal had nearly been wiped out.[4]

Instead, investors piled up their money into the so-called havens. As the interest rate on Spanish public bonds zoomed, the German two-year yield was lower, suggesting little confidence that European political leaders had set a path to fix Euroland. Four working days after the "summit," Madrid was obliged to offer investors a pickup in yields to induce them to buy in its auctions.

- The Spanish central government and the banks are not alone in confronting severe financial problems. The regions, too, run out of money. Catalonia, one of the richer Spanish regions, had a deficit of €16.5 billion in 2012 and asked Madrid to finance it. Other regions were not much better: The total deficit of the regions is €145 billion ($175 billion), and
- This amount of red ink represents 13.5 percent of the Spanish GDP.

As these statistics demonstrate, there are good reasons why Spain has become a basket case. Its economy is being battered by the deflating housing bubble, high debt, credit crunch, black holes in the banks, red ink in the regions, government bond market stress, and simultaneous fiscal austerity. The late budget revision in 2012 meant that the negative economic impact had been backloaded, with the second half of 2012 being worse than the first half.

Spain's negative economic momentum, a legacy of the departed socialist government, has been too strong, and nonperforming loans came back to levels not seen since the first half of the 1990s. Owing to likely budget slippages, economists expect additional austerity measures in 2013, leading to a GDP forecast of between -1.5 and -2.5 percent for 2013, subject to the bank bailout conditions, which continue being unclear.

The tile that fell on Mariano Rajoy's head is that the real estate momentum, under the socialist government, masked the many weaknesses of the Spanish economy. Few people appreciate the amount contributed to gross domestic product from intensive real estate construction. Spanish data is not available but guidance can be obtained from Chinese statistics.

The way an article in the *Financial Times* had it, real estate construction directly accounted for an estimated 11 percent of China's GDP in 2011. This very high number suggests that in 2012 growth in China was likely to falter if property construction did not start to accelerate again.

"It's hard to see how they can keep growth going over the next two or three years as property construction tapers off," said Nicholas Lardy, an economist at the Peterson Institute for International Economics and expert on the Chinese economy. "They can probably keep it all going for a couple more quarters but don't see how property can continue to be the big driver (of China's economy) that it has been over the last seven years or so."[5]

With a difference of a few years, because Spanish real estate blues preceded the Chinese, what Lardy said of China applies to Spain. The economy continues being squeezed by:

- The deflating housing bubble,
- Credit crunch,
- Government bond market issues, and
- Simultaneous fiscal austerity.

Right after having agreed with the EU on a 2012 deficit of about 4.5 percent, Mariano Rajoy unilaterally increased the 2012 deficit target, saying that he does not need anybody's approval to do so. The higher level of deficit Rajoy wanted has been again revised upward—and still the European Commission is doubtful if it will be possible for Spain to achieve its self-imposed deficit unless new taxes are levied.

In spite of a BBB- credit rating, analysts do not expect Spain to default on its debt within the next couple of years, but they point out that large structural deficits need to be reduced to achieve a stabilization of the debt-to-GDP ratio. Even so, they advise their clients to avoid Spanish national and local government bonds with maturities longer than two years as well as avoid bonds of Spanish banks.

The loan-to-deposit ratio of Spanish banks adds to the fragility of the country's financial industry. This ratio is the highest in Europe (2011 statistics). The loan-to-deposit ratio of Italian banks stands at 105 percent, of French banks at 101 percent, and of British banks at 102 percent versus 82 percent in the US and 74 percent in Japan.[6]

Aside from the much higher exposure by Spanish banks, there has also been a long tail of mismanagement that makes the Spanish banking industry so much more downbeat.[7] From May 2012, when the government stepped in to rescue Bankia, there have been mounting calls in Spain for an inquiry into what went wrong, but as usual politicians turned a deaf ear. Happily for Spain, the country's high court has opened a fraud probe into whether top executives falsified Bankia's accounts and misled investors during the bank's flotation. Among those indicted is Rodrigo Rato, former minister of finance, former governor of the IMF, and former chairman of Bankia.

The long list of reasons brought to the reader's attention explains why recapitalization alone would not save the Spanish banks. To expose the cozy links between politicians and bank management, as well as scams that usually spring up in such cases, it is necessary to investigate not only what went wrong in the system as a whole, but also to place emphasis on:

- What led Spain's savings banks to throw their money to the developers, helping to create a housing bubble with easy credit.

The *cajas* are known to be linked with local politicians. Banking and politics were clearly too close. What is less known is whether it was the politicians or the bankers who led the charge to deep red ink.

- Why did the Bank of Spain do so little to halt the lending spree? Was it also compromised at the political end?

If so, it will by no means be the only case. In the US by his own admission, Alan Greenspan, then chairman of the Federal Reserve, did not see the subprimes' bubble coming, but hedge fund managers had seen it and made big money by joining it.

- How well has the banking crisis been managed since its start? Was good money made to run after bad money?

For instance, the way Bankia was floated is a dark issue. Why did it take so long for politicians to admit the true extent of the losses and take decisive action to deal with them? Bankia is, in fact, only one example. The investigators should look into the Spanish banking industry individually bank by bank.

- Why is there a high level of total banking assets to GDP?
- Does this explain the Spanish banks super-revenues compared to managed banking assets?
- Or, does it have in the background an inordinate amount of risk?

This investigation plus the careful auditing of the Spanish banks books (and double books) should be a basic prerequisite to any recapitalization. It will also give a clearer picture of each Spanish bank's financial health than the unconvincing "stress tests" conducted by two external consultants and published by the Bank of Spain on June 21, 2012.

Notes

Preface

1. The parenthood of PSI is at best uncertain. According to anecdotal evidence it's the brainchild of Christine Lagarde and Nicolas Sarkozy, who convinced the Washington-based Institute of International Finance (IIF, the big banks' research facility and lobby) to act as the godfather (which it should not have done).
2. Though insured deposits have been finally exempt from the heavy hand of the ECB and of the state, even the fact that their status was waived for some time is enough to document that nothing can stop the ECB and Euroland's top brass from committing the great EU Bank Robbery any more (chapter 4).
3. http://www.cnbc.com/100600824; March 31, 2013.
4. Even if the US dollar is still a currency of refuge, like the euro and the yen, it is only a shadow of its past glory.
5. "Miracles are things we don't understand," said Isidor Isaac Rabi, the physicist of the Manhattan Project.
6. UBS, Wealth Management Research, Daily Forex Europe, May 4, 2012.
7. By contrast, identification is made when opinions have been already quoted by the financial media.

1   The Breakup of the Euro Is a Probable "Impossibility"

1. D. N. Chorafas, *Globalization's Limits: Conflicting National Interests in Trade and Finance* (London: Gower, 2009).
2. D. N. Chorafas, *Sovereign Debt Crisis: The New Normal and the New Poor* (London: Palgrave Macmillan, 2011).
3. In fact, a big amount went to the bankrupt Bankia that altogether was boosted by over €40 billion. On March 22, the Spanish government priced Bankia's shares by decree at euro 1 cent—effectively wiping out all shareholder equity.
4. It is no more everyone on his own. It is everybody against everybody else.
5. *Financial Times*, June 20, 2012.
6. While privatizations would have helped to reduce the debt level. The best strategy is to reindustrialize Greece, but this is not even talked about.

7. Jean de la Fontaine (1621–1695), a French poet, published a collection of fables largely drawn from Aesop.
8. *Financial Times*, May 18, 2012. The article makes reference to an FT/ Economist Global Business Barometer, a survey of more than 1,500 senior executives.
9. See also in chapter 8, *Lex Monetae*.
10. Through Spain's Fund for Orderly Bank Restructuring, a government-guaranteed body.
11. The chaos created the first two days by the IMF and ECB has also seen the circulation of several other versions of money grab: 10 percent and 9.9 percent for deposits below €100,000; 20 percent above that, and so on.
12. Which looked more like vengeance by Wolfgang Schäuble, the German finance minister, against Russian oligarchs than a sensible economic measure.
13. Which is a dramatic evidence that the EU, Euroland, ECB, and IMF are incapable of getting their act together.
14. *Guardian Weekly*, March 29–April 4, 2013.
15. By its statutes, the ECB has no right to give ultimatums. This has been another violation of the European Central Bank's statutory rules.
16. She proposed and effectively appointed him president of Ecofin.
17. Born on March 29, 1966, Dijsselbloem got a degree in agricultural economics, entered politics in March 2000, became the Dutch finance minister in November 2012, and president of Ecofin in January 2013.
18. UBS CIO WM March 23, 2013.
19. According to a former president of Cyprus (*Canard Enchaîné*, April 3, 2013). As a French cartoon had it, Luxembourg is too rich to be bothered.
20. *Financial Times*, March 28, 2013.
21. Under pressure from the ECB and other actors, Cyprus imposed losses of 60 percent on deposit accounts exceeding €100,000 ($128,000). Just in case anybody is interested in eleemosynary assistance, the official announcement states that customers will have 37.5 percent of their deposits above this amount converted into shares with full voting rights and access to any future Bank of Cyprus dividend. (Makes me laugh.) A further 22.5 percent will be temporarily withheld to ensure the lender meets the terms of its recapitalization. Instead of being a monolith stealing a wholesale 60 percent, it would have been better to apply an escalation clause. This is another example of the "I-don't-care" attitude reigning in Euroland.
22. *Bloomberg News*, March 26, 2013.
23. *Bloomberg News*, March 22, 2013.
24. Designed to crash Cyprus?
25. http://www.bloomberg.com/news/2013-03-27/cyprus-program-isn-t-templ ate-for-euro-area-bailouts-eu-says.html.
26. *The Economist*, March 30, 2013.
27. Including inflation, which is by no means a low cost action. In his deposition to the US Congress, Jamie Dimon, CEO of JPMorgan Chase, said that the cost of positioning his bank against inflation came to $1 billion.
28. Jouy-en-Josas, December 3, 1991, speech by Kohl on Franco-German relations.

29. Who followed Mitterrand as president of France.
30. Chorafas, *Sovereign Debt Crisis*.
31. It is interesting to note that in late nineteenth and early twentieth centuries the Latin Monetary Union invoked freely exchangeable coins minted in various countries, but it dissolved because the participants cheated in the precious metal content of the coins they made.
32. *UBS Investor's Guide*, June 22, 2012.
33. In the two decades preceding the ongoing economic financial and banking crisis, among some Western countries job creation was estimated at 17 percent of employment and job destruction at roughly 15 percent.
34. James P. Warburg, *The Money Muddle* (New York: Alfred Knopf, 1943).
35. Ibid.
36. *The Economist*, July 14, 2012. The term "summit" has been placed within quotation marks across the book to indicate that in Euroland, EU, G8, and G20 they have been costly and useless events.
37. The talks on the admission of Turkey in the EU are still going on.
38. *UBS Research Focus*, January 2012.
39. As the reader is already aware, the original Stability and Growth Pact was so much watered down that it became an exercise in absurdity.
40. Ben Bernanke tries to devalue the dollar through QE but the US currency is still a popular refuge.
41. Redenomination risk is the subject of chapter 8.
42. There were three in the second half of June 2012: G20 at Los Cabos, state summit in Rome, and the often-touted European "summit of last chance" in Brussels.
43. *Financial Times*, June 23–24, 2012.

2   The Lack of Leadership Is Deeply Felt in Western Countries

1. Bernard Connolly, *The Rotten Heart of Europe* (London: Faber and Faber, 1995).
2. Ibid.
3. What Pöhl predicted has happened, except that the German electorate's resistance came after a delay of nearly 22 years.
4. Guilio Andreotti, the then Italian prime minister, had a small fraction of the leadership qualities of his namesake Julius Caesar but a good part of Caesar's cunning.
5. With the possible exception of Eva and Juan Peron, in Argentina.
6. Which is an insult to the memory of John Maynard Keynes.
7. Rumor has it that the German demands for restructuring and cost control were not easy to implement by a socialist regime. Delors said so to Mitterrand but the president answered: "Do it!" It was done.
8. By the Federal Reserve.
9. By contrast, in Carthage, nobility was based above everything else on wealth.
10. *Virtue*, Socrates said to Protagoras, is *knowledge which cannot be taught.*

11. The EIB is a well-managed institution and it is not spending its money like that, at the whims of a politician. Its experts analyze projects to establish whether they are sensible, well-elaborated, and profitable.
12. It was quietly dropped from the socialist manifesto, but in March 2013 it resurfaced as a "solution" for Cyprus.
13. Which separated commercial banking from investment banking.
14. Rixey Smith and Norman Beasely, *Carter Glass* (New York: Ayer Publishing, 1970).
15. To put their house in order.
16. With Hollande's investiture have been plenty of festivities with a river of champagne to the cost of €4 million ($5.2 million) to the taxpayer.
17. *The Economist*, December 10, 2011.
18. *UBS Investor's Guide*, December 9, 2011.
19. This is true about what the political leadership needs to do both in America and in Europe.
20. D. N. Chorafas, *Business, Marketing and Management Principles for IT and Engineering* (London: Palgrave Macmillan, 2011).
21. According to this article, it is none other than Francesco Cossiga, former president of the Italian Republic, who, when told in 2008 that Draghi would become prime minister to replace Berlusconi, said: "Impossible. He is a *vil affairiste* who would sell the Italian economy to somebody he knows in his former business bank, director of the Treasury" (*Le Canard Enchainé*, November 23, 2011).
22. Appointed by Silvio Berlusconi.
23. As well as the Greek, Spanish, and French
24. Which is another characteristic of a casino society.
25. Military expenditures should be one of the first candidates for budget trimming. France, for instance, has a nuclear Force de Frappe, built in the Cold War years against the Soviet Union. Today there is no more a Soviet Union, but the Force de Frappe is still richly financed by taxpayers' money.
26. "Do you know how to recognize a speech by Jean Jaurés?" asked Clemenceau. "It is easy, all the verbs point to the future."
27. Monte dei Paschi is not quoted on the exchange. It is controlled by local "mutualist" foundations that fall under the control of leftist power brokers. They colonized the bank's board and devoted the bank's energy and money not to public service but to profits at any cost.
28. Of Banca Antonveneta. More on this later.
29. As if, otherwise this was easy and straightforward.
30. CNN, March 1, 2012.
31. *Financial Times*, March 3, 2012.
32. Ibid.
33. Like the US.
34. *Financial Times*, December 17, 2011
35. Spending more money than one has and getting deeper into debt is the socialists' classical big error. By overspending and living in debt, they penalize

both the economy and the economically weak members of society, rather than helping them.

36. Nikita Khrushchev, *Khrushchev Remembers: The Last Testament*, trans. S. Talbott (London: André Deutsch, 1974).
37. Oscar Wilde once wrote that the tragedy of old age is not that one is old, but that one is young.
38. Not to balance its budget, but to confirm its self-established deficit goal.
39. Respectively, with 4.5 percent deficit in 2012 and 3 percent deficit in 2013.
40. These are the official statistics. In real life the numbers are lower, though not dramatically so, because of the black economy.
41. *Financial Times*, January 9, 2012.
42. Euronews, July 31, 2012.
43. Jacques Attali, the French author, advisor to François Mitterrand and former president of the European Bank for Reconstruction and Development, says that fascism has been socialism's offshoot. Jacques Attali, *La Crise et Après?* (Paris: Fayard, 2008).

3   The Nineteenth "Summit's" Miracle Weapons: June 28–29, 2012

1. After having been a paper tiger for so long, the overpaid travelling European Parliament whose work habits beat those of unemployed persons is uniquely unqualified for that job.
2. The mutualization of all future debts would assure that the profligate continue enjoying a good life, while someone else pays for their pleasures.
3. A former prime minister of Belgium over a brief period of time.
4. The European Union has an inflation of presidents: Barroso, Van Rompuy, and the rotating chief of state who for six months supposedly heads the EU.
5. As already noted for 2012 Bankia posted a net loss of €19 billion ($24 billion).
6. Sixteen members of the Christian Democratic Union (CDU) and its Bavarian sister, the Christian Social Union (CSU), voted against the ESM. Ten members of its liberal ally, the Free Democrats (FDP), also voted no.
7. *Financial Times*, June 30–July 1, 2012.
8. Even if quite unwisely, after another telephone consultation, the Ecofin approved an advance of €30 billion to Spanish banks—essentially money thrown down the drain.
9. There have been as well question marks over whether ESM seniority would be waived for Italian bonds.
10. *Bloomberg News*, October 10, 2012.
11. It would be a bad idea to leave this function hanging on a fork by retaining the bank supervisors in each jurisdiction as integral entities, which is what Mario Draghi has suggested.

12. Because this is not going to happen overnight, there will be delays (probably major) in putting the June 28–29, 2012, agreement into practice, unless it is decided that bank supervision will be ultralight, which is counterproductive.
13. Though in a moment of weakness during the Brussels summit of June 28–29, 2012, Merkel accepted a one-off exception for the Spanish banks.
14. As it has happened on repeated occasions with the EU's agricultural subsidies and other projects, the list of TCRP scams will be enough to write a book.
15. *Financial Times*, June 30–31, 2012.
16. In France, the ruling socialist party has a strong anti-federalist wing. *Financial Times*, June 27, 2012.
17. *Le Canard Enchaîné*, July 4, 2012.
18. What France applied unilaterally a month later is a tax on equity purchases, not to be confused with the wide ranging tax on financial transactions.
19. *Financial Times*, July 10, 2012.
20. Ibid.
21. D. N. Chorafas, *Basel III, the Devil and Global Banking* (London: Palgrave Macmillan, 2012).
22. And I don't mean only the double books.
23. Gemina was one of the major financial holdings in Italy.
24. European Central Bank, *Financial Stability Review*, June 2012.
25. One option under discussion is to maintain the existing network of national bank supervisors under the authority of the ECB, which would have day-to-day responsibility for the biggest banks. In my judgment, this is a prescription for future frictions.
26. D. N. Chorafas, *Financial Boom and Gloom: The Credit and Banking Crisis of 2007–2009 and Beyond* (London: Palgrave Macmillan, 2009).
27. A soft form of PSI, a beginning, is consultations between concerned parties, but usually reference is made to the hard form that involves restructuring, rescheduling, reprofiling, and unavoidable debt writedowns.
28. According to the terminology of the ISDA, a credit event is a default. As such, it will launch the procedure for payment by protection sellers to protection buyers of credit default swaps (CDSs).
29. Harry Truman expressed his frustration with subordinate inaction in a different way. He once said: Here I am the commander in chief. I have given an order but nothing happens. (From memory, from one of Truman's biographies.)
30. *Financial Times*, April 4, 2013.
31. http://www.ecb.europa.eu/press/key/date/2011/html/sp110606.en.html
32. A research laboratory and lobby set up by big American and European banks.
33. Laiki and Bank of Cyprus lost €4.5 billion from PSI haircut on the Greek government bonds. Liaki also lost a guestimated €5.5 billion from deposits withdrawn from its branches in Greece.
34. This is not the only money that is curiously missing. Tim Worstall writes in *Forbes*: "There's Something Very Strange About the Cyprus Bank Haircut. Very Strange Indeed," http://forbes.com/sites/timworstall/2013/03/31/theres-something-very-strange-a...

35. D. R. Shackleton Bailey, *Cicero. Letters to Atticus. Volume 1* (Cambridge, MA: Harvard University Press, Cambridge, 1999).
36. Ibid.

4 ECB, EFSF, ESM, Eurobonds, and Political Horse Trading

1. But it started doing so in late 2011.
2. *Financial Times*, July 25, 2011.
3. At least on a temporary basis.
4. In December 2011, when it first put the EFSF on review for a downgrade, S&P stipulated that the fund's rating would slide in lockstep to the lowest level of its six underwriting governments.
5. It was planned to activate the ESM in July 2012, one year earlier than originally projected. This has changed waiting for the decision of the German Constitutional Court due in mid-September 2012.
6. Member countries had to satisfy it to have access to the European Stability Mechanism (ESM) and its bailouts.
7. *Bloomberg News*, March 26, 2012.
8. *The Daily Telegraph*, August 17, 2012.
9. Ibid.
10. Of other people's money.
11. The IMF is particularly afraid that the "Greek solution" will be extended to other Euroland countries "in need."
12. Just as an example, the total debt of Portugal—sovereign, corporate, and household—stands at 418 percent of the country's GDP.
13. *Financial Times*, November 14, 2011.
14. An independent member of the Irish House of Commons.
15. The EU court has fast-tracked its judgment in order to "remove uncertainty" on the "financial stability of the euro area" and pundits expect it to say no to Pringle.
16. "Future of ESM in EU court's hands," The Irish Times, EUobserver.com, October 23, 2012.
17. Fannie Mae and Freddie Mac were semi-guaranteed agencies of the American government, and after their bankruptcy the federal government took them over.
18. What Hollande further said is that *if* his growth pact is not adopted, *then* he would not be able to get the French Parliament vote for the fiscal compact.
19. Though they made a great deal of them.
20. UBS, Wealth Management Research, March 26, 2012.
21. For its ten-year bonds. Since then, as the Spanish condition deteriorates, the interest rate went up.
22. The socialist government also announced an increased tax on dividend payments and additional business taxes, even if they make French industry uncompetitive against its neighbors.

23. France lost 400,000 manufacturing jobs in five years as a result of rigidities in the social and labor structure, which led to high costs making its industry uncompetitive in the global market.
24. *BusinessWeek*, January 12, 2004.
25. D. N. Chorafas, *Financial Boom and Gloom: The Credit and Banking Crisis of 2007–2009 and Beyond* (London: Palgrave Macmillan, 2009).
26. Crédit Suisse's insurance subsidiary, an important economic unit in itself that in the end was sold for peanuts to AXA.
27. When it went under, Lehman Brothers was in debt to the tune of $660 billion. Lawrence G. McDonald with Patrick Robinson, *A Colossal Failure of Common Sense* (New York: Crown Business, 2009).
28. *International Herald Tribune*, December 14, 2009.

5   Throwing Money to the Four-Letter Wind: LTRO

1. Back in 2009, the ECB launched a similar operation on a much smaller scale, and European banking equities bounced up. That gain was short-lived.
2. In connection with the Private Sector Involvement (PSI) and CDSs associated with this credit risk.
3. Barclays had to pay $450 million to American and British regulators for its malfeasance. This large penalty, however, hit stockholders, not the men who profited from the massaged Libor and, through the illegal profits, made huge bonuses.
4. D. N. Chorafas, *The Changing Role of Central Banks* (London: Palgrave Macmillan, forthcoming).
5. *Bloomberg News*, May 1, 2012.
6. Italian banks have issued roughly €600 billion of retail bonds through branch networks in a way not reflected in the loans-to-deposits ratio, which is very high in Italy. The average ratio for Italian banking stands at about 150 percent, compared to levels of 100–120 percent considered as sustainable in the longer run.
7. Reportedly, some banks found the answer by using the ECB cash to enter a Mediterranean *carry trade*.
8. *Financial Times*, July 6, 2012.
9. Ibid.
10. UBS, Wealth Management Research, February 29, 2012.
11. Emphasis added.
12. The other usage of free cash was swapping shorter-term maturity.
13. March 2012.
14. *Financial Times*, March 3, 2012.
15. *International Herald Tribune*, March 5, 2012.
16. Bank for International Settlements, *82nd Annual Report*, Basel, June 24, 2012.
17. Emphasis added.
18. *Financial Times*, March 3, 2012.

19. France, experts say, has been living well beyond its means for over 30 years. Entitlements that got a boost under Giscard d'Estaing in the 1970s skyrocketed under Mitterrand in the 1980s. Since then no government has had the courage to bring them under control.
20. Silvio Berlusconi described the euro as "a strange currency that has convinced nobody."
21. Chorafas, *The Changing Role of Central Banks.*
22. *Financial Times*, July 12, 2012.
23. *Financial Times*, March 14, 2012, ft.com/alist.
24. The government recapitalized Nordea with Swedish Krona 60 million, which corresponded to the value of its holding transferred to Securum.
25. Bank for International Settlements, *82nd Annual Report.*

6 Fiscal Compact and Outright Monetary Transactions

1. After the name of the Dutch city where the "summit" took place and the common currency was negotiated.
2. The so-called Club Med.
3. The problems present in the way this is expected to be done are explained in section 2.
4. Not to be confused with the OMT, which stands for the ECB's Outright Monetary Transactions (sections 5 and 6).
5. An oxymoron.
6. An imprecise statement.
7. Just for the joke, these were the lightweight clauses François Hollande had pledged to renegotiate prior to being elected president of France. Then he ate his words, probably after it was explained to him that such clauses are practically worth nothing.
8. And may also violate other rules concerning occult government financing of selected private companies important to the economy.
9. For instance, on November 6, 2012, the French government announced a fund of €20 billion to help the country's companies reduce their social costs. Half that money will come from savings to be realized in 2014 through reduction of government expenses ("make me laugh"). But the fund will be open immediately therefore creating another hole in the budget.
10. *Bloomberg Businessweek*, September 24–30, 2012.
11. The order of statistical classification is different if accumulated public debt (the debt-to-GDP ratio) is taken into account. In this case, first position is taken by Japan.
12. A job comparable to governor of the Bank of England. Newton spent more years of his life as central banker than as physicist.
13. Of 1919 memories after World War I.
14. *Financial Times*, June 23–24, 2012.
15. The president of the ECB is Italian and the vice president Portuguese. Both Club Med; not a representative sample of the 17 member countries of Euroland.

16. Because of wrong-way interest rate policy over too long a timeframe.
17. This committee was established a year ago by Michel Barnier, the EU commissioner responsible for financial services, to look into reducing risk at Europe's big banks.
18. Dimitris N. Chorafas, *Stress Testing: Risk Management Strategies for Extreme Events* (London: Euromoney, 2003).
19. D. N. Chorafas, *The Changing Role of Central Banks* (London: Palgrave Macmillan, forthcoming).
20. Spain's nationalized Bankia among them.
21. Its recommendation on ringfencing trading is a "must" for sound governance, whether it becomes law or not.
22. With a 105 percent cost-to-income ratio.
23. The market for euro-denominated bonds reopened at the start of 2012.
24. Treaty of the Functioning of the European Union.
25. *Financial Times*, October 25, 2012.
26. Ibid.
27. *Financial Times*, October 1, 2012.
28. European Financial Stability Facility/European Stability Mechanism.
29. *Financial Times*, October 1, 2012.
30. Ibid.
31. *The Economist*, October 20, 2012.
32. A similar decision by the ECB was applicable between October 2008 and December 2010.
33. The reappointment of the central bank's governor is a form of government pressure. Chorafas, *The Changing Role of Central Banks*.
34. Spain, for example, is hesitating to accept the conditionality and supervision attached to a bailout program as long as bond yields remain affordable, and may only submit a request if yields for its bonds head for the stars.
35. Niall Ferguson, *The Ascent of Money* (London: Penguin Books, 2009).
36. *Financial Times*, October 17, 2012.
37. Martin Köhler, "Public Credit," in *Economic Systems and State Finance*, ed. Richard Bonney (Kettering: Oxford University Press/Clarendon Press, 1995).
38. Sarrazin assets that European countries without the euro have done better than those with it.

7   TARGET2: The Creeping Risk of a Financial Nuclear Bomb

1. Director, Ifo Institute, Munich.
2. Hans-Werner Sinn and Timo Wollmershäuser, "Target-Kredite, Leistungs bilanzsalden und Kapitalverkehr: Der Rettungsschirm der EZB," Ifo Institute, Munich, Working Paper No. 105, June 2011.
3. Another interesting statistic is that the ECB's debt with the Deutsche Bundesbank is over 330 percent of the total German federal tax revenues, which, in 2010, stood at €226 billion.

4. In March 2013 it has happened in Cyprus, and it was not a socialist government by a center-right president who enacted it albeit under pressure from Brussels, Ecofin, and ECB.
5. Which has been phased out when the OMT was introduced, but its accumulated toxic waste remains in the ECB's vaults.
6. Mariano Rajoy is not blind. He can look at Greece and appreciate the pain he and the Spanish citizens will go through.
7. Not the bonds of the member states of the union.
8. *Euronews*, October 27, 2012.
9. As well as Ben Bernanke at the Fed.
10. In Germany recent polls have shown a big majority against buying the bonds of Euroland's uneconomic sovereigns.
11. This is the amount owed to TARGET2 by the central bank of Spain, and the same is true of the other central banks.
12. UBS, Chief Investment Office WM, October 2012.
13. D. N. Chorafas, *IFRS, Fair Value and Corporate Governance: The Impact on Budgets, Balance Sheets and Management Accounts* (London and Boston: Butterworth-Heinemann, 2006).
14. Of the London School of Economics.
15. Paul de Grauwe and Yuemei Ji, "What Germany Should Fear Most Is Its Own Fear," CEPS Working Document, No. 368 (Brussels: Center for European Policy Studies, September 2012).
16. As far as global current account balances are concerned, countries with surpluses are Switzerland, Holland, Germany, Russia, Saudi Arabia, Taiwan, Kuwait, Luxembourg, Norway, and Sweden among others. Countries with large current account deficits are Britain, France, Spain, Brazil, Canada, Turkey, Italy, India, Mexico, Poland, Greece, Portugal, Argentina, and the US.
17. For instance, with their surplus dollars, Japanese companies bought the Rockefeller Center in New York, plenty of real estate in California and Hawaii, the Bank of California, and more.
18. Rajoy did not even touch them, in spite of his claims that he applies "austerity."
19. To this is provided as "evidence" an article by the same authors, de Grauwe and Ji (see note 15). This is a tautology.
20. De Grauwe and Ji, "What Germany Should Fear Most Is Its Own Fear,"
21. Low interest rates or high inflation will do the same.
22. Just prior to World War II, when the Germans steamrolled the Italians to join the Axis Powers, Count Ciano, then Rome's foreign minister, said to V. Ribbentrop, the German foreign minister, that Italy needs five years to rearm. V. Ribbentrop assured Ciano that this timeframe was a done deal. A little over a year later, Italy entered World War II and we know how that ended.
23. In mid-2011, a court in Milan sentenced Antonio Fazio to four years in prison for trying to block a Dutch bank's takeover of an Italian lender, an act against Euroland agreements. But the French and the Spanish did it repeatedly without their central bankers or chiefs of state being jailed. Moreover, Fazio's blocking was minor compared to the mistake of Italy's joining the euro, which was promoted by Rome's politicians.
24. D. N. Chorafas, *Risk Pricing* (London: Harriman House, 2010).

25. Compared to 65 percent in 2007.
26. Statistics by Deutsche Bundesbank, Monthly Report, March 2011.
27. "Yes" and "no."
28. Their case has been that the government had rammed the legislation through parliament in such haste that the Bundestag, the only federal organ of state that is directly elected, was in effect reduced to a rubberstamp.
29. *The Daily Telegraph*, May 20, 2012.
30. Marco Buti, "On the European Commission's Handling the Crisis: A Response to Paul de Grauwe," Euro Intelligence, June 4, 2012, http://www.eurointelligence.com/eurointelligence-news/comment/singleview/article/on-the-european-commissions-handling-the-crisis-a-response-to-paul-de-grauwe.html, accessed September 27, 2012.
31. Ibid.
32. *Bloomberg News*, October 28, 2012.
33. With plenty of legal risk associated to it.
34. Miguel Carrion Alvarez, "The Eurozone's Giant Sucking Sound," Euro Intelligence, August 28, 2012, http://www.eurointelligence.com/eurointelligence-news/home/singleview/article/the-eurozones-giant-sucking-sound.html, accessed September 27, 2012.
35. France has not been the only violator. In October 2012, Italy, too, came up with its violation of agreements when the Monti government unilaterally decided on a reduction in taxes "because of an improving economic situation." This has been strictly a political (and illogical) move. It is interesting to see if sometime down the line Italy sells its bonds to the ECB using the largesse of the OMT program in spite of having taken a wrong-way fiscal step.
36. If it ever sees the light.
37. *Euronews*, October 10, 2010.
38. Whose beginning has been postponed to January 2014, if it ever happens.
39. Who would be under the sway of the ECB.
40. http://www.ft.com/intl/cms/s/0/1e2f2cd0–064e-11e2-bd29–00144feabdcc0.html 27/09/2012
41. D. N. Chorafas, *The Changing Role of Central Banks* (London: Palgrave Macmillan, forthcoming).
42. *Bloomberg News*, October 11, 2012.
43. *Der Spiegel*, September 23, 2012.
44. *Financial Times*, October 1, 2012.
45. QE, OMT, LTRO, and the like.

8   Redenomination Risk Following a Euro Breakup

1. *Bloomberg News*, April 17, 2012.
2. Written in mid-2012, this projection was confirmed at the end of March 2013 with the case of Cyprus.

3. This is in accordance with Article 218(3) of the Treaty on the Functioning of the European Union.
4. *Financial Times*, August 7, 2012.
5. Deposits would need to be converted to create the necessary transaction demand for the new currency.
6. Hence, avoidance of an accumulating public debt. Fiscal policy and balanced budget correlate, but they are not the same thing.
7. The simplest way of defining the term *current account* is as a country's balance of payments: exports minus imports—including not only goods but also imported and exported tourism, licenses, and other assets.
8. A fiscal cliff is created by simultaneous tax increases and spending cuts by the government. In his deposition to Congress on July 18, 2012, Ben Bernanke said that the fiscal cliff could hit 5 percent of US GDP. (The US fiscal cliff was averted on New Year's Eve 2013.)
9. Not declared as taxes but which are really taxation. For instance, the price of gas and electricity includes a margin of taxation.
10. Negative taxes.
11. D. N. Chorafas, *Quality Control Applications* (London: Springer Verlag, 2013).
12. We have already seen the very negative reaction the surrender of part of sovereignty has got in France.
13. California presently has a deficit of $16.5 billion, and it is up to California itself to find a solution.
14. *Financial Times*, January 5, 2012.
15. UBS Wealth Management Research, February 3, 2012.
16. *Financial Times*, July 12, 2012.

Appendix

1. A recent unofficial figure is €2.5 trillion.
2. The funny part in Italian politics is the rapid political rise of Beppe Grillo, a critic of the establishment and shrewd comedian, who has talked of taking Italy out of Euroland and reneging on its debt.
3. But the payment of a thirteenth month remains because of fierce labor union opposition to eliminating it.
4. Spanish ten-year yields stood at 6.92 percent before the summit.
5. *Financial Times*, July 6, 2012.
6. UBS Chief Investment Office, Financial, June 25, 2012.
7. Mismanagement and high loan-to-deposit ratio correlate.

Index

Abe, 192
Ackermann, Josef, 105
Andreotti, Giulio, 14, 27, 119
Antonvenetta, 40
Apel, Philip, 62
Attali, Jacques, 14
Atticus, 73
Austerity, 5, 23, 33, 81, 163, 164

Bailout credits, 6
Bailout fatigue, 191
Bailout fund, 78
Bailout program, 52
Balance sheet recession, 165
Bank for International Settlements, 94
Bankia, 52, 200
Banking union, xvi, 5, 9, 25, 50, 60
Bank of England, 46, 95
Bank of Greece, 6
Bank of Italy, 27, 37, 39, 40
Bank of Japan, 95
Bank of Spain, 200, 201
Bank recapitalization, 72
Banque de France, 46
Baroin, François, 46
Barroso, Manuel, 49
Basel III, 102, 132, 133
Berlusconi, Silvio, 196
Bernanke, Ben, 16, 168, 169
Bismarck, Otto von, 41
Blind leveraging, 85
Boltzmann, Ludwig, 157
British Independent Commission on
    Banking, 132
Budgetary discipline, 45, 128

Budgetary independence, 60
Budgetary union, 50, 60, 65, 66
Budget deficits, 35
Budget overruns, 18
Bundesbank, 26, 68, 69, 135, 146, 147,
    149, 152, 156, 160, 174
Bush, George W., 16
Buti, Marco, 161, 162, 165

Caesar, 11
Cameron, David, 4, 41, 46
Capital ratios, 102
Casino society, xv, 36
Cheap funding, 36
China, 48
China's hyperinflation, 139
Chirac, Jacques, 14, 33, 119
Churchill, Winston, 194
Cicero, 73
Citigroup, 4
Clegg, Nick, 65
Club Med (countries), xvi, 81, 88, 106,
    107, 114
Collateralized-debt obligations
    (CDOs), 85
Comey, Jim, 95
Commodity Futures Trading
    Commission (CFTC), 3
Common currency, 25
Common fiscal discipline, 174
Conditionality of the OMT, 136, 140
Confederate bonds, 140, 141
Consolidation target, 52
Contingency plans, 6
Control of expenditures, 187

Convertibility, 181, 183
Cote, David, 49
Counterfeit money, 168
Creative accounting, 147, 150, 151
"Creative destruction," 16
Credit default swaps, 85
Credit event, 68
Credit inflation, 139
Credit-rating agencies, 46
Cross-border contagion, 165
Cross holdings, 64
Cuccia, Enrico, 64
Currency stability, 35
Cyprus, 8, 9, 11, 81, 84

Debt crisis, xv
Debt swap, 68
Deficit reduction targets, 33
de Gaulle, Charles, 28
Deglobalization, 4
de Grauwe, Paul, 153, 154, 157, 161
Delors, Jacques, 26
Deposit insurance, 8
Derivative financial instruments,
    36, 101
d'Estaing, Valérie Giscard, 26
Deutschmark, 174
Developed countries, 1
Dijsselbloem, Jeroen, 9–11
Disorderly currency, 8
Disorderly exit, 7
Dixon, Hugo, 38
Dobrindt, Alexander, 135
Doublebooks, 64
Dracos, 30
Draghi, Mario, xvi, 8, 11, 36, 38, 39,
    45, 103, 107, 108, 137, 141, 168
Dubious financial instruments, 83
Dumas, Charles, 168

Eased repo agreements, 197
Ecofin, 8, 11, 28, 84, 149
Economic and banking crisis, 171
Economic growth, 34
Economic realities, 49, Economic
    restructuring, 87

EFSF, xiii, 75, 76–78, 82, 83, 115, 196
Einstein, Albert, 89
Eisenhower, Dwight, 131
El-Erian, Mohamed, 113
Enhanced conditions credit line, 138
Entitlements, 35, 88, 115, 171, 195, 196
ESM, xiii, 54, 75–78, 82, 83, 115, 196
Eternity clause, 159
Euro, xiii
Eurobonds, 3, 31, 47, 50, 87–89, 91,
    104, 129
Euro break up, xvi, 6, 82, 173, 180
Euro-concessions, 54
Euro-denominated contracts, 180
Euro euphoria, 13
"Euro exit" mechanism, 20
Euroland, xvi, 3, 9, 13, 22, 27, 28, 35,
    39, 41, 43
Euroland breakup, 182
Euroland crisis, 6, 18, 19
European Banking Authority, 107, 108
European Bank Supervision, 57
European Central Bank (ECB), xiii,
    xv, xvi, 3, 5, 11, 12, 18, 31, 53, 57,
    60, 65–67, 75, 82, 83, 87, 95, 99, 106,
    107, 141, 142
European Commission, 25, 26, 28, 43,
    49, 55, 60, 80, 127, 199
European Council, 51, 123, 127
European Court of Auditors, 164
European Court of Justice (ECJ), 80,
    84, 123, 141
European debt crisis, 75
European Executive, 51, 163
European integration, 5
European Investment Bank (EIB),
    31, 75
European Monetary System (EMS), 26
European Monetary Union, 26
European Union (EU), xiv, 4, 11, 12,
    28, 32, 35, 49, 67
Eurozone breakup, 81
Exchange Rate Mechanism (ERM), 7
Exit option, 167
Exit strategy, 110
Expropriation, 20

Fabius, Laurent, 51, 61, 62
"Fat cat bankers," 97
Fazio, Antonio, 39
Federal Reserve, xiv, 95, 135, 137,
    148, 200
Feldman, Martin, 26
Ferguson, Niall, 141
Fillon, François, 46
Financial discipline, 128
Financial engineering, 84
Financial firewall, 78
Financial nuclear bomb, 147
Financial stability, 131
First Greek bailout, 66
Fiscal austerity, 15
Fiscal Compact Treaty, xvi, 33, 34, 54,
    79, 120–23, 125, 126, 135, 190
Fiscal discipline, 43, 129, 171
Fiscal equalization, 191
Fiscal imbalances, 121
Fiscal liabilities, 191
Fiscal sustainability risks, 128
Fiscal union, xvi, 5, 13, 16, 50, 114,
    171, 184, 185–87, 190, 191
France, 28, 34
Franc lourd, 28
French banks, 70
French public, 51
French sovereignty, 51

GAAP, 64
Gensler, Gary, 3
German Constitutional Court, 90,
    158, 160, 167
German monetary union, 176
German taxpayers, 60
Germany, 20, 47, 69
Germany's hyperinflation, 139
Glass, Carter, 32
Glass-Steagall Act, 32
Globalization of financial services, 4
Global nanny state, 101
Goethe, Johann-Wolfgang, 30
Gold bullion, 32
Gold clauses, 183
Goldman Sachs, 37

Government overspending, 114
Great EU Bank Robbery, 71–73
Greece, 5, 34, 41
Greek bonds, 6
Greek loans, 70
Greek PSI, 72, 100
Greek public debt, 42
Greenspan, Alan, 135, 200
Growth compact, 91

Haircut, 67–69, 71
Health care costs, 115
Höfert, Andreas, 9, 35, 87, 128, 193
Hollande, François, 4, 8, 31, 33, 47, 50,
    54, 55, 61, 62, 90, 91, 99
Hugh, Edward, 62

IFRS, 64
IMF, xiv, 11, 12, 67, 77, 152
Imprudent domestic lending and
    borrowing, 155
Imprudent international lending and
    borrowing, 155
Inflation, xv, 27
Institute for Economic Research, 59
Institute of International Finance
    (IIF), 7, 70, 71
Institutional reform, 43
Insured deposits, xiv
International monetary transfers, 19
Ireland, 5
Italian banks, 103
Italian miracle, 195
Italy, 5, 6, 8

Jenkins, Roy, 26
Ji, Yuemei, 153, 154, 157
JPMorgan Chase, 3
Junker, Jean-Claude, 9

Keynes, John Maynard, 16, 32, 173
Khrushchev, Nikita, 47
King, Mervyn, 46
Kohl, Helmut, 14, 15, 26, 27, 119
Kozlowksi, L. Dennis, 95–97
Kumm, Mattias, 84

Labor cost, 17
La Cour des Comptes, 47, 94
Lagarde, Christine, 8, 112
Lank, Kurt, 75
Laplace, Pierre-Simon, 31
"Last-chance summit," 41, 59
Latin monetary union, 176
Laxness of sovereigns, 193
Legacy cost, 17
Lender of last resort, 36
Less developed countries, 1
Leuthold, Steven, 180
Lex monetae, 177, 179
Liikanen, Erkki, 132
Liikanen Committee, 132, 133
Lisbon Treaty, 41, 136, 176, 178, 188
Loan to deposits ratio, 195, 199
LTRO, xiii, 19, 29, 36, 99, 105, 106, 115
Lycurgus, 30

Maastricht Treaty, 13, 14, 25, 119
Macmillan, Harold, 15, 47
Management of risk, 70
Mas-Colell, Andreu, 189
Medicaid, 131
Medicare, 131
Merkel, Angela, 9, 36, 43, 47, 51,
    53–55, 68, 71, 81, 90, 92, 99, 158,
    160, 168, 197
Military-industrial complex, 131
Mitterrand, François, 14, 15, 26, 27,
    52, 119, 160
Monetary stability, 120
Monetary union, 3, 5, 13, 14, 15
Monte dei Paschi di Siena, 12, 37, 108
Monti, Mario, 37, 38, 51, 54, 55, 61–63,
    90, 99, 196
Moral risk, 110, 111, 140
"More integration," 60
Mounting public debt, 15
Münchau, Wolfgang, 83, 137, 169
Mutualization of debt, 50

Neuger, James, 12
Neuro, 191
Nominal assets, 181, 182
Noyer, Christian, 46

Obama, Barack, 97
Off-balance sheet financing, 139
Offshore tax havens, 10
OMT, xiii, 134–37, 142, 145
Ortiz, Guillermo, 116
Osborne, George, 14, 46, 91

Paciolo, Luca, 151
Papademos, Lucas, 37
Papandreou Jr., George, 11
Parker, Bob, 78, 112
Pensions, 131
Per capita public debt, 44, 126, 127
Philip II of Macedon, 73
PIMCO, 12
Pissaridis, Christopher, 10
Plutarch, 30
Pöhl, Karl-Otto, 26
Political integration, 19
Political union, 15, 50, 51, 185, 188, 189
Pompidou, George, 31
Populism, 92
Portugal, 5
Pringle, Thomas, 83
Private bondholders, 58
PSI, xiii, 11, 41, 42, 67, 69–71
Public debt, 32
Public stability, 163

Quantitative counterfeiting, 139
Quantitative easing (QE), 29, 139
Quest, Richard, 112

Rajoy, Mariano, 41–43, 50, 54, 55, 62,
    63, 198, 199
Rato, Rodrigo, 200
Redenomination of banking
    deposits, 182
Redenomination risk, xvi, 171, 175, 181
Reinventing Bretton Woods
    Committee, 69
Restructuring, 23
Ring-fencing of trading, 132
Risk aversion, 93, 110
Risk management, 110
Risk-weighted assets, 17, 93
Rogers, Jim, 14

Romer, Christina D., 97
Roosevelt, Franklin D., 16
Russia's bankruptcy, 139

Sands, Peter, 117
Santander, 40
Sarkozy, Nicolas, 31, 33, 37, 42,
    68, 100
Sarrazin, Thilo, 143, 158
Scandinavian monetary union, 176
Schäffler, Frank, 135
Schäuble, Wolfgang, 168
Schmidt, Helmut, 26
Schneider, Carsten, 141
Second Greek bailout, 42, 79
Securities market program, 147
Seuro, 191
Sinn, Hans-Werner, 59, 145
Slovakia, 84
Smaghi, Lorenzo Bini, 69, 70
Smith, Simon, 33
Socrates, xv
Solon, 30
Soros, George, 20, 92, 172, 173, 192
Sound public finances, 163
Sovereign-big bank alliance, 97
Sovereign-big banks complex, 131
Sovereign bonds, 99, 100
Sovereign debt, 22, 67, 99
Sovereign guarantee, 56
Sovereign overruns, 22
Soviet Union, 48
Spain, 5, 6, 42
Spanish bailout package, 158
Spanish banks, 58
Spanish government bonds, 198
Spanish real estate blues, 199
Special investment vehicles (SIVs), 71
Special purpose vehicles, 86
Stability and Growth Pact, xvi, 3, 14,
    27, 35, 43, 114, 119, 120, 156
Standard & Poors, 32, 89
State capitalism, 48
Steinmann, Heinrich, 185, 186
Structural change, 48
Structural deficits, 79, 80, 124, 125
Structural reform, 16

Summers, Lawrence H., 97
"Summits," xiii, xvi, 29, 32–35, 43, 44,
    52, 55, 58, 59, 176, 197, 198
Swartz, Mark H., 95

Tail risk, 100
TARGET2, xiii, xvi, 6, 145–48
TCRP, xv, 53, 56, 57
"Template," 12
Thiel, Scott, 137
Too-big-to-fail, 132
Too-big-to-jail, 13
Transborder inspection, 63, 64
Transfer union, 115, 150, 168
Treaty of Rome, 4, 19, 114, 188
Trichet, Jean-Claude, xvi, 40, 116
Troika, 56, 58, 67, 137, 191
Tuomioja, Erkki, 81
Turner, Adair, 117
Twist, 29
Two-speed Euroland, 14, 78

Unaffordable debt, 33
United debts of Europe, 88
United States, 14, 34
Unsecured bonds, 102, 103
US bankruptcy, 49
US debt, xv

van Rompuy, Herman, 34, 51
Vienna Initiative, 68
Visco, Ignazio, 40
Volcker, Paul, xvi

Wage inflation, 157
Waksal, Samuel D., 95
Wall Street, 30, 97
Weber, Axel, 147
Webster, Daniel, 8
Weidmann, Jens, 109, 110, 160, 174
Wolf, Martin, 168
Wollmershäuser, Timo, 145
World Economic Forum, 116

Yardeni, Edward, 108

Zimbabwe's hyperinflation, 139

CPSIA information can be obtained at www.ICGtesting.com
Printed in the USA
LVOW11*2246070114

368462LV00014BA/984/P

0 1341 1571119 1